T0247859

BREAKING GLASS

BREAKING GLASS

Tales from the Witch of Wall Street

PATRICIA WALSH CHADWICK

A POST HILL PRESS BOOK
ISBN: 979-8-88845-286-8
ISBN (eBook): 979-8-88845-285-1

Breaking Glass:
Tales from the Witch of Wall Street
© 2024 by Patricia Walsh Chadwick
All Rights Reserved

Cover design by Fabien León

This is a work of nonfiction. All people, locations, events, and situations are portrayed to the best of the author's memory.

No part of this book may be reproduced, stored in a retrieval system, or transmitted by any means without the written permission of the author and publisher.

Post Hill Press
New York • Nashville
posthillpress.com

Published in the United States of America
1 2 3 4 5 6 7 8 9 10

Also by Patricia Walsh Chadwick

Little Sister: A Memoir

To the mentors who were instrumental in helping me forge my path in life, and to mentors around the world who play that role for so many others.

CONTENTS

A Prologue of Sorts

I am a birthday party girl—and always have been. As a child, I anticipated my birthday for weeks in advance and then made the most of being the center of attention for twenty-four hours.

So, when two of my closest friends from my days on Wall Street offered to throw me a birthday party—my seventieth birthday, to be precise. I said yes! It was to be August 8, 2018, in the Pool Lounge at the Four Seasons restaurant in New York City. Perfect!

The problem with birthdays for me was that they came to an end. My sixth birthday remains one of the most vivid memories of my childhood. The day had been perfect in every way—the weather was gorgeous, I got to pick my favorite games to play with my friends, and I blew out all six candles in one breath on my chocolate-frosted birthday cake.

But as the summer light faded and it was time to leave my chums, I was overcome with emotion. As the first tear welled in my eye, I blinked it away, but it was followed by more and more until a torrent was flowing down my cheeks and spilling onto my white cotton blouse. As I sobbed uncontrollably, my parents hovered over me, gently coaxing me to share with them what was breaking my heart.

But I refused, or better said, I was too embarrassed to let them in on the secret of my anguish. It was only as I sensed that their concern was turning into frustration that I blurted it out—"Because I have to wait three hundred and sixty-five days for my next birthday."

That's the kind of birthday girl I am.

Now a week before I stepped into my seventies, I was surrounded by eighty of my nearest and dearest—a medley of humanity from around the globe, ranging in age from twenty-four-year-olds, namely my twin children, to nearly eighty-five. Many of the guests were friends I'd made during my professional years, as I was making my way up the ladder in the "take no prisoners" world of Wall Street. For each person present, there was at least another who had been unable to attend for reasons (mostly) of geography.

Amidst chilled champagne and exquisite hors d'oeuvres, I made sure to have my picture taken with every person attending—a way to memorialize this once-in-a-lifetime event.

When the atmosphere reached its perfect state of cheer and relaxation, one of the guests reached for the microphone and for the next thirty minutes, as the mic was passed from one to another, my past life was laid bare (or so it felt). Some tales were endearing, some amusing, others even hilarious, and fortunately there were those who had the good grace to let the less glorious moments of my past remain just between us.

But there was one tale that stood out. A woman—another professional from my Wall Street days—was sharing with the audience how she and I came to know each other and eventually bond with a deep friendship. I can still hear her words. She dated the story to 1985, when I was a portfolio manager at Citibank.

"The head of institutional sales called me into his office," she started. "I was at Bear Stearns at the time. Behind closed doors, he spoke. 'Citibank is an important account for us, but we have a problem. A substantial portion of the assets is managed by a woman there who is difficult. I've put a number of different salesmen on the account, but the guys are all afraid of her. I'd like you to take over the account and see if you can build a strong relationship with her.'

"I was nervous," the woman told my birthday audience, "at just twenty-seven years old and because I knew of this woman only by her reputation. The traders on the block desk referred to her as 'the Witch of Wall Street,' so I wasn't sure what to expect."

The audience burst into laughter. My jaw dropped. Fortunately, I was sitting; otherwise, I might have simply fallen to the floor. *Me? The Witch of Wall Street?* I managed to keep my composure, but on the inside, I was horrified, mortified, and wanted to vanish.

This being a festive occasion, there was only one thing I could do— laugh it off and be grateful that I was in a room filled with friends.

In the aftermath of the birthday celebration, I couldn't get the moniker Witch of Wall Street out of my head. Witch was a loaded word— from the time I was a child, I had hated witches, much like I disliked goblins and gnomes and even giants. In fact, my distaste extended to anything that seemed unnatural. What I craved was normalcy because normal was a far cry from the environment in which I was growing up—a religious community in which children were separated from parents and not allowed to speak to each other.

For weeks after the party, I wondered why it was that I never knew I was called a witch. On Wall Street, there were no secrets—if Bear Stearns's traders had dubbed me as such, then I wondered if the same held true for Morgan Stanley, Goldman Sachs, Merrill Lynch, and a host of other firms. It was confounding to conceive of myself in that light.

Admittedly, I could be difficult in the never-ending pursuit of the best investment opportunities for my clients and the best execution on the trading desk. The decades-long journey up the corporate ladder until I touched the glass ceiling—and eventually cracked through it—was a steeling process, borne of pitfalls and successes as well as a few fiascos and triumphs.

Grit had been ingrained in my life almost since infancy; over time, it became an integral part of my personality. But wasn't that true of thousands and thousands of other women across hundreds of industries? Did they not also reach success in the corporate world through hard work? I was sure *they* weren't all called "witches." So, why me?

Reflection eventually drew me to my upbringing, which I had taken great pains to hide from both the guests at my seventieth birthday party and from the world at large for more than fifty years. The painful secret I'd hidden—that I was raised in a religious cult—was so shameful that I had concealed, even from myself, how much it influenced the way I faced the world and tackled challenges. But now that someone had indicated how fierce I could be in my professional life, I considered my history.

Born into Saint Benedict Center, a Catholic religious community turned cult, I had been separated from my parents at the vulnerable age of six—together with my four younger siblings—and raised in a repressive religious environment under the regime of a woman named Catherine Clarke, whom we called Sister Catherine, and a priest, Father Leonard Feeney. Obeying their edicts, my parents, who were active members of the community, forfeited their parental rights to the fiats of Sister Catherine, who oversaw the day-to-day management of the organization.

As the original founder of the community in 1940, she assumed leadership and charge of every facet of daily life—from the jobs assigned to the Big Brothers and Big Sisters, as the grown men and women were called, to the schooling and disciplining of the children, referred to as the Little Brothers and Little Sisters. She furthered her control over the activities of the members by imposing the rule of silence through-out the day.

Then, when I was only seventeen years old—twelve years after she had sundered our family—Sister Catherine cast me out, without money, without family, without anyone to advise me about a world I'd been taught to believe was full of sin and danger. The reason for my expulsion? I was not nun material!

Those childhood years of discipline and familial deprivation had shaped my character. In the last few years, and through the process of writing this book, I've asked myself the question: Did the ordeals of being separated from my parents and manipulated by the iron hand of Sister Catherine, my subsequent expulsion and my fight for survival, make me into the person on Wall Street that people dubbed a witch?

* * *

Now, in my eighth decade, as I look back at a thirty-year career on Wall Street during which I rose, step by step, from front desk receptionist at the Boston office of Ladenburg Thalmann at the age of nineteen to global partner at Invesco when I was forty-nine, I've come to appreciate the complex mosaic of my life.

Sister Catherine tossed me out of the only place I'd ever known as home because she was unable to mold me into the compliant role of a submissive nun. She discarded me, leaving me to pick up my shattered self and march forward on my own with ruthless determination to survive. And yet, I could not help but wonder whether subliminally—most assuredly, not wittingly—I modeled myself after her, a woman who let nothing stand in the way of achieving her goals.

With the benefit of maturity, I now appreciate that Sister Catherine was, ironically, one powerful reason that I survived and ultimately thrived on Wall Street, although that was certainly not her intent. Undeterred by the cultural norms of her gender at the time, she led warrior-style, and no one within the community dared to defy her. Admittedly, in my case, I had to start by tiptoeing into the world, but once I found steady footing, my own drive propelled me forward.

In looking back on the path of my career, I am reminded of a reality that I have come to accept in the hard-charging world of business. Qualities of leadership that are part of climbing the ladder to success in business—drive, perfectionism, impatience—are expected of men, who are rewarded for exhibiting them. Those same qualities, however, can get a woman branded as a "witch."

That's the real world, and in that real world, there is more than one road to success. This book is one witch's story about starting out on a journey—with no map or destination in mind—and achieving a level of success far beyond anything she could have imagined, and for which she had most certainly never planned.

A NOTE TO THE READER

*L*ittle Sister, my first memoir, was the inside story of growing up in a Catholic religious community that tragically morphed into a cult. When I published that book five years ago, I was breaking out of the shackles of my long-held secret by sharing, for the first time, a childhood that for decades I had hidden from friends, colleagues, and the world at large. The book chronicled an emotionally fraught childhood that included separation from my parents and expulsion at the age of seventeen, without a hint as to how to survive, much less thrive, in an unfamiliar and frightening world.

Breaking Glass moves forward from my childhood, but also revisits events of my bizarre upbringing through a different lens, offering insight into how the experiences of my early life influenced my character and helped me forge my path in the world of business. This is a story about resilience—how it helped me first to survive and then, starting at the bottom rung on the corporate ladder, to rise step by step until I was able to touch that glass ceiling and then break through it.

While *Little Sister* is my story of growing up in a religious community that tragically became a cult, *Breaking Glass* is a coming-of-age memoir and my story of breaking out on my own—from ingenue to successful businesswoman.

The names of a few of the people in *Breaking Glass* have been changed to respect family members who are still living.

CHAPTER 1

Reflections on Things Past

1996

From my corner office on the twenty-third floor of the Citicorp Center building at Fifty-Third Street and Lexington Avenue, the view of the sky was expansive. Whether the day was cloudy or sunny, foggy or snowy, I felt inspired by the presence of nature just beyond the glass.

The broad, open sky provided a calming environment, acting like a filter that sifted out the cacophony of Manhattan, allowing me to become oblivious to the honking of taxi horns, the sirens of police cars, and the wailing of ambulances some 300 feet below. I was in my cocoon, where I did my best thinking. Swiveling my chair to face the window and armed with a yellow legal pad and a pen, I'd put my feet up on the credenza and jot down my thoughts as they came to me.

This contemplative state was reminiscent of a time decades earlier when, as a twelve- and thirteen- and fourteen-year-old girl, I would lie for an hour at a time in the grassy fields of my home in the farm country in Still River, Massachusetts. That's where I lived as part of a religious community of one hundred members, including thirty-nine children, led by Leonard Feeney, an excommunicated Jesuit priest, and his spiritual alter ego, Catherine Clarke. Together, they created a monastic environment that demanded obedience, silence, chastity, and detachment from family.

To achieve those objectives, they separated parents from their children and then forbade family members from speaking to one another. Shortly thereafter, they manipulated parents into forsaking marriage for a life of celibacy and dedication to God. To prevent any worldly influence from seeping into our midst, Father and Sister Catherine—that was what we called Leonard Feeney and Catherine Clarke—forbade members to read newspapers, watch television, listen to the radio, or communicate in any way with family members who lived outside the community.

Gazing at the enveloping blanket of the blue sky, the teenage me wondered, *Are we the only thirty-nine children in the entire world living this way? Separated from our parents? Forbidden to call them "mom" and "dad" and forced to use their religious names—Sister Elizabeth Ann and Brother James Aloysius?* I craved an ordinary life, like the one I imagined children all over the world enjoyed.

In contemplation, I found myself taking the opposite point of view from what Father and Sister Catherine espoused when they'd say, over and over, "You are the luckiest thirty-nine children in the world because you were dedicated to God from the day you were born." The implication of that "good fortune" was that I would grow up to be the Bride of Christ and join the ranks of the grown members of the community as a nun. I wanted none of it. My dream was to marry a handsome prince and live with him in a castle where we'd have lots of children and beautiful gardens.

As I'd bask in the summer sun, with the long-bladed grass tickling my face, I'd escape to a different time in the years before I was six, when I was living in Cambridge with my parents and four younger siblings. The seven of us lived together in a bright, cheery apartment in Cambridge, Massachusetts. In the evenings, while my mother nursed the baby, Daddy gave us sponge baths, then told us bedtime stories, and just before tucking us into bed, he would sing a bedtime song—always in French. Life was perfect, particularly when he leaned over the bed to give me a kiss, with his "Good night, my little princess."

But one chilly day in November when I was six, our family life came to an end. My parents obeyed the order from Father and Sister Catherine to turn their children over to be raised under their dictates. So did the other eleven married couples in the community. As a curious child, I craved answers to questions that bombarded my brain—*Why can't I see my grandma anymore? Why is everyone out in the world going to hell?* But my curiosity remained unsated and my internal queries were left unvoiced and unanswered. That was the way it was in our community—no one questioned authority.

Once the children were wrested from their parents, the next step was to separate the parents from each other. Again, everyone conformed. And then, several years later, Sister Catherine unilaterally determined that the community would leave Cambridge and move to the hamlet of Still River, some thirty miles west of Boston, where she had purchased a twenty-acre farm and built housing and a school. Once there, she incorporated the rules of monasticism into daily life, and silence was enforced at all times but for a few hours of recreation each day.

Before long, what was once incomprehensible had become the norm, and while the questions of "why" never left my mind, I had come to accept the reality that was my life. And, despite its rules, its punishments, its familial deprivation, I loved that place—it was my home. I also found life in the country—raising chickens, riding horses, having my own pet heifer, growing fruits and vegetables, which we learned to can for the winter—a salutary distraction from what I could not change.

Our community hadn't always been that way. There was a time, before I was born, when Saint Benedict Center was a cheerful meeting place for Catholic students. The Center, as it came to be called, was founded in 1940 by Catherine Clarke and two young Harvard graduates and recent converts to Roman Catholicism—Avery Dulles, the son of John Foster Dulles, a Washington lawyer who would become President

Eisenhower's secretary of state, and Christopher Huntington, who hailed from a socially prominent family on Long Island. Catherine, a devout Catholic woman, and a manager of Saint Thomas More Bookshop in Harvard Square, wanted to expand outreach to young Catholic students at Harvard, Radcliffe, and other colleges in the Boston/Cambridge area. When Dulles and Huntington were called into service after the attack on Pearl Harbor, Clarke was left to oversee and manage the enterprise on her own. Throughout the duration of the war, the Center flourished, most particularly after Clarke was successful in convincing Richard Cushing, then archbishop of Boston, to allow Leonard Feeney, the renowned Jesuit priest teacher, writer, and poet, to serve as the Center's full-time chaplain.

Following the war, the ranks of students on the GI Bill in the Boston area swelled, as did those who came to the Center from colleges as far away as Holy Cross College in Worcester, an hour's drive west.

My parents met there in 1947. My father, Jim Walsh, a recently discharged naval officer, was studying for a master's degree in philosophy at Boston College, where he was also teaching mathematics. My mother, Betsy Ann McKinley, a freshman at Boston University, was a recent convert to Catholicism. Six months after their first meeting, Leonard Feeney married them, and, when I was born the following year, my parents asked Catherine Clarke to be my godmother. On most evenings, they could be seen dining with Feeney and Clarke in a local Cambridge or Boston restaurant.

However, from the peak of its popularity in 1946, the Center—within the span of two short years—experienced a dramatic fall from grace over a matter of church doctrine. In the aftermath of World War II, the archbishop of Boston, Richard Cushing, became a strong proponent of ecumenism—an effort to inspire collaboration among the many Christian religions. Leonard Feeney, to the contrary, railed against those who subscribed to a more benign interpretation of the path to get to heaven. As his rhetoric became increasingly strident and vitriolic, many of his followers abandoned him. Suffice to say, my parents were not among those defectors and remained part of a small group of stalwart supporters of Leonard Feeney in his fight against what he described as "liberalism."

In January 1949, that loyal group, totaling fifty-three young men and women—both students and academics—established a religious order that they named The Slaves of the Immaculate Heart of Mary. Feeney was their superior, and each member took a vow of obedience to him. Among them were my parents, as well as two other professors at Boston College. Three months later, my father and two other professors were fired by the president of Boston College for their outspoken support of Father Feeney. All three were married and had children.

In that moment of crisis, the community banded together, sharing financial resources. My parents sold the home they'd recently purchased on the GI Bill and gave the proceeds to Leonard Feeney. Over the next couple of years, the adult members adopted religious names and religious garb. Catherine Clarke became Sister Catherine, and my parents were now Brother James Aloysius and Sister Elizabeth Ann. I was no longer allowed to call them Mama and Daddy.

Sister Catherine purchased a cluster of simple homes in Cambridge for the twelve married couples and their children. To shield the community from what she deemed to be "the forces of evil in the outside world," she had the homes surrounded by an eight-foot-high stockade fence. The Center was now in a religious war with the hierarchy of the Catholic Church, one that would culminate with Feeney receiving a letter of excommunication from the Vatican.

The press, in derogatory fashion, referred to the organization and its members as "Feeneyites," and for several decades, that pejorative term was commonly used in the Boston area.

Within five or six years, there were thirty-nine children, and the community totaled one hundred men, women, and children. While Father was the religious head of the order, it was Sister Catherine who held the actual power. In short order, draconian style, she instituted rules that, little by little, controlled every aspect of life within the community, including parenting, education, discipline, and even recreation.

Then, when I was seventeen years old, Sister Catherine banished me. My crime? A chaste, teenage crush on one of the men within the community. The innocent behavior on my part—one that was unreciprocated by the Big Brother—posed a threat to Sister Catherine's ambition that every child would embrace the life of religious celibacy. To that end, she had separated the boys from the girls, forbidding them from having recreation together or speaking to each other. She prohibited any education regarding procreation. Menstruation was treated as an event that made us, in her words, "more like Our Blessed Mother." Chemistry replaced biology as the science taught in high school. It was as though she hoped that by revealing nothing on the subject, the course of nature could be manipulated. I proved her wrong, and she needed to discard me, lest my behavior become contagious.

I was a guileless teenager, but to her way of thinking, I was an evil influence that needed to be exorcised. Within a day of my expulsion, when members of the community flocked to Sister Catherine's office to ask why I was no longer around, her response was both obscure and derisive. "She was destroying the vocations of the men."

My parents were rendered voiceless in the decision to kick me out—having years earlier taken a vow to obey Father and Sister Catherine. Without money and bereft of parental guidance—my parents and four siblings would remain with the community for several more years—I was forced to fend for myself in a world Sister Catherine had warned for years would be the ruination of my soul. Armed with a high school diploma, but without the means to further my education, I was catapulted into the world.

Alone and unsure of myself, I had but one objective—survival. Failure was not an option, but I had not a clue how to describe success. Baby steps were all I could manage in the beginning. They led to longer strides, and eventually, to giant steps, although not without my full share of challenges, failures, and disappointments along the way. Fortunately, I learned to seize the lucky breaks that came into my life's path, and when they were scarce, I persevered with a steady dose of pluck.

While I had much to learn about the ways of the world, I was blessed with an array of invaluable tools—discipline, emotional fortitude, and perseverance—honed during my first seventeen years. Scholastic rigor and personal accountability were part of the bedrock of my upbringing, despite an environment of authoritarianism and religious zealotry. But while all that was important, it was *resilience* that saved me and an insatiable curiosity that propelled me forward.

CHAPTER 2

Silence Is Golden

1 9 6 6

Walking into Boston's Hickox Secretarial School at 367 Boylston Street for the first time, on a warm and sunny September morning, I was hit full force with the realization that I was more of a neophyte than I had anticipated.

Throngs of energetic eighteen- to twenty-year-old girls mingled in clusters in the classrooms—or in the hallways when they wanted to light up a cigarette. Any attempt on my part to blend in was futile. There was nothing—not a thing in my entire upbringing—that was relevant to what I was witnessing in my new life. I had been schooled for years in the art of fine diction and clear enunciation. My ears were unaccustomed to the rapid-fire, giggle-packed, high-pitched language that gushed unendingly from more girls than I had ever before encountered in one place.

In my eighteen years of living, I had never heard a single word of slang, much less a swear word. The names of people bandied about by the students were Greek to me—baseball players, movie stars, artists—I'd never heard of a single one. The only musicians I was familiar with were long-since dead—Mozart, Beethoven, Brahms, Schubert—and this gaggle didn't strike me as a classical music crowd.

It wasn't merely the language of the world that caused me angst. My clothing and my hairstyle were anything but hip. Fortunately, I had graduated by the time skirt lengths shrank to inches. But I didn't have a clue how to make my hair flip up or create one of those popular puffy dos.

So, I had to tiptoe my way into what felt like a jungle of wild beasts. For the first few weeks of the term, when anyone would engage with me with a friendly "hello," I experienced a sense of panic. While smiling shyly, I'd do my best to find a way to end the conversation. How could I know so little?

* * *

The stout, rectangular headmistress of the secretarial school seemed to take pride in her role. Wearing stiletto heels and sporting a white bouffant hairdo, she still barely came up to my shoulder, but that only buttressed my perception of her role as commander in chief of her army of future secretaries. Parading military style up and down the sixty-foot-long rows that separated dozens of girls seated in front of typewriters, she barked, "Straight backs, girls; hit that return with gusto." There was a hint of Sister Catherine in her demeanor. However, her stentorian voice belied a naughty sense of humor that she enjoyed sharing with both teachers and students, which, of course, went totally over my head.

The first seventeen years of my life were dominated by silence— Holy Silence, as we referred to it. The sudden freedom to express myself without constraint—to laugh at will, to query, to challenge, and to question—should have been alluring. But without the ability to understand, much less speak, the language of the world, I inevitably found myself taking refuge in that familiar rubric of silence.

One path to enlightenment in this new world was to cram dozens of strange words into my brain and use my lunch break to search for definitions in one of the several reference dictionaries in the typing room. This became a daily exercise, but often without success because this new vocabulary belonged to the language of slang and swearing, and there was, as yet, no Urban Dictionary.

Language was but one of a seemingly endless list of challenges I faced. Far more daunting was the fear that one of the students might figure out who I was—or better said, who I had been—a member of the hated Feeneyites. The Center was infamous in Boston and far beyond the city, and the only way I knew to prevent a slip of the tongue that might "out" me was to remain silent.

Classes ended around three o'clock each afternoon, and I'd head to the nearby Greyhound bus station. When Sister Catherine booted me from my home, she made one concession: for the duration of my nine-month secretarial course, I would be allowed to live in one of the guest houses on the Center's property in Still River and my mother could join me for dinner. But there was one proviso—I was to keep out of sight and to speak to no one within the community except my parents. Sister Catherine also approved a weekly allowance of $2.50 (equivalent to about $25 today,) nearly all of which I would hoard for the purchase of something I wanted—like the $12 transistor radio I'd been eyeing in the bus station.

That tiny device became my window into the outside world. Each evening after dinner, I'd retire to my bedroom, ostensibly to do my homework, but in fact, I'd spend several hours listening to the news and talk radio. In the morning, I'd slip the radio under my mattress before my father drove me to the bus station.

The twice-daily, hour-long bus commute between Still River and Boston was itself an education; commuter etiquette called for silence in the morning, a time for sleep and reading, while the return trip was more convivial.

It was on the afternoon trip home one day that the man sitting next to me asked in a soft and gentle tone, "Has anyone ever told you that you look like Lauren Bacall?"

My response was to edge closer to the window and stiffen my back as though creating a wall between him and me. *How dare he address me? He must be dangerous. Lauren Bacall? Never heard of her.* Of course, I hadn't. With a shy smile, I shook my head. But I was intrigued.

Lauren Bacall, Lauren Bacall. I repeated the name over and over. *Find out who she is. Lauren Bacall.*

At the dinner table that evening, I blurted the question out to my mother, not sure if she'd even know what I was talking about. "Sister Elizabeth Ann," I said, "who is Lauren Bacall? Someone mentioned her name today."

My mother's face lit up as she replied, "Oh, dahling, she was a beautiful actress." I was dying to hear more, but that was all she said.

"Beautiful actress"—not words I'd ever heard before. Had she made a slip, or was her simple statement deliberate? Was she possibly attempting to introduce me to a world she was still unwilling to reenter?

I was intrigued. Someone thought I was beautiful.

* * *

My daily bus ride was its own window on life "out in the world," as I thought of it. One afternoon, as I was riding the bus, an attractive young woman walked to the front of the bus and made an announcement. "I'd like to raffle off a watch," she said. "It's a brand-new Bulova, still in its box."

What's a raffle? I wondered. But I got the gist when she added, "All I need is a buck from whoever wants in." She started back down the aisle, displaying the stainless-steel watch with one hand as she held out a small basket to each of the riders. Some ignored her, but most fished out a single dollar bill.

My mind was in overdrive—is this illegal? Is it sinful to be part of a raffle? To gamble for something? As she approached my seat, I hunted in my wallet for change—a couple of quarters, dimes, and even pennies— dropped them into the basket, and then stared at the number twenty-seven on the ticket she handed me.

Now I was invested in the outcome, and I watched as the young lady strolled back to the front of the bus and stood next to the driver, who seemed oblivious to what was going on. She shuffled the tickets in her basket, picked one up, and called out, "Number twenty-seven is the winner."

What? Me? I've won? A watch? Without a hint of scruple, I accepted the watch in the box. Nothing like a little pluck that turns into good luck.

* * *

The girls at the Hickox School came from an array of local towns and a variety of socioeconomic backgrounds, but within a few weeks of arriving, I had begun to sort them into various groups. There were the coarse ones who smoked and wore lots of makeup, and their language was laden with swear words and accompanied by bawdy laughter.

Then there were the social ones, whose primary objective seemed evident, based on their vacuous conversations. They were in search of husbands—not that they would find one in an all-girls secretarial school. But perhaps that first job as a stenographer might land them the man of their dreams.

Finally, there was a contingent of girls whom I thought of as the "safe" crowd—graduates from nearby Catholic high schools, identifiable by their names (mostly Irish), their modulated voices, and their good manners. They were easy to engage, but I still had to remain on my guard at all times. An inadvertent lapse on my part could provide an opening for questions that might lead me to divulge the secret of my background.

It took some weeks, but little by little I started to grasp the language of the world. Their use of slang was an education, and I could almost decipher the meaning of a novel expression by the tone of voice used. But there was one word used regularly by a host of girls that stumped me. I sought help from a dictionary, but it wasn't there. I was stymied.

After several weeks of frustration, my only recourse was to ask someone. But whom?

Among the throngs of students, I singled out one girl, a prepossessing young woman, with delicate blond tresses that fell gently on her slender shoulders. There was something about her friendly smile as we passed each other in the hallway that encouraged me to engage with her. I learned that she was from Arlington Heights, and with her Irish surname, I was sure she was Catholic, which made her less daunting, and therefore the safest choice for a task that bordered on terrifying.

For days I procrastinated, and then as classes came to an end on a Friday, I approached her and asked timidly, "Could you help me with something?" Before she could answer, I just blurted out my question, "Do you know what the word 'shit' means?"

She looked at me quizzically and then responded in her disarming way, "It means shit."

I stood paralyzed—the one girl I'd hoped might be able to enlighten me without my becoming embarrassed had just failed on both counts, leaving me with the sense that I was an idiot. *How do I gracefully exit?* I wondered. I knew only one way. I smiled and said, "See you on Monday. Have a lovely weekend." And I walked out of the glass door.

That's it, I thought as I sped furiously across Boylston Street toward the bus depot. *I'm never asking another question. Not in my whole life. That's it, that's it, that's it. I'll figure everything out all on my own.*

CHAPTER 3

Where Do I Go from Here?

1967

C hild's play—that's what secretarial school was to me. Just months earlier, I had been a high school senior at the Center, and now I pined for the intellectual stimulation that had been so abundant there. Where were those speeches by Cicero in Latin? Where was the assignment to critique a paragraph in a Joseph Conrad short story? I longed for my etymology class, where words like "mellifluous" or "onomatopoeia" seemed three-dimensional, as though they had human qualities. My teachers had graduated from Radcliffe and Cornell, from Harvard and Boston College, whereas now I was being taught typing by someone who lacked a college degree.

For nearly eighteen years—that most formative time in life—while I'd been shut off from the outside world, I was fortunate to have received an exceptional education in its most traditional and classical form. It had played second fiddle only to the religious part of our lives, and I had seized on it with zest. Now that I was out on my own, I yearned for academic rigor and stimulation—something to engage my boundless cerebral energy and tax my cognitive stamina.

What I lacked was sophistication—the savoir faire that I could detect in others but knew I had yet to learn. My upbringing had been deliberately prescribed to keep me ignorant of the ways of the world. Manners I possessed; they'd been drilled into me from my earliest years. Poise I could affect, with as little as a smile. But I lacked even a modicum of worldliness, and I was at a loss as to how to attain it.

It was an odd juxtaposition—in matters of the world, I couldn't hold a candle to a single one of my classmates, but when it came to matters of the intellect, the reverse was true. I well enjoyed that feeling of moral and intellectual superiority. In time, I would come to learn what they knew, but they could never have access to the caliber of education I had received.

With my formative education behind me, it was now up to me to teach myself. Beyond my hand-sized transistor radio, my resources were scant, mostly the paperback books and magazines I purchased—often for as little as ten or fifteen cents—with my allowance. The thought of walking into the Boston Public Library, where I could have any book at no cost, and which was a mere three blocks from the Hickox Secretarial School, was too intimidating. While I had learned the mechanics of the Dewey Decimal System in school at the Center, I had yet to set foot in a library and was terrified that I wouldn't have a clue how to maneuver through the labyrinth of stacks and shelves.

So, it was at the kiosk in the bus station of the Back Bay that I'd skim the pages of books whose authors' names were foreign to me. Heading to the used paperback section, which was all I could afford, I searched for the words "Best Seller" in bold on the cover. I was on a catch-up mission to feed my hungry brain, and to do so meant I had to step outside the lines, metaphorically, and shatter the boundaries that had been imposed on me during the preceding seventeen years.

My two-hour daily bus commute provided ample opportunity for me to explore the world through the written word. Choosing a window seat toward the back of the bus, I cordoned myself off from the rest of the commuters and devoured a range of offerings in nearly every genre—with titles that ranged from *In Cold Blood* to *Rosemary's Baby* to *Native Son*; from *The Feminine Mystique* to Mary McCarthy's *The Group*; *The Agony and the Ecstasy* and *The Autobiography of Malcolm X*, as well as a smattering of steamy novels that were shockers—but not enough to abandon them—all in an attempt to uncover the language and the thinking of the world around me. At a book a week, in short order, I had consumed more than a year's worth of coursework that might have been titled "Introduction to the Real World 101."

My reading interest was honed over those first few months of forced independence, becoming a permanent fixture of my life that would change little over the next five decades. Compared to the stories of real life, fiction left me cold. I devoured memoir, biography, and history—books that included *The Kingdom and the Power* in 1969, the history of the *New York Times* told in brilliant prose by Gay Talese, and Robert Kennedy's posthumously published *Thirteen Days: A Memoir of the Cuban Missile Crisis.*

Some years later, it would be the 1973 publication of *Interview with History*, Italian journalist and war correspondent Oriana Fallaci's compilation of sixteen interviews with world leaders, including the shah of Iran, Golda Meir, Zulfikar Ali Bhutto, Henry Kissinger, Yasser Arafat, and Indira Gandhi that I found riveting. There was a fearlessness about Fallaci that I found inspiring, almost intoxicating—the way in which she could skewer world potentates with the genius of her questions. In a subliminal way, she became a role model, and over the ensuing years as my own career unfolded, her image would arise, séance-like, when I found myself preparing for a tough one-on-one session with a corporate CEO.

* * *

By March 1967, I'd finished the coursework at Hickox, and my achievements could be defined by two numbers: sixty-five, the number of words I could type in a single minute, and eighty-five, the number of words of shorthand I could take in a minute. OK, so now I had two skills. What was next?

With a sense of pride, the headmistress informed me that I held the record for completing the secretarial program in the shortest time, and she promptly offered me a position, following graduation in May, as a typing teacher.

Finding a job had been on my mind from the day I had set foot in the Hickox School. I was well aware that upon completion of the coursework, it would be up to me to find both a job and a place to live on my own. And suddenly there was a gift from heaven—employment. I accepted the position with a sense of relief. The familiar surroundings of the school would allow me to migrate from student to employee without the apprehension that still confronted me when I faced a new experience.

My first paycheck—for four weeks of work—grossed $320, an hourly rate of $2. At least, it was above the prevailing minimum wage of $1.40, I calculated. (In 2023 dollars, it amounted to $12.79 an hour.) After the government took its share, I received a check for $262.77, which was enough to afford a single room at the YWCA at the edge of the unfashionable South End neighborhood in Boston. A large plate glass window was the best feature of the small space that included a single bed, an old-fashioned radiator, and a narrow closet with a hollow fake-wood sliding door. The communal bathroom down the hall was shared by half a dozen girls. Not surprisingly, no men were allowed beyond the foyer on the ground floor.

I was now on my own, an independent eighteen-year-old, with a job and the responsibility for paying my rent. But I lacked what I most needed and craved—someone to whom I could turn for advice. Books were my only teachers. My parents were now less involved in my life, as I no longer was allowed to stay on the Center's property. From my point of view, that seemed better, inasmuch as I was now an avid explorer of the world from which the Center had, for nearly eighteen years, done its best to shield me.

It was not lost on me that my own mother, whom I still thought of as Sister Elizabeth Ann, had been exactly my age—eighteen years and ten months—when she got married, and eleven months later became a mother.

In the fall, I accepted the head mistress's offer of an additional $10 a week for teaching two evening classes. Almost immediately, I regretted my decision, when it became obvious that extending my workday would thwart my developing plan to attend college at night. But the commitment was made, and I wouldn't renege on it.

Suddenly I felt trapped—by my history, by my hasty decision to work evenings, by my lack of anyone to turn to for advice, and mostly by my inability to enroll in higher education. Without the opportunity to advance my schooling, I felt stymied—as though I was on a road to nowhere with no off-ramp.

CHAPTER 4

What Is This Thing Called Love?

1967

I was a teacher. Saying the words to myself had an upscale ring to it, like a profession that might even become my career, but I wasn't fooled. It was a job as a "typing teacher," not a teacher of mathematics and philosophy as my father had been at Boston College—that is, until he willingly sacrificed his career for the sake of his faith. But to me, he still was, and would always be, a "professor."

Nor were my students anything like those my father taught. From the vacuous conversations that spilled out of the young women's mouths, it was evident that most of them were whiling away time until they met the boy of their dreams, got married, and started the only career they were aiming for—that of a wife and mother.

There was a huge part of me that also wanted that life—in other words, a family, security, and children, for sure. Did I crave them as a young woman because they had been so painfully absent during my childhood? Perhaps. But there were endless other aspirations that tugged at my mind and heart—my journey was barely beginning. In short order, I would learn that marriage wasn't necessarily life's greatest gift.

One of my teaching associates, Donna, was a picture-perfect, slender, dark-haired, blue-eyed girl a couple of years my senior, and herself a Hickox graduate. She epitomized optimism and radiated happiness. She was a glass-half-full kind of girl, and we were kindred in that way. But I knew nothing of her social life, her family, or even where she lived.

One day she bounded into the staff lunchroom and breathlessly announced that she was going to Fort Lauderdale for a ten-day vacation with her parents. A little pang went through my heart. This was a vacation that was impossible for me to imagine, much less experience—the treat of my parents taking me for a week to a resort. My parents were still living in a religious order and going by the names of Sister Elizabeth Ann and Brother James Aloysius.

While Donna was basking in the Florida sun, she sent a postcard back to the school, describing what sounded like a heavenly vacation. She returned the following Monday, tanned and relaxed, and proudly displaying a diamond ring on her left hand. "I'm engaged," she gushed, beaming. "We're getting married in June!" That was just three months away.

Engaged? I was puzzled, having not a clue that she even had a boyfriend. "I met him in Florida," she replied when I asked. "He was the lifeguard at the resort."

I was speechless, but I knew to keep my mouth shut, lest I display my own naïveté about such matters. *Love must be wonderful*, I thought, harkening back to my own intense crush on Brother Basil at the Center. Nine months after being kicked out of my home, I still thought of him and always with a flutter of excitement.

We had a small bridal shower for Donna and wished her all the happiness in her new life, and she promised to bring back pictures.

Two weeks later, it was a somber and weary-looking bride who returned from her honeymoon. The spark of love was extinguished, replaced by the painful realization that she'd been duped by a cad, a man who had physically and emotionally abused her within hours of their wedding. She was now back living with her parents, bound for a divorce, and expecting a child.

My lack of sophistication made it difficult for me to grasp the complexity of her tragedy. But over the next fifty plus years, I would revisit that event in my mind hundreds of times and thank my guardian angel (yes, I still believed in guardian angels and do to this day) that I'd been saved a lesson as painful as hers and one that could so easily have befallen the young naïve woman I was.

Another teacher with whom I worked offered a more sanguine view on marriage. A few years older than I was, Mary Cudmore, with her jovial personality, was a relative newlywed and the breadwinner in her family, while her husband, Bob, was studying at Boston University. She found endless opportunities to bring him into our conversation, and her tenderness toward him gave me a warm feeling about what marriage could be like—a far cry from the disaster I'd just witnessed befall Donna.

"Come and meet him," Mary encouraged me one day as she was driving to pick up Bob at the end of his classes. And I did. He was a gentle, almost shy, bear of a man—a fascinating contrast to Mary's voluble and effervescent disposition. His adoration for her was palpable. Pragmatic, unafraid, filled with laughter and optimism, she made it easy for me to engage with her and admire her, and I was unsurprised when she told me she was Catholic. She made married life seem ecstatic, and I observed how solicitous she was of her husband.

Mary evolved into a role model for me—I observed the diligence with which she applied herself to her position as a typing teacher, shrugging off the antics of the headmistress. Never a cross word passed her lips, although her sense of humor could be charmingly biting. She exuded compassion, as well as common sense, which drew me to her.

I debated whether I should tell her my secret—the convoluted story of my upbringing. I was sure she'd be a friendly ear, and on a few occasions, I almost spilled the beans, but at the last moment, I froze, unable to craft an opening sentence for a life story as bizarre as mine.

* * *

I'd been teaching for a few months when, one day, a student suggested that I accompany her to the USO in downtown Boston, explaining that it was a good place to meet guys who were in the military. There was safety in numbers, I thought—even two—so I stuck my toe into what seemed like dangerous water.

This was the era when there was still a draft, and the war in Vietnam was accelerating, which meant that the USO was often teeming with men—and a few women—as well as staff members who had the air of chaperones. Ping-Pong became an ice breaker—a way to deflect too many questions, and I became a mean player. I even braved having a hamburger in a local pub with a guy on one occasion, and on another, I went with a group of girls and guys to the hit movie *Bonnie & Clyde*. But I could hardly call either of those excursions dates.

And then a few days before Christmas of 1967, I met Chris, a tall, blond, and exceptionally good-looking sailor from California. He asked me out on a date, but I told him I had plans to be with my family for Christmas. "I won't be back until December 30," I said.

"Are you doing anything for New Year's Eve?" he asked, and I admitted that I was free. "Want to meet me in Copley Square at ten p.m.?" he asked.

Brilliant idea, I thought. *I don't have to tell him where I live. And everyone will be out celebrating, so it will be safe.*

"Sounds great," I said, and I meant it. I had a date, a real date, on New Year's Eve!

* * *

By six o'clock on December 31, the snow had started to fall—soft and silent—lending an aura of romance to the brisk air. There were several inches on the ground a few hours later when I donned boots and my only winter coat—a long, black, gold-buttoned, double-breasted one. I

22

wore it with a fake white fur hat and white woolen gloves. I thought the look was sophisticated, something I was desperate to appear to be.

Copley Square was but a short walk from where I lived. It was also ground zero in Boston—everyone knew where it was. Pigeons and tourists flooded the small square in all seasons of the year, yet the atmosphere was peaceful. Its architectural centerpiece—Trinity Church—built nearly one hundred years earlier, sat majestically on the eastern edge of the square, bordered by the Boston Public Library to the west, with the Copley Plaza Hotel and the "original" John Hancock Building to the south. Trees and benches added a feeling of home.

Promptly at ten o'clock, I walked into the open square, hoping my date would be waiting for me. He wasn't—no big deal. I took in the crisp, frigid air and reveled in the stillness of the falling snow, and the hint of romance created by the glistening of the flakes as they gathered under the lighted lanterns that dotted the square. Couples, arm in arm, glided across the plaza, sometimes stopping to make out, something I had yet to do. I looked at my watch, the Bulova I'd won in the raffle on the bus; it read 10:30. Maybe his subway was delayed by the snow. I was ever the optimist.

By eleven o'clock, my toes were becoming numb. I stomped my feet a few times, trying to rev up some circulation, but stopped when passersby stared at me as though they thought I might be crazy or had a problem. They were right on that latter score. My problem was simple—I was waiting for someone whose first name was Chris, and who had provided no other information. Be patient, the ever-hopeful spirit inside me whispered.

It became eleven fifteen—the snow hadn't stopped falling, and the cold was now embedded in my fingers, my face, my whole body. I was shivering. By eleven thirty, my leather (or maybe it was fake leather) boots were soaked through, and my exhilaration of ninety minutes ago was evaporating.

I was beginning to feel like a fool when, off in the distance, I saw a lone figure coming toward the square. My heart gave a little flutter, and I squinted through the film of streetlight-lit snowflakes as his steps gathered speed. I could see that he was tall. A sense of elation filled my weary body, and I headed toward him. *He's made it—at least we'll enjoy a glass of champagne when the clock strikes midnight.*

Waving my hand, I tried to catch his attention, but he seemed oblivious to me, and then as he neared the square and the blurred silhouette came into sharper focus, I realized he was not my date. Making a sharp right, he headed to the elegantly lit Copley Square Hotel, which I imagined was crammed with couples awaiting the countdown to midnight, when they would drink and kiss and more.

The final minutes to the new year passed interminably—twenty, then fifteen, then ten, and finally five, four, three, two, and that final countdown to midnight. In the now drifting snow in the heart of Boston, I entered 1968 alone and dejected. I felt a sense of desertion—not for the first time in my life.

My first real date was a bust, and all I wanted was to get out of my ice-encrusted clothing and crawl into bed. I'd been stood up—an expression I'd heard of but never experienced.

If there was a lesson to be gleaned from that night's disappointment, it would have to reveal itself later. Pulling the blankets up around my still half-frozen body, I found a way to see the upside by telling myself that the new year would surely turn out better.

CHAPTER 5

A Bird in the Hand Is Worth Two in the Bush

1968

I was fired. Fired after only ten months on the job—my first job. The headmistress informed me—the words still sting—that "fraternizing with the students" was not appropriate for a teacher. It was true that I had made a few friends among the student body—where else could a nineteen-year-old girl with no family and no friends cultivate relationships?

Adrenaline, always lurking in the background of my psyche, shot through my body and catapulted my brain into overdrive. *Don't talk back. Don't ask her to change her mind. You've been here before. You'll be OK.* In moments of crisis, my instincts were usually right.

This was before the era of human resources departments and sit-downs with your boss, of performance reviews and setting goals in writing. The stentorian headmistress of stenography, as I liked to think of her, was the sole arbiter. She had established a rule, and I had broken it, but she was decent enough to pay me through the end of the month, which meant that I had a full two weeks to search for another job. And she provided me with a certificate that enumerated my skills with nothing more than those two numbers—the famous sixty-five words I could type in a minute, and the eighty-five I could take in shorthand. That was the sum total of my worth as a job seeker. It was hardly psychically rewarding, but it was more than nothing, and I was determined to make the best of it.

It was March 18, 1968, when I left 360 Boylston Street for the last time and headed home with a sense of mission. Home was now a small apartment in Cambridge, the benefit of frugality and the small raise I had received while employed in the secretarial school.

I'd been down this path before—well not *this* path, but that energy burst sure felt familiar. Time and time again, in the life I had been forced to leave behind, I'd been summoned to pull the proverbial rabbit out of a hat—SAT scores, college acceptances, interviews with strangers. Failure had never been an option then, and it most certainly wouldn't be now.

Alone in my apartment, I contemplated my objective. The task was straightforward—find a new job in one day. My strategy was uncomplicated—present my credentials at the employment agency on Newberry Street, a block from where I'd been teaching. That was simple enough: the certificate awarded to me for completing the secretarial course at the Hickox School was my ticket to ride.

Sifting through my wardrobe—a neither expansive nor expensive menagerie of late 1960s "junior" fashion pieces—I searched for what might pass as a professional-looking outfit and chose a modest A-line dress in a rose-pink and tan paisley print, a suede (fake, I'm guessing) handbag, and sensible shoes.

You can do it, I reassured myself as I laid each item of my ensemble on the far side of the bed.

Then I took a cue from my Grandmother McKinley, whom I'd come to know only in the past eighteen months. Standing barely five feet tall, with her white hair coiffed to perfection, her lipstick flawlessly applied, she was never without her eight-millimeter, choker-length pearl necklace, and she carried herself with an air of sophistication and elegance that I worked hard to emulate.

What other female role models did I have? I lacked maternal advice—my mother was still a nun—and I had yet to make serious friends. I was instinctively drawn to what appeared stylish, and my grandmother represented that better than anyone in my tiny circle of "people of the world." So, I added my own pearls to the outfit—the fake ones that had cost less than $2 in Filene's Basement.

You'll have a job by tomorrow, I encouraged myself as I slipped into bed early, to be rested for the challenge of the next day. In the darkness and quiet, it suddenly dawned on me that I did indeed have a source of support—my guardian angel.

It was from my mother that I learned, when I was no more than three or four years old, that God had assigned me my very own angel right at the moment of my birth. I gave her the name of Elizabeth—my mother's name.

The image I conjured up of my guardian angel as a small child has never changed. A delicate winged beauty, she was bathed in a soft glow, her long, light brown tresses falling over a multilayered diaphanous garment. Her sandaled feet never touched the ground as she hovered around me, warding off harm—ethereal and untouchable, but very much mine.

A constant and silent companion, she was, at times, the only resource on which I could rely. Until I was about ten years old, my pleas were mostly mundane—to win a game of marbles or come first in a spelling bee. As I matured into my teenage years, the intensity and frequency of my engagements increased, in direct proportion to the summonses to Sister Catherine's office. Angelic communication was one-way—my guardian angel was voiceless like all saints in heaven, but she was not deaf—of that, I was sure.

Truth be told, I'd given my guardian angel short shrift since I was unceremoniously vaulted from my home, but alone that evening in the throes of anxiety, I reached out to her and in the most pleasing tone of voice (in my head) asked her stay by my side until I had a job. And suddenly, it felt as though there were two of us on this mission.

* * *

It was a sunny and brisk morning when I confidently walked up the half-dozen steps into the employment agency on Newberry Street. The woman at the reception desk put me at ease with her friendly smile as I explained my mission. Handing her my certificate of graduation from Hickox, I took comfort in the nodding of her head. She seemed impressed.

"Will you take a seat, and I'll be back in a minute." The tone of her voice gave me optimism, and she returned a few moments later with good news.

"I have two excellent interview opportunities for a receptionist. One is just around the corner at *The Atlantic Monthly* and the other is at Ladenburg Thalmann on Franklin Street."

The Atlantic Monthly? My heart skipped a beat. Despite my lack of sophistication on nearly all matters worldly, I knew it by name and reputation and had passed its offices countless times, as it was within a block or two of Hickox. The name held a certain allure—on occasion, I'd purchased a copy of the magazine, and came away with the impression that it appealed to intellectuals. The thought flashed through my mind—maybe it was a way out. Out of where I was and toward a path to education, to a world of cerebral stimulation. The dream of attending college was never far from my mind, but quitting full-time work was a luxury I could not afford. That didn't diminish the desire in any way.

As for the other company, I'd never heard of it, and asked what they did. "It's a brokerage firm—they buy and sell stocks and bonds."

That expression—stocks and bonds—had a peculiar ring to it, and in an instant, I was brought back to the Center of my youth. I could hear the powerful—and anti-Semitic—voice of Father Feeney as he yelled from the altar during Mass. "Filthy lucre made by greedy kikes selling bonds and stocks. They get rich robbing poor people of their money."

By the time I was a young teenager, I had learned to give little heed to Feeney's rantings, which in this case, created a faint curiosity about what that world of "stocks and bonds" was all about.

The woman at the employment agency booked me for an interview at Ladenburg Thalmann for ten o'clock. "I'll be waiting for you when you're done. Good luck." I felt reassured.

The twenty-minute brisk walk in the bracing March air—through Boston Common, past the famed golden dome of the state capitol, and then down Franklin Street—bolstered my confidence, as I entered the elegant mahogany-paneled office of the two partners, George Burden and Godfrey Birkhead. The glass-framed bookshelves and elegant Persian rugs looked like something one might expect to find in the library of a stately home.

Much of the interview itself has faded from memory, but what has remained are several mental images—the faint hand tremor and the nervous, almost giggly, laugh from the slightly hunched, patrician and soft-spoken, Mr. Burden. It was as though he wasn't quite sure how to question a nineteen-year-old girl applying for the position of reception-ist. In contrast, his counterpart, Mr. Birkhead, had a booming voice accompanied by a hearty laugh.

How long does it take to be interviewed for a job that sits at the bottom rung of the ladder? I have no recollection, but what does remain as a pleasurable memory is Mr. Burden's cordial smile as he offered me the position of receptionist for $90 a week. And could I possibly start the next day?

"Yes, Mr. Burden."

If there was a rule of etiquette associated with the process of accept-ing a job offer, I was oblivious to it. But I was far from oblivious to the exhilaration bubbling inside me. I had a job—my guardian angel had come through. OK, I had come through, but sharing success was part of the ethic of my upbringing at the Center. My guardian angel deserved her credit as well.

In a flash, *The Atlantic Monthly* position faded into the background.

And thus began my career on Wall Street in March 1968. It may have been the first rung on the ladder, but in my mind, it was a giant step—a real job in the big, real world.

CHAPTER 6

Lessons in Grace from Sister Ann Mary

1966

E xhilarated—that was the best way to describe me. I had a new job—a real job, as I thought of it—a position I'd earned on my own. The state of euphoria brought me back to particular moments during my youth at the Center—those rare Sunday mornings when Sister Catherine would make an announcement as we ate breakfast in silence.

"There will be a community meeting in the living room starting right at ten thirty."

Those two words, "community meeting," were all I lived for. They meant that for forty-five minutes each of the twelve families at the Center would be allowed to spend time together—just parents and children. Brother James Aloysius and Sister Elizabeth Ann would always be seated side by side and engaged in conversation when the five of us arrived. Then, for the next blissful three-quarters of an hour, we'd be the Walsh family. It was a time to hug and kiss and share whatever was going on in our lives—but only the good things, because those minutes had to be happy ones.

My new position—as a receptionist—felt like the first inkling of success, and with it came a powerful sense of elation.

* * *

Nine months in secretarial school had provided me with the requisite skills for the position of receptionist, but it would be years before I had the sophistication and maturity to appreciate the other assets that I was bringing to the position.

As human beings, we are the product of our upbringing, wittingly or not. Experiences in our formative years—both those that we delight in recalling for decades and those we wish had never happened—influence how we approach life as adults. The people who shape our young lives—be they teachers, parents, or others in positions of power—leave their mark on us, for good or for bad.

At the Center, there were two members of the community—both women—who had an outsized impact on my life. Not surprisingly, one was Sister Catherine—she signified power and domination, and I feared her. The other was Sister Ann Mary, the Radcliffe-educated teacher whom Sister Catherine had appointed as the principal of our school. She manifested dignified sagacity and temperance, and I relished her counsel and took it to heart.

"Modulate your voice, dear," she would say when I'd get frazzled. "Don't let others see you rattled."

In the classroom, she would insert bits of wisdom throughout our lessons. "I want to hear beautiful diction from each of you. We must enunciate clearly, and we must speak pleasantly." "People can tell a lot about you from your manners and your diction." "Respect your elders; they know a lot more than you do." "Speak with a smile on your face. You'll get so much more accomplished."

Sister Ann Mary lived by the rules she taught—seldom raising her voice and delivering her guidance with perfect inflection, a heartwarming smile and genuine grace. She was an optimist, as only a great teacher can be, caring more about her students' efforts than their actual grades. She made me try harder, as I never wanted to let her down.

In my final days at the Center, with my impending eviction looming, Sister Ann Mary sought me out and ushered me into one of our small classrooms. She had been one of the few whom Sister Catherine let in on the secret of my expulsion. Even my siblings were unaware that I was about to be sent away.

Closing the door behind us, she spoke to me in the dulcet tone that was her hallmark. "You will go far, dear, because you have such intelligence and wonderful common sense. You have the best of Brother James Aloysius and Sister Elizabeth Ann"—referring to my parents. She spoke no harsh words about the evils of the world, nor did she imply that I was in any way a reprobate. She became my inspiration, and I saw her as a sophisticated woman who was making no judgments about me. Her words stayed with me, and to this day, I remain deeply grateful to her.

Long after I had reached the peak of my career, I would continue to visit her at least annually at the Center, and she never ceased to impress me with her humility, her erudition, and her enduring quiet leadership. When she died in 2019 at the age of ninety-eight, I softly wept. Throughout my childhood, and especially during my teenage years, no one had done more than Sister Ann Mary to offer me guidance and to exemplify the cardinal rules of decorum, grace and professionalism.

At the other end of the role model spectrum was the omnipotent Sister Catherine, who founded the Center and single-handedly controlled every aspect of life there—from how money was spent, to what roles were assigned to the men, women, and children, to what we ate and what we wore. All authority emanated from her, and there was no second-in-command. Her word was law, and she never gave any indication of having second thoughts regarding her vision her ambitions or the means to her end, which was the perpetuation of a community dedicated to the cause of "no salvation outside the Catholic Church."

During the decades of the 1950s and 1960s, the world was run by men—be it in business, finance, government, medicine, or science.

Within our community, however, Sister Catherine broke that mold. A nearly six-foot-tall woman, she epitomized power—she strode rather than walked, her green eyes surveying and analyzing everything that surrounded her. She ruled by decree, and no one within our community, not even Father, had the courage to stand up to her.

When she expelled me from the Center at the age of seventeen, it was without consulting my parents and without an invitation to return. She never reached out to me again, despite being my godmother. I've sometimes wondered in the decades since she banished me if she would have found satisfaction should I have been felled by some tragedy in my early years out on my own. Would she have viewed it as proof positive that God was punishing me for abandoning my religious vocation—a vocation in name only, given that she usurped God's role by telling me time and time again that God had selected me to lead a life of religious celibacy.

As I put my toe into the male-dominated world of business and finance, I must assume that those two women informed my unconscious. Each in her own way was a powerful influence. From Sister Ann Mary, I learned decorum, how to engage with my elders, to work collaboratively, and to think before I spoke. She proffered guidance that resonated with my yearning to succeed.

What I learned from Sister Catherine was of a different nature, and it was only with the writing of this book that it became evident to me. Throughout my childhood, it had been my fervent desire to please her and thus to be loved by her and to make her proud of me. After all, she was the only person at the Center who was allowed to dispense love or show affection. I failed on all those scores, and as a result, I lived in constant fear of her. But what I gleaned from her—subconsciously—was that being a woman was no obstacle to success. In that regard, she was a powerful role model. Despite my own status as a neophyte in the world of business, I felt unencumbered by my gender.

CHAPTER 7

The First Rung on the Ladder

1 9 6 8

I was dressed to impress on the first day at my new job—cork platform shoes, a gray miniskirt topped with a white cable-knit turtleneck. My hair, long and straight, made it all the way to my waist. As I stepped off the elevator a full thirty minutes before the office opened, it became apparent that there was no one to impress. The foyer was pitch black, except for a sliver of triangular light that pierced the darkness, emanating from a partially opened door into a windowed office. I felt along the wall for a switch, turned on the lights, and settled at my desk with a sense of responsibility.

In my optimistic and youthful mind, I relished the idea that I was starting a brand-new life. What had come before was history, albeit a secret one, and I prayed that I wouldn't inadvertently let others know about it.

I was bursting with enthusiasm and dying to prove myself in my new position. I would challenge my ability to be the finest receptionist in the world, despite not fully knowing what the job entailed.

In addition to the two partners who had hired me and who shared a spacious office, there was a handful of brokers, each with his own clients, a trader who executed the buy and sell orders, and only one other woman, the secretary to the partners. In short order, I became everyone's "Gal Friday."

"I'm happy to get your lunches," I told the brokers, when they asked me timidly if I might do them that favor. They were busy, and I was available—and thus I did it every day, and as the office expanded, so did the list of sandwiches.

"Let me copy that for you," I offered, as one broker headed to the Xerox machine.

"I need twenty copies," he said almost apologetically.

"No problem, I can manage it."

In 1968, collation was not yet an option on copying machines, so I set up a table adjacent to the machine and as the first twenty copies of page one rolled into a tray, I placed them face down, side by side, building up the piles as the remaining copies were printed. By the time the last sheet was printed, the project was fully collated, and all I had to do was staple twenty times. Not an intellectually stimulating project, for sure, but I took pleasure in keeping up with the machine.

A broker was bemoaning that his telephone needed to be moved. "Let me try," I volunteered, and armed with a small screwdriver, I was his hero in about four minutes. From that day on, I was the office's go-to telephone repair girl.

Keeping active was the best antidote to boredom, and I engaged with passion, to the point of knowing the voice of every customer who called—all of whom were men, many of whom had little patience.

"Gimme Teddy" were the only words I ever heard from one man.

I wanted to say, "It would be nice if you said, 'Good morning,' or 'Please,'" but I'd hold my tongue and reply, "I'll put you through to him right now." I never laid eyes on the man, but in my imagination, I crafted an image of what a rude man looked like.

A regular customer called one day and lit into me because I had taken too long to answer the phone. I responded, "I'm sorry, but I was with another customer, and I couldn't cut him off."

I surprised myself with my boldness, and when he responded petulantly with, "Do you know who I am?" I said, "Yes, Mr. King." A brief silence ensued, and I smiled to myself. The caller was Ed King, then the executive director of the Massachusetts Port Authority. Ten years later, he would become the governor of Massachusetts.

I put the incident out of my head. There was no use getting upset with irksome or even irate customers, and more to the point, I knew that he knew that I was in the right, which provided its own satisfaction.

Months later, as Christmas was nearing, a messenger stepped off the elevator carrying two packages, which he put on my desk and quickly disappeared back into the elevator. To my amazement, each of them was addressed to me. *Me? Who would send me something? Who even knows me?*

Birthday girl that I am, I love presents, and I could hardly wait until there was a lull in the stream of telephone calls to cut through the tape and packaging and then to discover a bottle of champagne in one box and in the other six smoky, low-ball glasses embossed in gold with the words: Massachusetts Port Authority. The accompanying note read, "I'm sorry I was rude to you. Have a Merry Christmas."

A win.

* * *

Fifty-five years ago—when I was breaking into the world of Wall Street—the internet was not even a pipe dream. Paper was the only official medium of news communication, and it came in the form of "the tape"—an endless stream of five-inch-wide reels of financial news that had the staccato chop of Morse code all day long as they were printed. The tape included thousands of bits of the most current information regarding every stock that was traded, from earnings reports to takeovers, from bankruptcies and scandals to investigations. Hour after hour, the news spilled onto the floor in ever-mounting ribbons of paper—information that was of value to someone.

Requests came in the form of a yell from a broker. "I need everything on RCA," might be one broker's request, and I'd stand in front of the "printing press" scanning what seemed like miles of paper, eyes peeled for the letters RCA.

Another might call out, "There's news coming out on Polaroid today—keep an eye out for it." That meant checking the tape every few minutes for any tidbits on the company.

There was little gentility in the demands, but that was the way of Wall Street—information was money. But before long, I came to know all the brokers' favorite stocks, and I'd cut out anything I thought might be of interest to them. They may have been brusque, but I won them over with my anticipation of their needs. In return, they'd occasionally pay for my sandwich when I returned from the deli with their lunch order. I felt the winner in that exchange.

Perhaps the most tedious chore that was assigned to me was updating what were known as S&P tear sheets—some thirty-odd three-ring binders, produced by Standard & Poor's, with a page for each stock on the NYSE, the American Stock Exchange, and the over-the-counter market (as the NASDAQ was called back then)—each of which was updated on a quarterly basis. It was a cycle of mindless substitution—replacing the old tear sheet with the new one. To ward off the boredom, I took to memorizing the symbol for every listed stock. They were filed alphabetically, so I learned them a letter at a time.

My childhood had been replete with memory lessons. Father Feeney would encourage us with one of his favorite quips. "Your memory is a muscle—you need to use it to keep it in shape," and from the altar, he would speak in Latin, *"Repetitio est mater studiorum"* (Repetition is the mother of studies). I took his coaching to heart, memorizing the entire Catholic calendar of feast days of the saints—all 365 of them.

Now as I sat at my desk, engaged in the tedious process of removing outdated pages and replacing them, I'd stare at the name at the top and its stock symbol, while reading the short paragraph that described the company's business:

Cabot Corp.	CBT
Canadian Pacific Railway	CP
Caterpillar Tractor	CAT
CBS	CBS
Chicago Bridge & Iron	CBI
Chrysler	C
Citicorp	CCC
Coca Cola	KO
Corning Glass Work	GLW

And on and on and on.

During lulls in the day, I'd head to the trading room and watch the electric ticker symbols scroll across the top of the wall. This was my test, and before long I had memorized the symbol for every stock listed on the New York Stock Exchange.

* * *

The challenge to my brain had its appeal, but as an intellectual exercise, it failed. Despite my increasing comfort with life in the world, I couldn't dismiss the gaping hole I knew I had to address—my education. I yearned for a scholastic environment, to be a student in a classroom, surrounded by fellow students and stimulated by a professor teaching philosophy, history, or French.

There was no internet on which I could do research, but one thing was certain—I had nothing close to the financial resources required to quit work and attend college. The good news was that my evenings were free—I seldom had to stay late at the office. So that summer—just as I was turning twenty years old—I researched local colleges to see which ones offered evening courses.

By the end of August, I had completed my application for enrollment at Boston State College, soon to merge into the University of Massachusetts. During my lunch hour, I took the trolley to the school and selected my four freshmen courses—English Composition, Western Civilization, Physical Science, and Introduction to Psychology, which was of particular interest, as the subject was treated with disdain in the community where I was raised.

As I walked out into the sunlight, I was rapturous. *I've done it!* I thought. *I'm in college now. I'll be learning the same things all those millions of other college students are learning. What difference does it make that I'm going at night?*

I so ached to share the good news with my parents, whom I still thought of as Brother James Aloysius and Sister Elizabeth Ann. I was sure he would be happy for me, but I didn't dare call the Center. Someone might eavesdrop on our conversation and spread the word within the community that I had renounced my faith by going to college.

With no family and no friend in whom I could confide, I did the next best thing. As I stepped off the elevator into the reception area, I walked past my desk, through the trading room, and into George Burden's office.

"Hello," he said as I bounded up to his desk.

"I'm so excited," I told him. "I've just signed up for evening courses at Boston State College." To reassure him, lest he think I was quitting my job, I added, "I won't have to leave until five o'clock. My classes all start at six."

"Wonderful," was George's reply, and still high on my own excitement, I returned to my desk. A couple of hours later, as George was leaving for the day, he stopped by my desk. "I spoke to Godfrey," he said, referring to the other office partner, "and we have agreed to reimburse you for half the cost of your coursework at the end of each semester."

His words were like a miracle. "Thank you," I replied. As the elevator door closed behind him, I thought, *Why am I always so lucky?*

The three-hour classes each evening made for a long day, but I was energized by the experience of once again being in the classroom. It was as though the day was starting again at six o'clock, as I sat in the front row and crammed my notebook with copious notes. Modern American poetry—works by Sylvia Plath, W. H. Auden, and William Carlos Williams—brought me particular pleasure and was reminiscent of my senior year in high school when we studied the eighteenth- and nineteenth-century English poets under the tutelage of Sister Mary Clare, the brilliant Radcliffe graduate who brought vitality and life into the study of English literature.

The scholastic environment enhanced the opportunity for social engagement, but seldom during the week, as my homework often took me past midnight. The intellectual excitement that came with the onset of my studies far outweighed the burden of twelve-hour days of work and school. There was nothing more intoxicating than the intellectual stimulation associated with my coursework.

*　*　*

It was six months, almost to the day, in my new job, when the lead partner, George Burden, approached me at the front desk. I was becoming used to his mannerisms, which were peculiar to the situation in which he found himself. The half-smile indicated he was in a good mood—he seldom displayed a broad one, unless the market was roaring ahead—and he was rubbing his fingers and thumb together, which told me that he was nervous. So, I waited for him to speak.

"We're so pleased with your work here," he started, "that we're raising your pay from ninety dollars to one hundred dollars a week."

I was caught off guard—a raise was the furthest thing from my mind, but I thanked him with the manners and grace I'd been taught, all the while calculating in my head—11 percent after six months was the equivalent of a 22 percent annualized increase in income. He returned to his office, while I reveled in what felt like another step in the right direction.

I have a habit of holding on to things—I keep sweaters long after they should have been thrown in the dumpster. I've kept every scholastic record from my past and every note from a professor. Where that habit came from, I don't know—could it have been a response to being raised in an environment in which nothing was my own? I don't know. But having retained every pay stub from my first jobs has been useful in telling my story half a century later.

Barely had I adjusted to my new take-home pay of $74 when George Burden called me on the intercom, asking that I come to his office. Assuming it was a matter of business, I grabbed my steno pad and a pen. As I approached his desk, he stood up and walked toward me, with that "good news" smile unfolding across his face.

"I hope you're enjoying it here," he said, and before I could respond, he continued. "This is the time of year when we give out bonuses."

That statement was foreign to me. *A bonus? For what? The employment agency never mentioned that.* And then he handed me a check for $1,500. He must have seen my astonished look because his face brightened up.

"Thank you, Mr. Burden," was all I could find to say, as I did a split-second calculation: *That's almost a third of my yearly salary!*

"You're welcome," he said, "and Merry Christmas." And then fiddling with his tie, as though embarrassed about what he was about to say, he added, "And you can call me George." I did from then on.

I was euphoric with the realization that I was wanted, and needed, and even rewarded—sentiments that still felt new. One thing felt sure—my feet were firmly on the ladder to somewhere.

CHAPTER 8

Learning to Fly

1968–1969

Even with a generous raise in pay and an astonishing bonus, I was reluctant to relinquish the frugality that was a necessary part of my daily life. Aware that I had only myself to turn to should an emergency cash need arise, I took scrupulous care to create my own rainy-day kitty, by keeping a weekly ledger of every expense incurred and how much was left in the bank at month's end.

When an unexpected windfall of $3,100 (equivalent to about $27,000 in 2023) fell into my lap from my great aunt's estate, I promptly opened an account in a savings bank and forbade myself to spend a dime of that inheritance. There was one exception—it could be a source of investment capital with which to buy stocks; that is, if I could get one of the brokers in the office to help me open an account and give me some "tips," as they seem to be called.

There was something addictive about saving—for someone who never had a piggy bank, or an allowance, or the opportunity to earn babysitting money as a teenager. Watching the cash grow, albeit in minuscule increments, brought a sense of accomplishment.

As the months went by and I didn't have to bail myself out of an unforeseen crisis, I thought of cash as a resource that would help me fulfill a childhood dream of traveling to places around the world.

Geography and arithmetic had been my favorite subjects in grade school. Perhaps it was the closeted nature of my upbringing that made me long to know how others around the world lived and dressed, the foods they ate and the names they had. The lives of the saints, a daily part of my education, also brought the outside world to life—not only did I want to visit Rome and London, but also the more esoteric places that included Avignon and Fiesole, Assisi and Beirut, Constantinople and Cairo. Of course, in post-Center life, I had added New York as a must-visit destination as well.

Now at twenty, I was desperate to convert my grand dreams of exploration into reality. One of the back-office guys from the firm's New York office arrived in Boston, and, despite his beatnik-style beard and long curly hair, I couldn't resist accepting his offer to take me to New York and to the hottest show on Broadway—*Hair*.

It was a weekend of firsts—a train from Boston to New York City; a Broadway show with a chorus of naked performers who were gyrating and singing with their arms in the air; an overnight in a sleeping bag at the guy's dingy Brooklyn apartment where I made sure there was no hint of romance; a refusal of his offer to try LSD, but a cautious first drag of marijuana, and wondering why everyone thought it was so great, when all it did was burn my throat.

By Sunday afternoon, I was on the train back to Boston. Despite the less than appealing accommodations, a spark had been lit, and I was yearning to revisit and explore "the Big Apple," as everyone seemed to call it—why, I had no idea. But my next trip, I told myself, would be to what I fantasized was the "real" New York—Manhattan, where there were fancy restaurants, and fancy stores, and fancy places like Central Park and Lincoln Center. I just had to find a fancy man to take me.

* * *

With my improved salary and monthly cash flow, I indulged in one splurge—the purchase of a used record player and a few records of the hottest rock bands of the day. For hours into the late night, sitting on the pumpkin-colored, secondhand shag rug that covered my living room floor, and with my ear no more than six inches from the spinning turntable, I played the Beatles, the Monkees, the Four Seasons, and an endless list of other groups, singing the words aloud, despite barely comprehending their meaning.

What was "Yellow Submarine" about? And "Lucy in the Sky with Diamonds"? But at that early stage of my self-education in the world of rock 'n' roll, I cared only about how I could blend into the world that everyone else took for granted.

As my social circle widened, so did invitations to parties—typical late sixties weekend affairs with thumping rock 'n' roll, flowing alcohol, and blinding strobe lights that enhanced the marijuana haze in the living room of someone's apartment in Cambridge or Boston—the ideal environment in which to hone both my dancing skills and my kissing skills. The louder the music, the better, in my mind. It prevented me from hearing questions that might lead to a slip of the tongue regarding my past life as a Feeneyite.

Sporadic dating. And the occasional glimmer of romance that generally flamed out within a few weeks was the norm. Romantic inclinations on my part had a way of being ephemeral. Was it my own doing? Was I afraid of tying myself down when my dream was to explore the world that I was just coming to know?

Perhaps it was the effect of being tossed unprepared into the world, unschooled on the societal norms regarding love and marriage, but I seldom was anxious to convert romance into more than that. Subconsciously—or was it more likely deliberately?—I'd let a relationship fizzle out by becoming bored and convincing myself that marriage with this one or that one would never work. Attending a wedding, which I did on a few occasions, was confirmation that being tied down to one person for the rest of my life was not what I wanted—at least not yet. Despite that wariness, I held a deep desire to one day have a family of my own—a husband and children who couldn't be taken away from me. In the far recesses of my mind, I envisioned a time when I would be a mother, but at the age of twenty, my dreams for the future were amorphous.

A student at the Harvard Business School was intriguing for a few months. Originally from Texas, he showed up at a Halloween party with his roommate, both dressed up as diapered babies in a supermarket cart. On our second date, he told me that he'd been in the Marines and had spent time in prison and was now getting his graduate degree. Without sharing my own bizarre childhood, I took heart that his past didn't have to define his future, and I admired his willingness to divulge his shameful—to my way of thinking—past, but I lacked the courage to follow his lead. After a few more dates, I told myself it was time to bring the relationship to an end. He was smart and driven, but intellectually vapid, and I had tired of him. After all, my raison d'etre was to complete my college education and to explore the world.

* * *

It was at a weekend cocktail party in the early months of 1969 that a young lawyer introduced himself to me. The place has faded from my memory but not the man. With red hair and eyeglasses, he wasn't a knockout, but there was something about his outstretched hand as he greeted me—a gesture almost too old-fashioned for the hippie-dominated culture of the late 1960s—that I found appealing. *He's a gentleman*, was my thought.

As if to break the awkward first engagement, I asked him where he worked, to which he replied, "Hill & Barlow," as though I should be familiar with the firm. I wasn't and was thus too unsophisticated to be impressed with his reply, but I could sense a level of worldliness that was far beyond that of the Friday night party crowd that increasingly bored me.

When he, in turn, asked about my work, I silently chastised myself. *Why didn't you keep your mouth shut?* I thought, as I tried my best to dance around the fact that I was going to college in the evening, rather than full-time, as was the norm. He seemed unfazed, and before the evening was over, he had asked, and I had accepted, an invitation to dinner that weekend.

"I'll pick you up in my car," he offered. That was a first. I was used to meeting friends or going on a date at a prearranged restaurant. No one had ever come to get me. *What royal treatment*, I thought, as I willingly gave him my address.

If he meant to impress with his sporty convertible, he was successful. As we drove through the streets of Cambridge, my hair was caught by the wind in the chilly open air. What a far cry from my New Year's Eve experience in Copley Square, barely a year earlier!

Over a scrumptious dinner, during which he happily dominated the conversation, and I willingly let him, I created a picture of my date— much like putting together a jigsaw puzzle—from his vocabulary, his accent (or rather his non-accent), and his exquisite manners. When he responded to my question about where he went to college—Williams College and UVA for law school—I concluded that his pedigree far outshone mine. *What does he see in me?* I wondered, and was flattered when he asked me out again, and then again.

There seemed no end to his graciousness—we skied together in Vermont on weekends at a lodge he shared with a pack of his friends, mostly couples either married or lovers. The sleeping accommodation was one room per couple, so there we were together, a tight squeeze in a not very wide bed. I appreciated that there was no expected quid pro quo on his part for bringing me as his weekend date. I wished deeply that I could find him romantic, but it wasn't happening.

His words at one memorable dinner still come back to me. The setting was intimate—a French restaurant in the tony Back Bay section of Boston. In the soft light that flickered from a candle, he asked about my life, my job, my schooling. Then unexpectedly, he changed the subject. "I'd be happy to pay for all your courses until you finish your education."

I was taken aback. *He really cares about me.* I had never met anyone like him, and to this day, I can relive the sentiment that came over me—that feeling of being wanted for nothing more than the person I was. I had no response—I couldn't thank him because I knew I couldn't accept his offer. The romance was one-sided. If I had been able to make the emotional commitment, I would willingly have become his girlfriend and availed myself of his generosity. But the chemistry simply was not there for me.

In the late spring, he took me to visit his parents in the Pennsylvania countryside, on a property that included an orchid greenhouse where his mother spent much of her day. It was almost too perfect. I loved the idea of this man, just a few years older than I was, taking such an interest in me, but I knew we couldn't go on this way much longer.

* * *

On a bright and balmy early summer evening in June, he brought me, as his date, to a dinner dance at the prestigious Eastern Yacht Club in Marblehead. Was he offering me, unwittingly or perhaps knowingly, a glimpse of the life we might enjoy were we a married couple?

He had friends—lots of them it seemed—and, cocktail in his hand, was engaged in animated conversation with people who lived a life I had yet to experience. For my part, with my own gin and tonic, I was no longer a fish out of water. While it would be many years before his way of life would become mine, I moved effortlessly among a crowd that epitomized sophistication, basking in a new world—all thanks to the man whom I admired but with whom I was unable to fall in love.

The sun was slowly setting in the west. Turning my back to the harbor and the glorious array of boats at their moorings, I nearly collided with a man who was blocking my way to the bar and the replenishment of my gin and tonic.

"Hi," he said, "I'm Josh. Who are you?" It was evident he could tell this wasn't my home turf. The tanned face looking down at me was smiling, and as our eyes met, my heart nearly stopped. Who was this Adonis in the blue blazer, white chinos, and sockless feet in penny loafers?

I introduced myself. "Where do you live?" he wanted to know. "And what do you do?" I told him in the vaguest of terms. When he asked whom I was with, I shared that too. His rapid-fire questioning as we sipped our cocktails felt more like a dance than an inquisition. And I wanted to dance, physically and metaphorically.

In no time, he was introducing me to his friends, as though I was *his* date for the evening. But he'd forgotten my name, and cool dude that he was, he simply made up one. When I quietly pointed out his error, he laughed aloud, and that was the magic that sealed our fate.

As the evening was coming to a close and I was preparing to leave with my lawyer date—who would deposit me safely back at my apartment in Cambridge before returning to his house in Marblehead—my newfound interest sought me out. I didn't dare look him in the eye, as he said softly, "Meet me at Logan Airport tomorrow morning at nine."

"OK," I said. And I did. Together, we flew to Long Island.

It was the start of a rollercoaster ride—a romance that swept me off my feet and brought out the wild in me, which suited us both. We were a great match. He would appear and reappear in my life for decades to come, while the gentleman lawyer faded into the past.

* * *

At a Friday night bash in early August, I signed up for a group trip to the Woodstock Festival. *Why not?* I thought. It was being touted as the biggest concert in the history of the world, and I reasoned, in a moment of utter madness, that it would be a fabulous way to celebrate my twenty-first birthday. The who's who of music would be there— Jimi Hendrix, Joan Baez, Jefferson Airplane, Janis Joplin, and hundreds more.

Buried in the far recesses of my mind were the questions I was deliberately ignoring, despite daily reports on television that were providing the answers: there were no hotels, motels, or even shacks; toilet facilities were grossly inadequate; and there was no running water. Day by day, the number of expected attendees grew—from 50,000, which I thought had to be exaggerated, to an estimated 200,000 people.

Then, on August 9, a week before our departure for Woodstock, the shocking news was blasted across the country and the world—Charles Manson, leading his cult of teenage girls—had gruesomely stabbed to death the eight-month pregnant Sharon Tate and the friends staying with her in her home in Beverly Hills.

My already waning appetite for the adventure of Woodstock evaporated with that news. Visions of the Boston Strangler, the notorious murderer in my hometown a few years earlier, and Richard Speck who had murdered eight student nurses in Chicago in 1966, brought nightmares. "Let's not go," I recommended to the group, but I was the lone wimp. No one else seemed fazed.

In the end, I was saved by the weather forecast, which called for torrential rain and mudslides. I begged off, forfeiting whatever money I had put down. Camping had never been my thing—I liked the comfort of my own bed and a warm shower.

When reports of the Woodstock phenomenon filled the evening news, showing nearly half a million attendees sloshing together in a sea of mud as the heavens opened up on them for days on end, I congratulated myself on my pragmatism, even if it did deprive me of a wild setting for celebrating my twenty-first birthday. But the party girl in me found a way to get invited to a summer weekend bash on the Cape, one that left me with a much-deserved hangover.

Now, some fifty-five years later, I admit that there is a small part of me that wishes I could tell my children and grandchildren that I had been part of that phenomenon called Woodstock.

For a girl who found the counterculture of the late 1960s not to her taste, I did my fair share of dancing at its periphery, soaking up the marijuana haze at weekend parties, reveling in the freedoms that were part of the avant-garde baby boomers, notably the ability to shun the world of marriage and children.

Was I influenced in this matter by my own upbringing? Did I realize the counterculture nature of the community in which I was raised, where, on a daily basis, we were proud to be as we claimed, "contra mundum" (against the world)? Where our favorite slogan was, from the New Testament Epistle of James, "I have fought the good fight"? Those words were the lifeblood of our mission at the Center, and under the leadership of Leonard Feeney and Catherine Clarke, we stood ready to die for the dogma: no salvation outside the Catholic Church. That "we" did not include me. I felt like the lone, but necessarily silent, dissenter, a traitor to the cause. The pragmatist in me could find no logic for the case that we—one hundred people in a world of some three billion people—were the only souls that would get to heaven when we died.

As I approached my twenty-first birthday, I didn't yet have the sophistication to grasp that I, too, had been brought up on the fringe of society. Now, half a century later, clarity emerges. The seeds of my own path to independence were likely sown early in my childhood. When it came to physical danger, I was a wimp. On the other hand, I was an intellectual rebel, the product, no doubt, of my parents and my upbringing.

CHAPTER 9

Hard Landing

1969

"Down seven points!"

The gasp came from senior partner George Burden as the two of us stood side by side, our eyes glued to the stock market tape running across the far wall of the trading room. It was a solid sea of red—the telltale indication that stock prices were falling. Not a green uptick among them. On Wall Street, they called it a bloodbath.

A pin-drop moment might have been the way to describe the scene in what was normally a raucous trading room, with brokers yelling—even screaming—orders to buy and sell stocks. The tension was palpable as those brokers now stood in silence. From the corner of my eye, I glanced at George's hands—they were shaking as he rubbed his fingertips together.

I did a quick calculation—seven points was a bit more than 1 percent. *Wow*, I thought, *it's fallen a whole percent in just an hour.* I didn't dare extrapolate that trend for a day, much less for a week or a month.

This was how 1969 opened—a far cry from the bull market of the year before.

The Dow was, at that time, the bellwether index for the US stock market—a time when the country's economy was fueled by manufacturing giants that included General Motors, Goodyear Tire and Rubber, International Harvester, and Bethlehem Steel. The Dow had peaked at close to 1,000 points at the end of 1965 and was hovering around that level when I joined Ladenburg Thalmann a little over two years later, although there had been a marked increase in its volatility.

The postwar decades of the fifties and sixties had been robust years for the US economy, and for nearly twenty years, the stock market had reflected a sense of economic euphoria. By the midsixties, however, the environment had changed, as the increasing financial and human capital expended on the unpopular and unsuccessful war in Vietnam led to rising inflation and growing social unrest.

The highflying stocks of the prior decade had been dubbed "the Nifty Fifty." They included Avon, General Electric, Merck, and Disney, as well as plenty of now-defunct companies such as Polaroid, Kresge, Simplicity Pattern, Control Data, Teledyne, University Computing, LTV, and more.

The combination of the inheritance from my great aunt and my bonus check was the impetus for me to explore making an investment in stocks—but which ones? I queried an elderly broker about what tips he had for me if I wanted to buy a stock. He seemed more than happy to offer his advice and strongly recommended Commonwealth United Entertainment, a company about which I knew nothing and that was far from a household name.

Thus, my first foray into the world of investing was based on trust—a purchase of fifty shares of the stock for a total of $1,210.69. In a matter of a week or two, my investment was in the red. Uncertain about what to do, I went back to the elderly broker who had displayed an air of wisdom. "What should I do with my stock?" was my plaintiff query. The shrug of his shoulders told me all I needed to know—I was on my own.

Fearful that I might lose all my money, I sold the stock a mere three months after purchasing it and incurred a loss of more than $300. Welcome to the world of investing.

The experience was painful but not enough to kill my appetite. Over the next few weeks and months, I talked to other brokers in the office. Each was ready to offer ideas, and I put my toe back into the water—not always with success, but I'd been bitten by the investment bug. My portfolio was anything but sophisticated, replete with names of now long-defunct companies like Riker-Maxson and Computer Learning Systems.

Trading was expensive—commissions were 2 to 3 percent on each trade, and that was with the discount I got for being an employee. Before long, I had my own small portfolio of stocks—an array of ideas I'd solicited from the now growing team of brokers in the firm. With a turbulent market, my performance was far from stellar, but I was learning—learning to pick up the pieces and try again if I made a mistake.

Investing made me feel like more than just the receptionist, and I wondered about becoming a broker. Convinced that I could pass the exam, I approached George Burden to get his permission. The worst that could happen was that he'd say no.

"I'd like to apply for my license as a New York Stock Exchange broker," I said. "I'll study hard, and I'm sure I can pass."

George, as though not to dampen my perpetual enthusiasm, responded with a cheerful yes. "I'm sure you will pass."

And so it was that I took a first step in the right direction for a girl who was destined to be buying and selling stocks for the next fifty years. During the next few weeks, I studied feverishly and felt confident on exam day. My memory of the exam itself has faded, but the notice I received some weeks later is clear. I was now a licensed stockbroker, at the age of twenty-one.

CHAPTER 10

The Five-Million-Dollar Challenge

1969

George was once again standing in front of my desk. Guessing what he wanted was a game I was learning to play well. If he hesitated before starting to speak, I knew the matter was important to him.

"Umm, would you please come to my office?" he asked in the reserved and respectful way that was his nature.

Following him as he shuffled through the trading room, I wondered what it might be this time. I was his go-to person for an array of matters unrelated to the business of finance—a true Gal Friday—a role quite different from the one played by his personable secretary.

Had the light bulb in his lamp burned out once again? I wondered. *Or had his multibuttoned telephone gone on the blink, and he knew I could jiggle a few things and get it working again? Or perhaps he wanted to discuss a present for his wife?* It floored and flattered me that this mature and proper businessman valued the opinion of a twenty-year-old on such a personal matter, and it gave me a growing sense of confidence that I must be assimilating myself pretty well into the real world.

"We're closing a deal in a couple of days," he started, once he'd sat down and I was standing in front of his desk, "and we'd like you to go to New York and collect five million dollars, from five separate investors. Would you be willing to do that?"

His almost fragile smile, I had come to recognize, was his way of saying please.

My response was instantaneous—of course I would. It didn't trouble me that I wasn't quite sure what a "deal" was. I was still on a steep learning curve about stocks, stock symbols, the electronic "tape" that ran endlessly around the perimeter of the trading room, and the scads of ticker tape I had to sort through for an array of brokers.

George gave me no time to rethink my answer and presented me with all that was needed for the assignment—a ticket from Boston to New York on the Eastern Shuttle, the names and addresses of the individuals I was to meet, the last of whom was north of the city in Westchester County, and a return plane ticket to Boston. Almost as an afterthought he said, "The limousine driver will meet you as you exit the airplane. Do you have any questions?"

Limousine driver? Not a taxi? My mind drifted but came back in time to say, with confidence, "I've got it."

"We'll be here whenever you get back tomorrow evening," were his farewell words.

The surge of excitement brought me back to a time some three years earlier, when I'd been called upon by Sister Catherine to apply to Vassar College and Bates College. Not that she had any intention of allowing me to attend either college upon my graduation from high school. Rather, she was responding to criticisms from anti-Feeneyites who argued that our education within the cult was not on a par with what was offered at the local public school.

Sister Catherine needed an impressive rebuttal, and I was her ammunition. It was a challenge—an opportunity to prove myself, to shine, and maybe to be in her good graces for a few days. I fulfilled my duty by being accepted at both colleges. In short order, our tiny school received its accreditation from the State of Massachusetts.

Now, again, I was being asked to take on a task—a significant one, it seemed to me—and I relished the challenge. I also appreciated the trust that the partners—George and Godfrey—were putting in me.

That evening, I picked out my dress—the same one I'd worn for my interview just a year earlier. The tan and soft-pink paisley, bias-cut, long-sleeve dress fitted the bill. It was stylish but not overly so. Paired with my fake pearls, cream handbag, and matching high-heeled shoes, it seemed appropriate for a trip to New York.

I could hardly sleep. *My second trip to New York. A limousine. Five checks for one million dollars?*

It went like clockwork—the flight, the driver, the long limousine ride through the narrow streets of lower Manhattan, the stares that came my way as I exited in my pretty-close-to-miniskirt and five-inch heels. Did I have lunch? I have no recollection, but by early afternoon, I had four of the five checks—a total of $4 million—securely zipped inside a pocket of my handbag.

The drive to Westchester for the last meeting of the day took me on winding lanes that ran through bucolic countryside—reminiscent of the town of Still River, where I'd grown up. But the houses in this town were mansions, far more elegant than the colonial-style farmhouses of my hometown, and an introduction to a side of life I had yet to encounter.

A long tree-lined driveway led up to the sprawling stucco house of Mr. Rosenberg, my final stop of the day. As I stepped out of the limousine and took the few steps to the elegant front door, it opened, as though I was expected. Mr. Rosenberg, a slender and refined elderly man, supported by an attendant, greeted me.

"Come in," he said as though I were a friend. "Please join me for tea."

I couldn't resist the invitation. Afternoon tea brought back fond memories of those Thursday afternoon tea parties at the Center. Hosted by Sister Catherine, they were intended as a lesson in manners, but they offered a blissful half hour when I had the pleasure of serving tea and cookies to my parents.

Mr. Rosenberg was garrulous and spent much of our time together educating me on the history of his house. When he inquired about my interests, I froze for a moment, before gaining my composure and providing innocuous responses, all the while beseeching my guardian angel and the whole court of Heaven not to let him ask me about where I grew up. I'd have had to lie if he did—I couldn't let this charming Jewish gentleman find out that I was a Feeneyite.

My inward gasps of prayer were answered. When we had exhausted our pleasantries, Mr. Rosenberg produced the certified check for $1 million, and with a chuckle, he said, "Now don't lose it, honey."

I gave him my word and tucked the precious cargo into the zippered compartment in my handbag, where it brought the total of my day's collection to $5 million.

As the limousine took me on the final leg of my trip—back to LaGuardia for the flight to Boston—I tried to imagine what that much money could buy. What kind of a "deal" was it that needed five million bucks?

Once in the air, I furtively removed the five certified checks from their hiding place. Six zeros—I stared at each one of them. I'd never even seen $10,000, much less $1 million. Fingering them allowed me to lapse into a moment of reverie—what if these $5 million were my own money? I'd be rich and could buy anything I wanted in the entire world.

The plane touched down at Logan Airport and brought me out of my daydreams. Half an hour later, I was in George Burden's office, my heart beating a bit harder than normal as I handed over the $5 million. This was 1968, eons before the advent of cell phones, much less the ability to send a text message. We'd been out of contact for a full day.

His elation was almost childlike—had he been worried that I might fall down on the job? He'd put his trust in a twenty-year-old receptionist who'd been at the firm for just a year, and I hadn't let him down. I'd expected that much of myself, but it was gratifying to observe his pleasure. If this was a test, I had just gotten an A+.

"Let's celebrate," he said with the wide smile that he seldom shared. "I've made a reservation at the Ritz-Carlton. Godfrey will join us."

I seldom went to restaurants because frugality was an essential part of my life on a receptionist's salary, and something of the grandeur and scale of the Ritz dining room was far beyond my means.

"Order whatever you'd like," George said, as he sipped his martini. The pleasure in his voice was more congratulatory than I expected or needed.

As we ate and chatted, I took note of my surroundings—the blue-domed ceiling edged in gold leaf and the magnificent chandelier that hung from its crown, the wall sconces, the elegant place settings, the blue velvet seat covers and chair backs, the white-gloved service, and the exquisite French cuisine.

So, this is how the partners live, I thought.

In the quiet of my apartment later that night, as I relived the events of that day, I could not help but envision how far removed that life was from the role of receptionist.

My quest for a college degree was becoming increasingly urgent.

CHAPTER 11

Nightmare

1969

W ith a new spring in my step, I headed to the office the next morning, carrying the sixth sense that there would be more opportunities to prove myself.

Despite the volatility in the stock market, the office seemed to be thriving—to judge by the expanded space and the growing number of brokers. One, in particular, seemed to outrank the others—he'd been offered a large corner office and brought two secretaries, while the rest of the team shared support staff. I welcomed the new staff of young women close to my age. Until they arrived, I'd been the only person in the office under the age of twenty-five. My days may have been crammed with the hectic nature of buying and selling stocks, but there was always time for a bit of small talk with the two new secretaries.

The broker looked to be in his forties—with a bit of a paunch and dark-rimmed glasses that had lenses so thick they made his eyes look small. What he lacked in physical appeal, he seemed to make up for with a jolly sense of Irish humor. His desk was arrayed with pictures of his children; someone said he was on his third wife.

Our paths didn't cross much except when he used the elevator that was just feet from the reception desk. From time to time, he'd invite the secretaries in the office out for an after-work drink. Those excursions mostly excluded me unless it was Friday—college classwork absorbed four evenings each week. Such was the price I happily paid to earn my degree.

One afternoon in early summer, he stopped by my desk as he was about to head down the elevator. "Want to have a drink at five?"

I was taking an evening course in political philosophy at the Phillips Brooks School at Harvard that started at six o'clock. "Sure," I replied, in the way that New Englanders say it—as an "OK, I guess so." I adored this course, given by Professor Riley, the prototypical professor who had little in the way of interpersonal skills but was a genius at the podium. There was no way I would allow myself to be late for the class, so my acquiescence was tempered by the understanding it would have to be a quick one.

"Meet me at the Nines," he said, referring to The 99 Club, a popular hangout for people who worked in the world of finance, from traders to salesmen to brokers and often a gaggle of young receptionists, secretaries, and the rare female stock trader. Given my coursework, I hardly frequented the place except on the occasional Friday, when I could take part in the end-of-week drinking ritual—a raucous affair that tended to last too long and result in a well-deserved headache the following morning.

Promptly at five o'clock, I walked into the Nines, which was eerily quiet. The drinking hour was still thirty or so minutes away. Fine with me—it would make for quick service and a fast exit. The broker sat at the bar, wearing a broad grin as he chatted with the bartender. Two drinks sat on the bar—each in a large martini glass. I didn't drink martinis, but that didn't mean I wasn't willing to try.

I tried it—or did I? I must have, but I have no recollection of that or of anything beyond seeing the two men in a jolly mood and the two cocktails on the bar. That much is clearly memorable. Nothing else.

I awoke in the darkness of my bedroom, unaware of the time. I was on my back, and I was naked—that was not the way I slept. I lay motionless, stunned and trying to grasp the situation.

Am I awake? Is this a dream? Why am I naked? What time is it?

I became aware of pain. And then a motion as though something bumped the bed. Terrified, I let my eyes glide slowly to the left without moving my head. It took a few moments to become accustomed to the darkness around me. In the black that slowly turned to gray, I was able to make out the shape of a figure—his back was to me. Slowly, silently, he was moving. My eyes, now adjusted to the lightless room, allowed me to watch as he dressed himself. I couldn't see his face.

He turned as he brought his eyeglasses to his face, and in an instant, I realized that this was no dream. The man was the broker who'd invited me for a drink. As I stared in horror, he stealthily picked up his shoes in his left hand and tiptoed out of my bedroom into the living room. A moment later, the door clicked shut behind him.

I lay on my back as though paralyzed—for how long I don't know—while trying to re-create the events of the evening, but I couldn't remember a thing. It was clear to me that I had never gone to class, which for me was equivalent to a mortal sin. Something happened, but I couldn't put the pieces together.

My mind was in turmoil. I started to blame myself—but for what? *How did this happen? How did I let it happen? But…what happened?*

By dawn, I was no longer in a fog, but I was no clearer about what had transpired before I awoke. All I knew was that I needed to get up and get dressed and be at my desk before nine o'clock. The clothes I had worn to work the day before lay strewn on the floor, and the sight of them made me cringe—it looked like the crime scene it was. I left them there.

Questions turned over and over in my head. *How did he do it? Why didn't I wake up? How did he know my address?*

Still in shock, I rose, showered, and washed my hair—almost as an act of exorcism. Then I dressed for the day, trying to put behind me the grotesqueness of the night. The tortured feeling that was gripping my insides had a familiar ring to it—one that used to come over me when I was in trouble. It was a sensation of being powerless. There was no one to help me, no one to whom I could turn.

My only recourse was to soldier on, and that's what I did. Leaving the apartment, I walked the six or seven minutes to Harvard Square, took the Red Line to Park Street Station and walked another five minutes to my office. I was sitting at my desk before nine o'clock.

When will he arrive? The thought nauseated me. I wanted to hide—to extinguish my shame and embarrassment. The elevator made the whirring sound—it was coming up. I grabbed the phone as if to make a call as he stepped off the elevator and strode past me without his habitual good morning. That was good. He knew I knew—and he knew he would get away with it.

I wanted to kill him—stab him in the heart—watch him die. To scream out to everyone what he'd done. But deep inside me, I knew that wasn't how it worked—he was the big producer, and I was the pretty receptionist at the front desk who wore miniskirts.

Sister Catherine had been right. Her enigmatic words—ones she had repeated over and over—now rang in my head, "Don't ever let yourself be alone with a man. Terrible things can happen."

But she had never explained what those terrible things were. There had been no need to share them with me because she had determined that my destiny was to be the Bride of Christ.

Now I had another secret that, once again, I dared not share with anyone. But as the day wore on, I decided to reach out to one person—Annabel, one of his secretaries, an English gal who had become a good friend. She worked in a little cubby, a bit removed from the hustle and bustle of the office. The words spilled out—whispering what I knew and what I didn't know.

It was then that she let me in on her own secret—he had tried to rape her one evening when he offered her a ride home. In that moment, we went from being chums to bonding together emotionally. She was luckier than I, but she'd nonetheless been traumatized.

Next, I did what I had to do to survive. I buried that dreadful night as far back in the recesses of my mind as I could. Nothing was to be gained by dwelling on it—that's what I told myself. *Don't be his victim. Move on as though last night never happened.* I also vowed to myself that nothing like that would ever happen again. Vigilance became the armor that would protect me.

Decades passed before I found the courage to share the events of that night with my parents and my sisters. I thought my experience was perhaps one in a million, or even less than that, at least in this country. My naïveté was shattered in 2014 when the allegations about Bill Cosby came to light. It was only then that I faced the reality that date rape— or in my case invitation-for-one-drink rape—had a long and evil history. Then with the subsequent exposure of Harvey Weinstein's deplorable behavior and a seemingly unending list of powerful men abusing (mostly) young women, I became less ashamed of sharing my story, of adding my voice to those millions—yes, millions—of young women who have been subjected to the ignominy of rape.

* * *

A few weeks later, George called me into his office, and once again, I was unprepared for what was to come. It was a promotion—to the role of secretary from receptionist. He had recently hired a stock analyst— not a broker, mind you, but someone who did in-depth research that would appeal to the powerful mutual fund portfolio managers who ran billions of dollars in Boston. I acknowledged my appreciation and was smiling both inside and out. It was a relief to escape the reception area where I had to confront, often several times a day, the man who had drugged and assaulted me. Now I would be at the opposite end of the office suite, between George's office and that of my new boss.

Another step forward and I was excited about this new responsibility, and curious to find out where it might lead me.

CHAPTER 12

Thank You, Edwin

1969–1971

By the twenty-first century, the word secretary had all but disappeared from the American lexicon, supplanted with titles such as administrative assistant or even the acronym PA (i.e., personal assistant, although it could perhaps be better noted as professional assistant). Gone were the days when a boss might ask his PA to pick up a package for his wife at Bloomingdale's. Nowadays, the term secretary seems antiquated.

There are no more secretarial schools, as such. The two key component skills for a traditional secretary—typing and shorthand—are no longer relevant. Children today learn to type by the time they're entering middle school, and there is no longer any need to dictate a letter, either because the administrative assistant is capable of drafting such letter or because executives use the technology of the day, transcribing voice to word.

However, as recently as a handful of decades ago, the position of secretary was often a full life's career. A good secretary was an invaluable asset for a businessperson—admittedly, the preponderance of them were men—and a good man took care to treat his secretary with respect and good pay. She often held the keys to his own success.

That said, the roles that each played were vastly different. It was an *Upstairs, Downstairs* arrangement, regardless of its duration—unless, of course, the relationship made the metamorphosis to a romantic one, and the secretary became wife, with all the repercussions of *sturm und drang* that came with such a transition. My story, however, has no such trajectory.

The promotion to secretary in the summer of 1969 brought that same excitement I had brought to the role of receptionist. The added thrill was the prestige of working for a single person, rather than a gaggle of brokers, and the added benefit was my new space—a cozy cubicle not more than ten feet by eight feet but sharing the same mahogany wood-paneled walls and bookcases that the partners had.

Edwin Taff was now my boss. A recently hired graduate from the Harvard Business School, he came to our firm by way of IBM. Ed stood out from the ranks of the brokers with his exquisitely tailored navy-blue suits—even my as-yet untrained eye was impressed with how his wardrobe defined him. He was conservatively fashionable in a way that caught one's eye. He seemed to me reserved and yet engaged as I observed him from my secretary's desk. His demeanor was the same, whether he was conversing with one of the staff or the partners. I felt honored to be his secretary.

He was a far cry from the ever-expanding team of stockbrokers who spent their days with their jackets off, barking buy and sell orders at the trading desk. That was how they earned their income—every trade meant dollars in their pockets. But Ed was different. Even when he shed his jacket, which wasn't often, he had the air of professionalism—a crisply ironed shirt, every hair in place, but without any airs of grandeur.

In my world of hope and optimism, I aspired to have Ed's credentials, but for the moment, I was still attending college in the evening after work. The chasm between our education and experience was not lost on me—I understood my role and respected his. From the beginning of our working relationship, we formed a partnership. He beamed energy, enthusiasm, hard work, and an entrepreneurial spirit, and my vivacity made us a forceful team.

I typed his research reports on an array of technology stocks—not the hot names like IBM, Digital Equipment, and Control Data that were coming under pressure in the market—small, undervalued companies that appealed to savvy and sophisticated institutional investors. I was curious about his work, and he'd answer my questions, however unsophisticated they might be.

Ed's job seemed far more interesting than what the retail brokers did—making cold calls and generating commissions by peddling "new ideas" based often on what they referred to as "hot tips." Although I had passed the New York Stock Exchange brokerage exam, I became more intrigued by what Ed did—it was a more intellectually appealing path.

Outside the office, Ed was an entrepreneur, investing his own money into start-ups that he created. I offered to help him, if only for the opportunity to earn some extra money, but earning soon turned into learning. There was no question he wouldn't take the time to answer.

* * *

Looking back on the world of investing in 1969, it feels like a millennium away from today's technology, which runs at warp speed and allows for—or rather, forces—nanosecond decision-making. High-speed computers and other tools of the trade in the twenty-first century had yet to be envisioned, much less invented and utilized.

But, high speed or low speed, that booming stock market decade of the 1960s produced a generation of young, powerful, and driven fund managers. They were the financial world's celebrities of the day, and they hailed not just from New York—Boston had more than its share of aggressive mutual fund managers. A handful of them—in their early thirties and largely with Ivy League credentials—were partners at the investment firm of Thorndike, Doran, Paine & Lewis (TDP&L) and, together with their team of analysts and portfolio managers, they ran hard and fast in the growth stock environment.

The most important question on a money manager's mind at the end of each day is: Did I beat the market today, or did it beat me? But in the late 1960s, there was no way to get that answer. Portfolio valuation statements and performance reports were available only at quarter end, in other words, only four times a year.

Ed devised a solution for those competitive TDP&L fund managers by creating a computer program in BASIC—the most commonly used computer language at the time—that would value their portfolios on a weekly basis. In order to work with him on this project, I took an evening course at Boston University, where I was enrolled in the College of General Studies.

We were a team, and there was a third member—the head trader at TDP&L—Susan Harburger, an exceptionally bright young woman just a few years older than I was. Every Friday afternoon when the market closed at three thirty, it was Susan who sent us the portfolio holdings and for the next two hours, Ed and I worked feverishly together. Sometimes there were coding errors, lodged in what seemed like miles of inch-wide, key-punched yellow strips of paper, and I became particularly adept at spotting them.

By five o'clock, we sent back up-to-date performance reports, giving those hard-driving managers a leg up on their competitors. Knowledge is power.

It wasn't long before the TDP&L portfolio managers were directing their highly profitable stock transactions to our trading desk. A win-win for a scrappy fund firm and a small brokerage house in the cut-throat business of Wall Street.

Those Friday afternoon marathon sessions often ended with Susan and me heading out for a drink or even dinner together.

Throughout my years of working for Ed, it felt more like working with him. He personified generosity of time and of spirit, encouraging and supporting every step I took to advance my education and my career.

Decades after our lives had taken different paths, as I look back on the trajectory of my career, I have come to realize, with a deep sense of appreciation, the role that Ed played in shaping the earliest years of my career. Always supportive, endlessly willing to let me have as much rope as I wanted, he was the consummate mentor—generous with his time, happy to teach and guide, and proud of my achievements.

It would be many years before I was able to thank him in person. In the spring of 2019, I reached out to let him know of my memoir, *Little Sister*, and to try, over the phone, to summarize the story in fifteen minutes. He was flabbergasted, and we agreed to meet for lunch in Boston.

It had been half a century since we'd worked together, and as I awaited his arrival at a restaurant on Boylston Steet in Boston, I found myself intensely curious. *Will I recognize him? Will he have changed—be feeble or bent over?* I hoped not. And then he was looking at me with the magical smile that was his signature. I could have been back at the office on Franklin Street. Except for the black hair having turned white—it was the same Ed, elegant as ever in now casual attire. We caught up on life—he still played tennis, and he still golfed. Why was I unsurprised? For more than an hour, we covered the span of half a century.

As lunch came to an end, he presented me with his copy of my memoir, asking me to sign it. It was a touching moment for me as I inscribed with gratitude: "To Ed, thank you for being my first mentor."

CHAPTER 13

Fast Friends

1969–1970

Friendships have a way of evolving from unusual stimuli. What brought Susan and me close to each other? Was it the pressure of those Friday afternoons, followed by the opportunity to kick back and share a cocktail, that became the nucleus of our friendship? We may never know the reason, but some fifty years later, she and I can still engage as though we're in our twenties, sharing inner thoughts, giggling about our misbehaviors half a century behind us. We've always kept each other's secrets—the indication of a true friendship.

On the surface, there was little reason to think that Susan and I had much in common. Four years older than I was, she had graduated from college a year before I was kicked out of my home in Still River.

By the time I met her four years later, she had a degree in sociology from the University of Maine and had traveled to London, Paris, Rome, and Madrid. As she liked to describe it, she had no typing skills, which made her inadequate for the role of secretary. After applying to

Keystone Investments, a renowned mutual fund company in Boston, she was assigned to the trading desk and became hooked.

A year later, she was sought out by TDP&L, a new asset management firm that was started by a small group of young, brainy portfolio managers. They were progressive for their time and were happy to hire women in professional positions. Susan was the eighteenth employee hired, and she hit the ground running.

When our paths first crossed, she was already a respected woman in what was the most masculine of roles in the world of finance—an equity trader—perhaps the only woman in Boston with that title. She was responsible and accountable for every stock trade that was made by the team of portfolio managers at her firm—guys such as Bob Doran, Nick Thorndike, and John Gooch with a reputation as the best in the business.

In the vernacular of trading, "She fought for every eighth." That's how stocks were traded then—in eighths, quarters, and halves of a dollar—a far cry from the pennies of today.

We first met on the phone—as part of that Friday afternoon rush to get portfolio valuations completed by five o'clock. Even though we had yet to meet in person, I sensed we were kindred spirits. She had a palpable vivacity and a can-do attitude. Her voice communicated confidence, without a whiff of arrogance; her infectious laugh was magical and her sense of humor wicked.

Meeting her in person was impressive—not because she was a flashy dresser: she wasn't. It was the recognition that the personality I'd come to love on the telephone was even more fun-loving and spirited in the flesh.

I can still see her as she came around the corner into my little office—her short, dark, wavy hair and stylish eyeglasses were incidental to her natural cordiality and conviviality. And she brought everyone around her into her orbit.

Except for weekends, when we could socialize, our engagement was mostly by phone—neither of us took time off at lunch. On one occasion, in the middle of a conversation, her voice changed, and she barked, "Hold on—I'll be back" and in the background, I could hear her yelling at someone—was it some big-wig broker at Merrill Lynch, or maybe Goldman Sachs or Lehman Brothers? I took note that she ran her desk far more aggressively than our head trader. I liked that.

Stock trading was the fast lane in a fast-paced industry—where success meant beating the other guy on every trade—and Susan was as good as it got. She could take, and she could give, and she wasn't shy about ranting when people got in her way.

She'd often laugh softly into the phone as she'd share snippets of information about hotshot traders she'd outwitted. The picture was electric in my mind—Susan hunched over the phone like an eighth-grade girl confiding in her best friend that she had a crush on the gorgeous freshman quarterback.

On many a call, she'd suddenly change her tone midsentence, "Gotta go. Gotta take this trade." And the phone would go "click," leaving me to imagine the remaining fragment of her sentence. She read people fast, and her categorization was binary, which I found delightful—they were either seriously fabulous or seriously not.

Susan was smarter than any woman I had met since leaving the Center. I was almost envious of the power she wielded in the all-male world we both inhabited. Likely, it was our shared characteristics—the strongest of which may have been that we were fearless—that made her company so delightful.

Before long, the two of us were inseparable. It was then that I toyed with the idea of sharing my secret with her, but each time I came to the verge of opening my mouth, I froze, unable to find a way to start the conversation. Susan's engagement with the world was polished and sophisticated in the way that I longed to be, and I feared that sharing with her my dark side would give her second thoughts about me. So, I buttoned up, and the longer I held my story from her, the more it seemed impossible to break my silence.

As I look back to those early days of our friendship, I have come to realize with gratitude that Susan was the first role model since my days at the Center. I wasn't worldly enough at the time to make that connection—perhaps it is most often with the benefit of hindsight that such influence becomes evident. Confident, controlled, and comfortable in the all-male world of stocks and bonds, she proved that women could play the game as hard and as well as men without discord.

* * *

It wasn't long before TDP&L was one of our firm's largest customers, as defined by the commission dollars that flowed to the trading desk. Those Friday afternoon valuation reports were proving to be an invaluable service in the volatile bear market of 1969. That was how business was done—commissions from trades were the only way brokerage firms were paid.

Sometime in the middle of the mayhem that defined the stock market that year, George Burden, the senior partner, came to my secretarial nook, accompanied by Ed. In his slightly nervous way, George fidgeted with his fingers and then blurted out what was on his mind, his face lighting up as he spoke. "How would you like to take Susan Harburger to lunch? She's a really good client, and you know her so well."

I looked at him and then at Ed. *Take Susan out for lunch?* Secretaries barely left their desks, let alone went to a restaurant in the middle of the workday.

The 1960s was an era when white men dominated the world of Wall Street and finance, and women seldom broke out of their role as support staff. Susan, in my mind, was a rare exception, but I did not feel the same way about myself.

It was also the era of the three-martini lunch. I had noticed, almost from my first day on the job when I sat at the reception desk in the foyer off the elevators, that both senior partners left the office at ten minutes before noon—often with a friendly "I'll be back a bit after two"—and I'd wonder what transpired during those two plus hours.

George went on. "I think the Ritz-Carlton might be a wonderful place to go."

The Ritz-Carlton? The image of that evening some months earlier when George had taken me to dinner there floated back into my mind—that elegant, blue-domed ceiling.

"Yes," I replied, because that was what was expected, even though I was trying to sort out what to make of this request. "Should I call her up and invite her?"

In moments, Susan and I were on the phone. "George says that I should take you out for lunch at the Ritz."

She responded with a lively "Fabulous!" or something similar, as though it was a perfectly natural request. As the head trader of a renowned money management firm, she was an enviable client, and every trader from the sell side of the street—the brokerage firms that wanted her business—was invariably trying to take her out to dinner. What they discussed, I had no idea, nor did I have a clue as to what *I* was supposed to talk to her about. But she was my best friend, and the client part didn't mean anything. So, I just looked forward to having a fancy lunch.

And that's what we had. Over a gourmet meal that has now faded from memory, we did what we always did—chat endlessly in hushed tones, lest others around us hear our secrets, about what twentysomething girls have talked for millennia, with a preponderance of our time devoted to our latest romantic interests. We didn't rush back to the office. Our lunch could best be described as "anything but business."

Back at my desk, I reflected on George Burden's confidence in me. *I'm making progress,* I told myself. Where that would take me, I had no idea, nor did I have a plan. For the time being, I was thrilled to tumble forward and enjoy the reward of being in the good graces of my bosses—a dramatic stride from my lot in life just a few years earlier.

* * *

The camaraderie between Susan and me soon became a close friendship—no doubt enhanced by the compatibility of our personalities. On the spur of the moment, we took a long weekend trip to Bermuda, and despite our misfortunes—her motorbike accident and my sunburned body—the trip was divine. We were meant to be traveling companions—adventuresome and willing to hang out over our skis, as long as we did it together.

The late 1960s was the era of miniskirts, or better said micro-mini-skirts, and tall black or white leather boots, which became an instant status symbol when Joan Kennedy, wife of Sen. Edward Kennedy, was photographed walking through Heathrow airport in miniskirt and boots.

In the spring of 1970, the fashion world was turned on its head when a handful of designers introduced the midi-skirt, which could best be described as an unsightly cross between the maxi-skirt—a garment worn mostly by hippies—and its polar opposite, the micromini-skirt that was all the rage with the twenty-something crowd.

As spring turned to summer, the windows of Boston's most fashionable stores—Bonwit Teller, Lord & Taylor, Saks Fifth Avenue—were sporting the midi. One weekend, over the course of a few hours, while Susan and I lay on the beach, our conversation went something like this.

"The midi is hideous." "I wouldn't be caught dead in it." "It's disgusting that they're forcing working women to spend money for that trash." "Let's fight back." "Let's have a demonstration." "Why not?" "The whole country's demonstrating, so let's have a demonstration of our own against the dictates of the fashion industry."

By Sunday evening, we had a plan—we'd stage a demonstration in front of Bonwit Teller on August 19. For the next two days, we enlisted women within our circle of friends—mostly secretaries from our offices, as well as Susan's sister—all of whom eagerly accepted the task of creating placards with clever slogans that included: "Middies Are for Biddies." "Stop Designer Dictation." "No Midi in This Bare Market!" "Legs Have Made America Great," "Seventh Avenue Is One Way—the Wrong Way."

During the lunch hour, a troop of about a dozen of us—working women in our twenties—marched in front of Bonwit Teller on Berkeley Street in the heart of the fashionable Back Bay section of Boston, wearing miniskirts and carrying banners. Crowds gathered and cheered us on—mostly male office workers also on their lunch break. It wasn't long before both a photographer and a local reporter for the *Record American*—the hot tabloid of the time—had descended on us. So did Pat Collins, the Boston entertainment television reporter, who did an interview with Susan.

Some forty minutes later, it was time to return to our respective offices. That's when the photographer approached me. "Do you think I could take a picture of the girls from behind you and through your legs?" he asked.

"What?" I nearly screamed the word.

"I promise it will be decent," he responded quickly.

I grabbed Susan by the arm, seeking her advice. "Go for it," she laughed, and with her blessing, I let the photographer use his creativity, praying that he would keep his word.

The event was covered on the evening news and made for a few laughs. But in the middle of the night, I awoke in a state of anxiety. *What's that photograph going to look like? On the front page of the* Record American! I whispered to my guardian angel, *Please, please let the picture be decent.*

And there it was in the morning—a nearly full-page photo of my back side and legs that framed the cheerful gaggle of young women with a point of view. I breathed a sigh of relief—it could have been worse.

Cloudy,
In 80's
Page 20

Record American

Largest daily circulation in New England

10 Cents   Thursday, August 20, 1970   72 Pages

Home
★ ★
Closing Stocks

Rate Row Puting New Squeeze on Motorists

— Story on Page Two —

Oil Shortage Seen Hiking Electric Rates

— Story on Page Four —

Mary Jo's Mother Backs Ted, Raps Judge Charge He 'Lied'

Story on Page Three

Legs like these are as good a reason as any for girls—and guys—to protest encroachment of midi-skirt. (Story Page 2)
—Record American Photo, Mike Andersen

Record American, Boston, Thursday, August 20, 1970

2

No Fault Penalizes 'First Car' Owners

Rate Law Seen Threat to Auto Sales

By MIKE BENNETT

Anyone trying to put a car on the road for the first time in Massachusetts will probably end up in the assigned risk pool for personal liability insurance and have to pay up to three times the fixed rate for fire-theft-collision coverage.

"Just about everyone has to go into the pool because the companies aren't writing new business," a sales representative of a large agency specializing in auto insurance said Wednesday.

The insurance companies are refusing business not only because of the no-fault bill, but also because of spiraling accidents and claims, allegedly insufficient rates and costlier settlements.

The almost chaotic conditions resulting were revealed by the Record American in surveying insurance agents and underwriters, auto dealers and business associations across the state.

"We will take care of a transfer where a present customer buys a new car, but probably won't cover him if he buys a "second car," said Payson Langely, general manager of the Aetna Casualty and Insurance Company.

That consideration and the fact several large companies have notified customers policies will not be renewed at the end of the year has had a marked effect on the new and used car market.

"It's bound to have an effect on sales and our people are hurting," William Plunkett, executive secretary of the Massachusetts State Auto Dealers' Ass'n, said.

Plunkett believes a compromise acceptable to the Governor, the Legislature and the insurance companies can be worked out "in the next few days," because the alternative is "an end to the auto business."

"If you can't put a car on the road, you can't sell it," he said. Plunkett's association represents 613 of the approximately 860 dealers in the state. He estimates 250,000 new cars and 375,000 used ones are sold in Massachusetts annually. "Total sales are $1,400,000, or 14-percent of all the sales in the state," he said, "and the dealers employ almost 20,000 people, 6.1 percent of all the employes in the state."

The effect on one small dealership was described by Charles H. Norcross, president of one in North Adams and a director of the dealer's association. "We've sold three new cars but can't deliver them because no one will sell the buyers the necessary insurance," he said. "If this keeps up we'll have to lay off salesmen right off the bat. In two or three months we could forget about it and close the doors."

C. Eugene Farnan, state insurance commissioner, cannot say what percentage of the approximately 120 companies writing auto policies are refusing to issue new ones.

"But there are a number," he said.

Among the companies are several of the largest in the state. Liberty Mutual, for example, insures 175,000 motorists in Massachusetts, and has been "deliberately slowing down the growth of new business we've had in the past four or five years," according to a spokesman.

The company has laid of some "200 salesmen a few months ago, mostly the younger men who we found were bringing in newer business which

Turn to Page 11, Col. 1

Mini- and micro-skirted young women protest the coming of the midi-skirt during a lunch-hour march outside an exclusive Boston women's store.
—*Record American Photo, Mike Anderson*

'Don't Hide Your Assets!'

Minis Bare All-Out War on Midis

By DAVID O'BRIAN

When you stage a protest demonstration before a crowd of balding, conservative businessmen, and they respond with shouts of "Right On!", then you've got to have something going for you.

About 20 young mini- and micro-mini-skirted girls had more going for them than clever slogans Wednesday when they took to the streets to display their wrath against that ultimate of fashion-dictated absurdities—the midi-skirt.

The site of this noon-time demonstration for all that the healthy American male holds dear was the sidewalk in front of Bonwit Teller.

"We aren't picketing Bonwit Teller," stressed Pat Walsh, a secretary with great legs—and one of the organizers of the protest. "But we are calling for a boycott against the midi. We're hoping that if enough people see us demonstrating," it might give them the courage to stand up for the mini."

No courage was lacking among those who participated, mini as well as midi. The girls made their feelings—and legs—public in no uncertain terms with signs bearing slogans such as:

"Legs Have Made America Great."

"No Midi In This Bare Market."

"Don't Hide Your Assets."

"Don't Be Midi-Evil."

"Seventh Ave. Is One Way —The Wrong Way."

"It's not the midis themselves I object to," explained Susan Harburger, another organizer, "so much as the idea of being forced to wear them."

Both girls insisted that by October, unless something is done, minis will not be available in the stores at all. "Already," Miss Walsh claimed, "most of the window displays are featuring midis."

"I personally feel that the midi is unattractive," added Miss Harburger. "I feel that men like to see legs." Right On!

Warren N. H. Speaker

CONCORD, N.H. (AP)—Former U.S. Supreme Court Chief Justice Earl Warren will be the principal speaker at the Sept. 16 dedication ceremonies for New Hampshire's new state Supreme Court building.

ABM Expansion Gets Clear-Cut Victory, Brooke Bid Fails

WASHINGTON (UPI) — The Senat voted Wednesday for expansion of the Safeguard antiballistic missile (ABM) system — a clear-cut legislative victory for President Nixon.

The vote, rejecting a move to block expansion, was 53 to 45.

The administration victory was assured when ABM opponents failed in their second and final attempt to confine deployment of the defense weapon to two sites authorized last year in North Dakota and Montana.

The vote, on an amendment by Sen. Edward W. Brooke, R-Mass., gave the administration what it felt was an important bargaining wedge in the soviet-American arms control talks. It will enable the administration to build two new Safeguard sites to protect strategic missiles and bombers in Missouri and Wyoming.

Opponents of the ABM picked up three votes from a similar test vote last week with Sens. Clinton Anderson (D-N. M.), Thomas J. McIntyre (D-N. H.), and Marlow Cook (R-Ky.) switching over.

But the administration gained four — Sen. Allen J. Ellender (D-La.), Charles H. Percy (R-Ill.), Margaret Chase Smith (R-Me.) and Jennings Randolph (D-W. Va.).

Sen. William Saxbe (D-Ohio), an ABM opponent, did not vote.

Safeguard is designed to protect Minuteman missiles and B52 bomber bases from a possible surprise Soviet strike that would paralyze the U. S. land-based nuclear arsenal.

The Brooke amendment would have prevented deployment of ABM radars, computers and missile-interceptors at the new sites proposed for Whiteman AFB, Mo., and Warren AFB, Wyo.

A tougher amendment that would have sliced the $322 million for Whiteman and Warren was defeated 52 to 47 last week.

Just before the vote, Defense Secretary Melvin R. Laird warned the senate that adoption of the Brooke amendment would pose a threat to U.S. bomber bases.

In a last-minute administration appeal before the Senate voted on a restrictive amend-

ment, Laird also said the proposal would raise the ultimate cost of the ABM and delay completion of the defense system by 15 months.

His letter was read by Chairman John Stennis of the Senate Armed Services Committee in final debate before the Senate vote on the issue.

"The Department of Defense cannot support, and is opposed, to the Brooke amendment," Laird said. "It is the view of the department that adoption of the amendment would both increase the cost and reduce the effectiveness of the Safeguard defense of Minuteman (offensive missiles)."

He then said the measure would eliminate protection to a substantial number of strategic bomber bases.

A similar amendment sponsored by Sens. Philip A. Hart (D-Mich.), and also Sherman Cooper (R-Ky.), was rejected last Wednesday. But unlike the Brooke amendment, it would have cut $322 million earmarked for new Safeguard installation at Whiteman AFB, Mo., and Warren AFB, Wyo.

The Brooke amendment would allow the entire $1.3 billion requested by the administration, freeing the extra $322 million to be used for more radars and computers at Grand Forks and Malmstrom.

Brooke contended his proposal would create a "defense in depth" of the Minuteman fields at Malmstrom and Grand Forks.

But Sen. Henry M. Jackson (D-Wash.), who has led the fight for Safeguard, said the number of Minuteman silos protected by Brooke's proposal would be less than a third of those guarded if the system were expanded to Whiteman and Warren.

As with the Cooper-Hart amendment, the key argument was the effect of the proposal on the Strategic (SALT).

RECORD AMERICAN

August 20, 1970   Vol. 9—No. 278

Published daily except Sunday ...

It may be a stretch to claim that our demonstration killed the midi, but it never became a fashion statement. Even *Newsweek* referred to "the midi debacle of 1970."

CHAPTER 14

A Family Reunited

1969

I was eager to leave my hometown, to abandon Boston and escape to a city where no one knew me. The heartthrob Monkees' hit song said it all: I wanna be free like the bluebirds... Picture perfect.

It was three years since I'd found myself a cultural orphan in an alien world. The runway to normalcy had been long and the takeoff slow, but I had learned to fly and was emerging from ingenue to worldly, if not yet altogether sophisticated. But my past still haunted me, and I went to great pains to keep the tale of my upbringing a secret. A new wrinkle associated with my convoluted past kept me from taking flight from Boston and making a home in a place where there was little likelihood anyone would have heard of Father Leonard Feeney or knew of my story. I was trapped by a burden that I took upon myself, unrelated to my ongoing education or my job. I was trapped by my family.

* * *

The stage had been set a year earlier, in May 1968, when Sister Catherine died of cancer. She was sixty-seven years old, and despite having been struck with non-Hodgkin's lymphoma a year earlier, she had refused to accept a death sentence and continued managing every detail of the day-to-day spiritual and material lives of the community's members—until she fell into a final coma.

With her death came the almost instantaneous disintegration of what had been her powerfully controlled domain. Two of my siblings, ages sixteen and twelve, let it be known that they wanted to leave the place. My mother already had one foot out in the world, and my father accepted it as his responsibility to leave with his children in June 1969, when my brother would be graduating from high school.

There was risk in his decision. At the age of fifty-one, he had not held a conventional job for twenty years. The stress of leaving the Center, and the realization that he would now face the daunting task of supporting his family, was a source of anxiety for him. For two decades, he'd worked every day within the community. At home, he was responsible for repairing the cars and farm vehicles. In addition, he was a regular fundraiser for the organization, an activity that took him to cities across the country, as he peddled the Catholic books authored by Father and Sister Catherine.

Throughout that time, he'd been forced by Sister Catherine to abandon his secular profession—that of teaching mathematics and philosophy. In cultlike fashion, she had deliberately hindered his ability to find employment in the outside world, by depriving him of the occupation for which he had studied and been trained. The stress associated with the realization that he would soon be responsible for the financial support of his family wreaked havoc on his health, bringing on bouts of colitis in those final months leading up to his departure.

A year earlier, my mother, while splitting her time between the Center and Cambridge, had found a three-bedroom apartment on the ground floor of a two-family house in North Cambridge. The apartment was light and airy, spacious in the way that prewar multifamily houses tended to be in Cambridge—constructed with the expectation that families would come with four, five, and even more children. Was it foresight? Did she anticipate the day when she, my dad, and my siblings would exit the Center?

For a woman who'd lived the life of a religious nun for the prior eighteen years, my mother emerged from the convent with her sophistication and worldliness intact. Tall and slender, she carried herself with poise; the sophistication of her vocabulary astounded me. She had an eye for style and a homemaker's practical touch.

"Dahling, will you help me rearrange the furniture?" she asked one evening. "I think we can make the place look cozier." At the Goodwill store, we found a mahogany bookcase and end tables, and soon the apartment had a sense of warmth—it felt like a home.

"Some blue drapes will tie everything together," she said, perusing the living room. I took pleasure in watching her slip seamlessly into the role of mother, wife, and housekeeper.

In the final months leading up to my father's departure from the Center, her mood was euphoric; her exhilaration was palpable.

For my part, I worried about how my parents would survive financially, and took the bold step of addressing the issue with my mother. "The Center needs to give you some money. You've both worked there for twenty years—going on bookselling trips every three weeks, sewing all the children's clothes, cooking, and repairing the cars. You sold the house you bought on the G.I. Bill and gave them the proceeds! You can't leave with nothing."

Mother nodded, deep in thought. Some weeks later, she told me quietly one evening, "They've agreed to lend us nine thousand dollars when we leave in June."

"Lend?" I was fuming. "They owe you that money and more! I'll make sure you never have to pay it back." And I meant it. In a sudden role reversal, the child had become the parent.

My mother quickly responded, "We'll be fine, dahling, I promise you."

In my mind, my parents were now the newbies and I saw it as my responsibility to get them settled into their new life. While I couldn't help but worry about them, I was, at the same time, ecstatic over the realization that my family would now be free from the bondage of the Center and would reenter the world—a place I found teeming with challenge and opportunity.

Happy as I was to see my parents leave the Center, their departure also presented a personal dilemma. For three years I'd been making every decision about my life on my own—some wise and others sorely lacking in good judgment—but without parental guidance or interference. Now, nearing the age of twenty-one, the idea of a head of the household who might invade my space was more than I could countenance.

The solution came on an impulse, and the day after my father, together with my youngest sister and my brother, settled into the large first-floor apartment of the two-family house I'd been calling home for over a year, I signed a lease on a simple one-bedroom apartment on the other side of Harvard Square—far enough away to ensure my privacy yet close enough to be a caring presence.

Each day, my father scoured the newspapers, making appointments for interviews, without as much as a résumé, and within a month he was employed at Volvo as a new car salesman. For a man whose passion was to study, one might have expected him to regret his new role. But always the optimist, he saw the upside. In his own words, "Volvos are bought by intellectuals."

My mother was cut from different cloth—pragmatism, problem-solving, and sleuthing characterized her approach to business. Within two years of leaving the Center, she rose from bank teller to bank manager and constituted the entire lending department at North Cambridge Savings Bank. She reveled in her role and enjoyed sharing her decision-making techniques as a loan officer. "I work on instinct," was an expression she used. "I didn't like how he was dressed," she told me one time. "If you need a loan, you need to look respectable."

A monastic existence for twenty years did nothing to inhibit my parents' love of life once they were back in the world. They made friends with the neighbors and with the local parish priest, and they reconnected with friends from their days before the Center. My mother was a sophisticated, if not quite fashionable, dresser, and she saw to it that my father's wardrobe complemented her own. There was no way to tell they had "a past."

* * *

Little by little, as financial concerns for my parents gradually became less pressing, my vision for them expanded—they needed to become homeowners. Truth be told, my motivation was selfish. As I was moving up in the world, I wanted my parents to seem like all other Americans, and owning a house was the best way I could think to make them part of "the middle class."

"You need to buy a house," I said to my mother one day. "Paying rent is just a waste of money."

"I know, dear," she responded, nodding.

"You can afford it," I told her. "Why don't we look together?"

Mother brightened up, and it wasn't long before she took the lead in the search for a house. She knew what she wanted. "It's got to have four bedrooms, a dining room that can seat a dozen, and ample space to entertain company. And I want a garden so that I can putter."

Her words about the garden conjured up an image—my mother dressed in her nun's habit, kneeling in the garden, a small pillow under her knees. At the Center, her primary responsibilities had been as seamstress (within the community, all of our clothes, including lingerie, were homemade) as well as dessert cook. But many an evening, I could look out my cubicle window and watch her as she weeded the long slender strips of garden that edged the bluestone pathways surrounding the house. She seemed at peace, although I will never know what thoughts were going through her head.

Mother found the house she wanted without my help, and she called one day.

"I think you're going to like it," she said with the conviction of someone who knew her own mind. In other words, *Like it or not, I've got my house.*

She was right. It was perfect in every way—set on a large corner lot that overlooked the third hole at the Oakley Country Club in Watertown. It had a cottage look and a backyard that was perfect for cookouts. The price was right—$39,000. ($295,000 in today's dollars.)

"The mortgage rate is high at seven and a half percent, but we can afford it," Mother said with pride.

Hardly had my parents moved into their new house when I asked if I might invite Susan there for dinner. Their becoming homeowners meant, to me, that they were now respectable, they were middle-class, they were all-American, and I could show them off.

My ever-cordial dad embraced Susan as though he knew her, which was close to true, given how often I mentioned her. "What may I get you to drink?" was his opening salutation, which endeared him to Susan. I loved seeing my father in a social role. His confinement as a celibate member of a religious order for twenty years did nothing to inhibit his naturally gregarious personality.

As dinner progressed, I enjoyed being the outsider, observing Susan while she engaged with my parents and siblings. There were no faux pas on the part of my family—no slips of the tongue that would divulge anything about our prior lives. Wine, which was consumed by all in more than adequate quantity, had a salubrious effect on the rapport it engendered.

My family embraced Susan, and she embraced them back. She became a frequent guest—or perhaps better said, a member of the family.

CHAPTER 15

Behind the Iron Curtain

1971

To explore the world—that had been my most ardent childhood ambition, imbued no doubt by the endless stories of the saints that were my earliest recollections. Descriptive phrases—the rolling hills of Umbria, the holy Isle of Lindisfarne, the towering cedars of Lebanon—each was stamped with a vivid self-created image in my mind, a place beckoning to be part of my journey through life.

Third grade had introduced me to my favorite subject—geography—and over the next several years, I memorized the capital of every country in the world, even the ever-changing names and shapes of the many countries in the center of Africa. From Baffin Island to Albania, from the Belgian Congo to Thailand—I reveled in memorizing details about the customs, the weather, the languages, and most particularly the native attire of millions of people living around the world. No matter that I was also learning that most of the people living in those fascinating and faraway places were on their way to hell for all eternity because they weren't Roman Catholics.

Was it the claustrophobia of my own childhood—the forced segregation from a world that clearly existed all around me—that made the notion of flight and exploration so magical?

My first trip overseas was to London—in the fall of 1970—at the invitation of Annabel, the English office girlfriend who had returned to the UK. Her home was a large window-filled, multibedroom flat off Sloane Square that she shared with three roommates, and where we spent not more than a few hours a night sleeping. Our days were packed with visits to palaces, museums, and cathedrals, and outings that included punting on the Cam and picnicking in the Malvern Hills that looked down on the River Wye. Evenings found us in the theatre and barhopping till the wee hours of the morning, accompanied by Annie's slightly wild, but trustworthy, friend Dominic. As a farewell present, he took us to the sights and smells of the boisterous wholesale meat market in the darkness before dawn. Three marvelous, sleep-deprived weeks added fuel to the travel flame within me.

* * *

Back in the States, it was the spring of 1971 when Susan said, seemingly out of the blue one day, "Let's go to Europe."

"But to places that are out of the ordinary," was my response. "We can go to Rome and Paris any time." Susan was more than up for that, having already visited both places on a number of occasions. We bounced ideas off each other in ten-second snippets over the phone during work hours.

Vienna was at the top of my wish list. My childhood was replete with stories that sang the praises of the city as a beacon of Catholicism—how the Counter-Reformation, in the middle of the sixteenth century, eradicated Lutheranism and restored Vienna to a power in league with Pope Pius V, a canonized Catholic saint. The Romanesque/Gothic cathedral of Saint Stephen was among a number of Catholic churches I dreamt of visiting. Susan, an Episcopalian with a liberal attitude toward church attendance, was more than game. In addition, both of us craved chocolate and pastries, for which the city was renowned.

"And let's end up in the Greek Islands for a whole week." That was Susan's idea—she'd been to both Mykonos and Santorini, while I had merely read about them. Greece meant the Acropolis and the Parthenon to me—I had yet to be introduced to the exotic beauty and the sybaritic life of the Aegean Islands.

Susan had a mere four years on me in age, but they had been packed with world travel. One couldn't ask for a better friend and travel mate. When it came to the parts in between Austria and Greece, I suggested to Susan—or did we mutually arrive at the idea?—that it would be cool to visit some countries behind the Iron Curtain. We pounced on the idea of Hungary—Budapest to be precise.

The closest Susan and I had come to Hungary was the Café Budapest, a swish Hungarian restaurant that occupied the lower level of the Copley Plaza Hotel in Boston. Elegant, expensive, and with an exotic menu, it was the kind of place I could afford only if I had a date who was paying. Susan, on the other hand, by virtue of being a major client of almost every brokerage firm in Boston and New York, knew the menu far better than I. But we agreed on one thing: Hungarian food was worth a stop in Budapest.

How we landed on Dubrovnik, Croatia, remains a mystery, but we congratulated ourselves for decades afterward.

* * *

Arriving in Vienna, our first mission was to procure two tickets to the opera. We lucked out, even if the only available seats were on the gallery level—in other words, the nosebleed section—of the Staatsoper for that night's performance of Puccini's *La Bohème*. The aria-rich melodrama tells the tale of the on-again, off-again romance in nineteenth-century Paris between the impoverished poet Rodolfo and the young Mimi, a seamstress who is dying of tuberculosis.

Susan, so much more culturally sophisticated than I was, had attended the opera in Boston—this was my first experience. Even without binoculars, I could make out from a great height the splendid sets and costumes. Almost as engrossing was the opulence of the attendees who packed the multitiered theatre, while the extraordinary acoustics allowed the orchestra and sublime voices to soar with perfection to our standing-room seats in the rafters.

Intermission provided the opportunity to splurge on a glass of champagne, and with our Europe-on-$5-a-day kind of budget, it was stretching to say the least. And then it was back to our seats near the ceiling of the opera house.

But where were our seats? Unlike Hansel and Gretel, we had left no crumb trail in the maze of levels and sections, and we soon realized we were lost in a sea of ten-foot-high, crimson-red velvet curtains. Which one opened to our assigned places? Again and again, we struck out, until, possibly egged on by a bit of champagne, travel fatigue, and the annoyance of patrons as we peered into the wrong seats, we got a case of the giggles. No usher seemed interested in our plight—could they tell we were "ugly Americans?"

Fortunately, Mimi had not yet succumbed when we spied our seats and slipped into them. Our giggles soon turned to tears as she and her estranged lover Rodolfo made up, expressing their love and reminiscing about their first meeting just moments before she expired. We hit the pillows on day one of our two-week vacation delightfully exhausted.

We woke up to a warm and sunny spring day in late May. It was Pentecost Sunday, fifty days after Easter and a major holy day in the Catholic Church. By now nearly five years after leaving the Center, my frame of reference was still very much the church calendar. While I'd long ago given up attending daily Mass and skipped many a Sunday as well, I was constantly drawn to the music and liturgy of the Catholic High Mass. Holy days, such as Pentecost, were especially appealing—an opportunity to hear the Mass sung in the traditional Gregorian chant, so much a part of my religious and cultural upbringing. Susan, a seasoned Episcopalian, was all in for the event.

Flowering fruit trees and a sea of lemon-yellow daffodils and boldly variegated tulips greeted us as we walked to the cathedral. Arriving early, we found seats that offered a broad view of the sanctuary. For the occasion of Pentecost, it was the renowned Vienna Boys' Choir that sang the Mass—in Latin, rather than in the Viennese vernacular. A too-short ninety minutes later, we exited the cathedral, uplifted by the grandeur of the ceremony and the beauty of the music.

It was now time to get the coveted chocolates, a close second to a religious experience for the two of us. From the cathedral, we made a beeline for the renowned pastry shop across the Stephansplatz. A line had already formed, and we joined it, only to find mothers and their daughters cutting in front of us as though we didn't exist. It took but a few minutes to conclude that our appropriate but unfashionable attire couldn't hold a candle to the array of elegant hats and crinolines that the Viennese ladies and their young daughters were sporting. Susan and I were aghast as we fell farther behind in the line, and as customers exiting the shop with boxes of pastries drove off in their Mercedes Benz.

"Let's get out of here," I said, nudging Susan. "We can find another shop." And we did, only to discover that a single chocolate in Vienna cost practically what we had allowed ourselves for an entire meal.

Was it the feeling of being poor? Or perhaps, worse, being treated like dirt because we weren't fancy, wealthy, or Viennese? A sense of disgust for both the city and its haughty citizens billowed up inside me. I couldn't wait to depart both Vienna and Austria, and I promised myself that I'd never return, a promise I have kept, perhaps unwisely.

By eight o'clock the following morning, Vienna was in our past as we boarded the train at Wien Hauptbahnhof for the three-hour ride to Budapest. This was 1971, and the United States was still in the thick of the Cold War—for us, that was part of the fun and the challenge of going behind the Iron Curtain.

As we neared the Hungarian border, the train slowed, and the screeching sound of metal on metal brought an instant romantic flashback to the movie *Doctor Zhivago*, which I must have seen more than a dozen times. Once we thudded to a dead stop, any semblance of romance evaporated. The heavy metal door slid open, and four Hungarian soldiers stomped aboard our car. Adrenaline shot through my body—I was looking for drama but not sure I really wanted it. As long as Susan and I stayed together—that was all that mattered. But what if they separated us? They wouldn't do that—or would they? Had I read too many espionage thrillers by Graham Greene and John le Carré?

Of course, they spoke not a word of English, but their outstretched hands told us what they wanted—our passports. There wasn't a humorous bone among them all—what a shame, as we tried to catch the eye of at least one of them for a flirtatious moment. No chance. Our passports posed no crisis, so our first engagement with Soviet-era military was short-lived and uneventful.

If the residents of Vienna were a disappointment, the reception we received in Budapest more than made up for it. The city still showed the scars of battle from twenty-five years earlier during World War II, and its citizens lived in stark contrast to their Austrian neighbors. But what the Hungarians lacked in worldly goods, they more than made up for with their grace, joy, and generosity.

Hardly were we off the train when we wandered into the marketplace—sparsely dotted with vendor stalls and local residents selling goods that were far from fancy. We were chatting softly together when one of the vendors, an old woman dressed in crumpled attire, recognized us as Americans. Grabbing my hand and looking into my eyes, she proclaimed, "Thank God for you Americans," as she offered me a small bag of peanuts. When I tried to pay her, she slapped my hand and then patted my face with her own calloused hand.

Hammered-silver jewelry—bracelets, necklaces, and bangles—was the most fashionable item for sale. For one dollar, I bought a necklace—a round silver sculpture that I decided was a modern representation of a fish. Instinctively, I thought, *If this were in a shop in Vienna, I could never afford it.* I wear the necklace to this day.

Our miniature room in a miniature hotel at least came with our own bathroom. What we were saving on accommodations we had every intention of splurging on meals, and on our second and last night in the city, we headed out to treat ourselves to what we hoped would be the best Hungarian food in town.

We were sipping a cocktail before dinner when a gentleman approached and asked to join us. As he treated us to a second drink, we queried him to discover that he was a Viennese businessman. His impeccable English made that believable as he explained that he was a salesman whose customers were Hungarian construction companies.

"I'd like to take you girls to dinner," he said. Susan and I looked at each other—no way to whisper or "run to the ladies' room"—but we relied on our pact that as long as we stuck together, we'd be willing to dare a few things.

And no ordinary dinner it was—at the Moulin Rouge of Budapest! Who knew that behind the Iron Curtain there was a nightclub that rivaled the bawdy decadence of its namesake in Paris? Throughout the long evening, the Viennese businessman remained a gentleman, and we returned to our miniature hotel in time for a couple of winks before packing our bags and heading for the airport on our way to Dubrovnik.

That medieval paradise on the Adriatic coast in southern (now former) Yugoslavia was a far cry from what we expected of a Soviet satellite country. The friendly guide in the tourist booth at the airport found us room and board for three nights in an elegant white stucco house, owned by a couple whose two daughters were away at medical school in Vienna, giving us the luxury of each having our own bedroom. The cost was one dollar per night.

The man of the house—we had but a fleeting glance at his wife— made up for his lack of English with unending hospitality. Breakfast was hearty, if not exactly identifiable on our first morning, and as we headed out the door to explore the town, our host chased after us carrying two miniature glasses, each filled with a yellowish liquid. Unable to converse, he shoved the drinks into our hands, and we had no option but to down them, doing our best not to gag. The "treat" was a peach liqueur—at nine o'clock in the morning!

If doing our best to remain sober at breakfast was how our day started, it ended on a sublime note, as we sat in Luza piazza in the center of Old Town Dubrovnik at dusk, sipping a glass of wine and being ser-enaded by a stringed quartet that played Schubert and Mozart. The familiar music had a magical way of dissolving the Iron Curtain and creating a cultural bond with the townspeople.

This is Communist Yugoslavia? I kept repeating to myself. Well-dressed couples, arm in arm, strolling along the old wall that overlooked the Adriatic Sea, were a far cry from what I had imagined a "communist country" to be. Prosperous was the best way to describe the town, with its impeccably maintained buildings and its myriad churches—open and inviting.

Some memories fade with the years; others remain vivid for a lifetime. Dubrovnik is uniquely enthroned among my most beloved recollections.

Athens offered the opportunity to use the one year of Ancient Greek I had taken in high school, which came in handy, if only for the ability to read signs and phonetically sound out street names, guaranteeing that Susan and I never got lost. However, that classical education was of no value for conversing in modern Greek.

In the Agora, we bought the two items we discovered were bar-gains—fur coats (in June) and gold jewelry. A pair of gold cufflinks for my father set me back $25, or $185, adjusted for fifty years of inflation. They now belong to my son, while the fox fur eventually bit the dust.

A climb up the back side of the steep hill that led to the Acropolis proved almost fatal, but the reward was beyond spectacular—a free and open walk through the Parthenon, decades before such a luxury became prohibited.

After two action-packed days, we boarded a ship at Piraeus Harbor for the island of Spetses. Our plan was to spend a couple of nights there and then take the ferry to Mykonos, a popular destination for tourists. But the Greek gods foretold otherwise, and we spent seven self-indul-gent days reveling in everything that was idyllic about Spetses—which, in essence, meant having no plans at all. Our hotel room, which we sim-ply lucked into, looked over the blue Aegean Sea. For $5 a night, it was a five-star experience. Mykonos was forgotten.

Our social life was directed by a cadre of young Greek men—all of whom were gay and very safe. They swam with us during the day and escorted us to the local taverna for roasted lamb and its accoutrements, accompanied with endless servings of retsina—with the smell of turpentine, I thought. But Susan and I managed to dance it off night after night, often crashing into our idyllic hotel room moments before dawn. Sleeping through the morning, we'd hit the beach by early afternoon and repeat the daily cycle.

Two friends on vacation and sharing accommodations for a full sixteen days is one sure way to assess the soundness of a relationship. Susan and I returned to Boston closer than ever. Nearly fifty years later, we revisited our trip—I brought the photos, and she shared the diary she kept—reminiscing about a time that seemed like yesterday.

* * *

Sometime in early 1972, I was assigned to work for Jimmy Sullivan, who had recently joined the firm as the airline industry analyst. Jimmy was as Irish and as Catholic as his name. His demeanor was reserved—that is, until he had an opportunity to talk about his two loves.

First and foremost was his six-year-old daughter who, he was eager to tell me, was born after fourteen years of marriage and many novenas. Over and over, he'd say, "I can't believe it. I'm fifty-two, with a little girl who's just six."

His pride in her was immeasurable. "She's brighter than any child I've ever seen," he'd say at least a few times a week. "She's taking ballet lessons, and I've got to leave early to see her recital." "She's the best math student in her class." I got the sense that he believed in miracles and that she was his.

His second love was the airline industry, about which he could talk for hours, his sotto voce belying his passion. He could recite endless statistics on every airline—at a time when there were far more than there are today, including Eastern Airlines, Braniff, Pan Am, TWA, Ozark, Midwest, Mohawk. Northeast, Northwest, Frontier, and on and on.

In an undeterminable order (to me), his other passions were golf, whiskey, and his dog, with whom he loved to play catch, until a fast-thrown ball got caught in the dog's throat one evening and he fell down dead. It was without tears, but with a sense of shock, that Jimmy told the story the next morning and then again and again for days, as though he couldn't grasp the loss. Something died in him when he lost his dog.

Jimmy was a guy's guy, far more comfortable in the company of men than women. While he could be pleasant and even jovial from time to time, there wasn't an ounce of flirtation in him. He played golf with the same fellows, week after week, and his client rolodex was full of names of men. He had no pictures of his family on his desk, and he never spoke of his wife but made up for it with his incessant adulation of his daughter.

For hours each day, he'd sit at his desk, with an array of large, pale-green ledger sheets spread out in front of him and stacks of airline annual reports cramming the remaining space on his sizable desk. A box of No. 2 pencils, a pencil sharpener, several large rubber erasers, a simple calculator, a spinning rolodex, a telephone, and a desk lamp filled the remaining space.

His secretarial needs were de minimis, and finding myself with time on my hands that I was craving to pack with projects, I approached him. "Could I help you with the numbers you're working on? I've got lots of time, and I'd like to learn about what you do."

Jimmy looked up and stared at me—well not directly into my eyes but with a faraway look I had come to recognize meant that he was cogitating. After a few seconds, I interrupted, "If you show me what you need, I know I can do it." Still no response.

Does he think I'm incapable? I've watched what he does—copying numbers from the annual reports and the government data sheets, and then using the calculator to come up with ratios. I can do that.

Then he uttered a soft, "I suppose so."

Jimmy's engagement was in sharp contrast to that of Ed, who had encouraged and supported me in my never-ending quest to take on more responsibility. Ed had made me feel as though we were partners. Jimmy was not the teaching sort, but he had an eager student on his hands and he made a genuine effort to show me the ropes, which I absorbed easily.

In short order, I took over nearly all the number crunching on a broad array of airline companies. The alphabet soup of acronyms became part of my vocabulary—revenue passenger miles (RPM), available seat miles (ASM), load factor (LF). I calculated them for each airline and then ranked them from most successful to least successful, and soon I had a vivid three-dimensional picture of the drivers of profitability, and thus the prices, of airline stocks.

* * *

Susan was on the phone. "I've got some fabulous news," she whispered.

"What?" I asked.

"I've been offered a fantastic job as the head trader for a new fund that Cab Smith is starting."

Cab was one of the hotshot portfolio managers at her firm and was capitalizing on his success by breaking out on his own. That he wanted Susan as his trader was a tribute to her professionalism.

"Wow," I said, "that's great."

When she added excitedly, "It's in Philadelphia," my heart sank. What would I do without Susan as part of my life? She knew me better than anyone in the world—despite my inability to share with her any details of my bizarre childhood.

"Are you going to take it?" I asked, trying to mask my disappointment.

The words were barely out of my mouth when she asked, "Will you come with me?"

"Yes," was out of my mouth without a thought. Ever since we'd returned from our trip to Europe, I'd been hankering to get out of Boston, to escape from a city where people knew me as a receptionist and then a secretary. I needed a challenge, an opportunity to take a giant step in the world, to prove myself. Now that my parents had ceased being "my children," I was free to fly the coop, and the opportunity had just been laid in my lap.

The plan was set—we were moving to Philadelphia in June—Susan with a job, I without one. But at the age of twenty-three, I wasn't worried.

With still a couple of months before June, I broke the news to Jimmy Sullivan of my impending departure. He took it in stride, as though he was indifferent to my leaving. *Why?* I wondered. Puzzled, and even offended by his lack of curiosity about why I was leaving and where I might be going, I followed up with an unambiguous question of my own.

"Have you been happy with my work? Have I done a good job?"

In typical Jimmy fashion, he paused and gazed into space before responding, "You've been OK."

I was stunned, hurt, and deep down inside I was fuming.

Is it because I'm a girl? Does he think I can't do the same work as a man? Is his daughter the only smart girl in the world?

CHAPTER 16

Twenty-Three and Free

1972

F ree from angst, free from responsibility, free to be daring, free to fly the coop, free to be me.

Annie Martindale, the ever-optimistic and vivacious advisor of my studies at Boston University, solved the only thing that could have held me back from leaving Boston for Philadelphia—how would I continue my studies?

"Go to Philadelphia," she said emphatically when I presented my predicament. "We'll accept every course you take at either Wharton or at Penn's liberal arts college." What more did I need?

* * *

A few weeks before Susan's new job was to begin, she and I drove to Philadelphia in my "new" car—an aquamarine '63 Buick, with a white leather interior in impeccable condition—that I acquired for $300 from a schoolteacher neighbor of my parents. She must have lived within a mile or two of where she taught, as there were barely 10,000 miles on the odometer. The car was broad and heavy, the way cars were built before the onset of the quadrupling of the price of oil. Not fashionable but safe, and that pleased my father.

Susan had a singular mission—to find an apartment. Mine on the other hand was twofold—I needed a job, as well as a place to live. My guardian angel did her part—in a single day, we found a spacious and light-filled two-bedroom apartment on the third floor of a prewar building—a euphemism for less modern, but with the advantages of lofty ceilings, large windows, and cheaper rent. Our apartment overlooked the blossoming trees and flowers of Rittenhouse Square, bursting with variegated shades of green and myriad colors at the end of May.

Susan had a job, and together we had an apartment. Now I needed to find a job. I was dying for a challenge, something that would keep on stimulating my mind—not that I knew how to describe that position, but I loved the business of working on stocks, pulling the numbers together, and observing trends that developed over time. The stock market was the only business I knew.

The phone rang—it was Susan. "Good news," she said, and in her rapid-fire way, she filled me in on the details—her new employer had reached out to a brokerage firm whose research he valued.

"You've got an interview. It's with The Pennsylvania Group. They're a research boutique in Bala Cynwyd, just fifteen minutes from our apartment. I'm not sure just what they want you to do, but you've got to go."

Research boutique—the term conjured up an elite entity, one that provided something special, and that's just what it was and what it did. In the late 1960s, the retail brokerage business emerged into a growth market, as individuals, in massive numbers, became small investors. The resulting back-office congestion wreaked havoc on Wall Street, and over a handful of years, one in every six brokerage firms in the country was either merged into oblivion or went bankrupt.

The downsizing of the brokerage industry offered an opportunity for new firms—research boutiques, as they came to be called—to spawn. They were structured to eschew the crowded retail arena. Rather, they chose to serve the institutional market—firms that managed mutual funds, endowments, and the pension plans of corporate America. Their appeal was their product, which they termed "proprietary" research. Without the front-office cost of retail brokers that resulted in back-of-fice bottlenecks, they sank their capital into hiring a small group of specialty analysts, each with responsibility for but one small sector of the market.

The Pennsylvania Group was one such firm—its three founders, Ivy Leaguers from Philadelphia and St. Louis, started the company in 1970. Within a couple of years, the firm had hired six highly reputable research analysts, a couple of stock traders, a few institutional salesmen (yes, they all were men), and an all-female support staff. In the spring of 1972, they were looking for someone who could assist the team of analysts in their research. That was the job for which I was to be interviewed.

* * *

The interview was memorable. I sat in a semicircle with four of the firm's six analysts, each of whom was a man attired in the uniform of Wall Street—a Brooks Brothers suit, a white button-down shirt, and a diagonal-striped tie. Except for one of them who wore a blue shirt, which I noticed.

For the first few minutes the analysts described their areas of exper-tise. "I cover the trucking stocks"—that was John Cook—"and I'd like you to update my spreadsheets with the data on the industry." Mike Conn explained the insurance industry and what he needed. Sherif Nada followed the hospitality industry, and Jack Smith covered IBM. They explained that the other two analysts covered the railroad and the airline industries.

What had started off as a series of monologues, with each analyst explaining what he expected of me, soon became an engagement in which I took the lead. "I can do all of that," I told them with assurance, explaining the role I had played supporting Jimmy Sullivan. Copying numbers and calculating ratios with my trusty slide rule—yes, this was an era before the HP scientific calculator, and a slide rule fit nicely into a slim bag—was child's play. As the interview progressed, I was envisioning a role that I could grow into—an opportunity to take a leap forward. When the moment came, I chose my words carefully.

"I'd like to do more than just crunch numbers for you," I said, addressing all four of them. "Are you willing to answer the questions I might have so that I can understand how each of the industries you cover works?" I got it out and waited for their response. I was willing to look elsewhere for a job if this position was going to become boring.

Their response was unanimously encouraging, and I leapt at their offer of a salary of $10,800 (a little over $73,000 in 2023 terms), a $2,000 increase over what I had been making in Boston. Even better, it was a salary—no longer would I be paid by the hour. It felt like a giant step forward.

Four years earlier, I had been offered $2.25 as the receptionist at Ladenburg Thalmann, and now, at the age of twenty-three, I was making well more than double that amount, and I still had some years to go before finishing my undergraduate degree in economics.

* * *

In short order, I was immersed in the world of trucking, lodging, insurance, airlines, and railroads. Evenings remained dedicated to my college studies, taking courses in economics and finance at the Wharton School. In a treat to myself, I enrolled in a course at the University of Pennsylvania entitled Art History. That course inspired a lifelong love of art that would lead to a passion for collecting.

Philadelphia was freedom, but it was also a city so unlike Boston. By the time I got home from work and my evening courses at Wharton, the city was close to shutting down. There were no pubs, no clubs for disco dancing, none of the helter-skelter that was part of the life of Boston. Everyone seemed to live on what they called "the Main Line." It sounded like a railroad line, and that's just what it represented—all those upscale suburbs to and from which commuters traveled into the heart of Philadelphia each morning. *Boring beyond imagination*—that was my thought.

As the year wore on, I found myself heading to New York, if only for a night on the town, mostly on the weekends. I was soon a fixture at P. J. Clarke's, the Irish saloon in the shadow of 919 Third Avenue, the address of our New York office. It was a magnet for celebrities, including Jackie Kennedy, Elaine Stritch, and the ever-boisterous TV sports producers. However reckless I might have been, however long into the wee hours I might have stayed up, I'd catch a train back to Thirtieth Street station that ensured I'd be at my desk by seven thirty the next morning.

Susan was better than the best roommate—compatibility was our first and last name, and while she was wined and dined by brokers from New York, a treat I had yet to experience, she was anything but high and mighty. We were soulmates in a hundred ways—sharing the same sense of humor, the same love of food, and the willingness to keep each other's secrets, including the details of our love lives.

Our language was salty—two girls with no rules. The "f" word was simply an adjective used to describe just about everything—the laundry, the salt and pepper, the ticket on my car windshield. One day, we made a pact—it's hard to remember which one of us thought it up. "Why don't we stop using the 'f' word as a regular adjective?" And that day we ended our juvenile habit. It was comical to realize that a mere six years earlier, I'd had no idea what the word "shit" meant.

We didn't have too much time to practice our more refined vocabulary because Susan came home one evening with news. "I'm moving back to Boston to be with Frank."

I wasn't surprised, but I *was* heartbroken. Frank, who'd been courting Susan for several years, proved himself by never giving up on her when she left Boston for Philadelphia. As often as three times a week, he'd fly down to take her out to dinner and spend the night at our apartment. He was perfect for her—smarter than almost anyone we knew; witty, in that Boston Irish way; and a great gourmand. It took a year of separation, but he finally won her love.

It was almost impossible to imagine daily life without Susan, but I knew that Frank was the right man for her, and that proved to be true for the next nearly forty years. I downsized to a one-bedroom apartment a few blocks away at Seventeenth and Locust.

* * *

A year into my job at The Pennsylvania Group, I was promoted, with the title of statistician. It was empowering, and I reveled in the growing role I was playing. That gang of six—the research analysts to whom I reported—had kept their word, and it wasn't long before I was making trips to Harrisburg with Mike Conn, the insurance analyst, to pore over reams of insurance company filings with the State of Pennsylvania. Mike knew the industry inside and out, and I soon had a solid grasp on what differentiated the strong from the weak companies.

An even greater leap forward came a few months later when Sherif Nada invited me to work with him on a new company he was covering—Hartz Mountain, the bird food company turned global supplier of pet products. A family enterprise, it was founded by Max Stern in 1934 as a seller of bird food and canaries. By 1973, it was being run by his son Leonard. Still in his thirties, Leonard was responsible for turning the company into the largest global pet care establishment in the world.

In preparation for our upcoming trip to New York, Sherif instructed me to work up a spreadsheet of forecasts for revenue, costs, and income for the company. I was flattered, but more importantly, I grateful that he was enlarging my role—allowing me to graduate from statistician to junior analyst.

It was October 1973, and stock markets around the world were in turmoil because Egypt and Syria had attacked Israel during the solemn holy day of Yom Kippur. At the same time OPEC imposed an embargo on oil exports to the United States.

Sherif Nada and I were preparing to take the train to New York for a meeting with Hartz Mountain. He had grown up in Egypt, and following the events surrounding the Suez Crisis in late 1956, his parents decided to send him to the US for an education. Leonard Stern's family was Jewish and hailed from Austria.

As the two of us were heading out of the office to catch the train to New York, John Gillan, the witty lead partner at the firm, turned to Sherif and said, "Hey, my boy, listen up. When you introduce yourself to Leonard Stern, I suggest you tell him your name is Sherman Nothing."

The joke was not lost on me. Even with my limited knowledge of Spanish, I made the connection that Nada translated into "nothing." Sherif laughed and was happy to ignore the sophomoric advice.

As Sherif interviewed the chief financial officer and then Leonard Stern, I took copious notes, the benefit of my shorthand training at the Hickox School. Upon our return to Philadelphia, Sherif allowed me to coauthor with him the Hartz Mountain research report he sent out to clients.

Looking back more than fifty years later, I appreciate how easy it might have been for Sherif (or Mike Conn or John Cook for that matter) to have reneged on their promise to give me all the rope I wanted. Each of us fulfilled our part of the bargain, and each of us was a winner.

* * *

I had not taken a day of vacation since joining the firm eighteen months earlier, accumulating vacation days so that I could go to Australia for Christmas in 1973 to visit friends I had made while on the Greek Island of Spetses with Susan.

After the challenges of language in Eastern Europe, I was looking forward to vacationing in English-speaking Australia, oblivious to the vernacular nuances of the language. At a fancy Christmas Eve dinner for about twenty people, I was seated next to the host.

"Would you like a second helping of turkey?" he asked me.

"No thank you," I replied. "I'm stuffed."

The room turned uncomfortably silent—there were a few stares in my direction and I could feel my face becoming flush. Whatever faux pas I'd committed, I was oblivious to it and could only hope that my

American accent would act as an apology. It was only after dinner that a friend shared with me—all the while laughing—"In Australia, if you say you're stuffed, it means you've been laid." Nice way to start a Christmas holiday with strangers.

Fortunately, I would discover that Australians have a rocking good sense of humor, as they willingly overlooked similar gaffes over the next two weeks of sailing, swimming in the shark-infested sea, and non-stop partying.

By the time I returned to Philadelphia in early 1974, global economies were tumbling into recession. Lines at gas stations across the country were hours long, as drivers topped off their cars every few days, fearful that the country might run out of gasoline. The resulting surge in inflation and soaring unemployment were wreaking havoc on the stock prices, and a full bear market unfolded as the year wore on. The Pennsylvania Group was caught in the maelstrom and was soon operating in the red.

By May, I found myself the victim of the firm's dire straits—unemployed. Being laid off didn't come as a shock to me. I'd heard enough moaning among the partners and in the banter at the trading desk.

Suddenly, I wasn't ready to leave Philadelphia. After living a full year and a half in what had seemed like romantic limbo, I met Ryan, a student at the Wharton School, on the first evening of the second semester of the 1973–1974 scholastic year—we were both enrolled in a course on insurance finance, I as an undergraduate and he in pursuit of a master's degree. What remains with me of that first impression was his smile and his jovial sense of humor. We shared our backgrounds—better said, he shared his, the divorced father of a three-year-old daughter, and I did my best at obfuscation. He was too much of a gentleman to probe, and it wasn't long before a beer and a burger after class evolved into more romantic dates on the weekends. What he may have lacked in intellectual curiosity, he more than made up for with a joie de vivre and an optimism that matched my own.

Over dinner that weekend I shared my plight and my plan—I would be heading back to Boston. He understood. Our last few weeks together were memorable, and I was touched when he gave me John Denver's new album—crammed with songs that were part of our romantic life.

We promised to stay in touch and we did—for a while, and then sporadically, and then every year or two. It must have been close to ten years later when he reached out to say he was coming to New York in the near future and wondered if we might have a drink together. A great idea, I said. When some months went by, and I didn't hear from him, I called his office. His assistant was silent when I asked to speak to him. After a long. long pause, she spoke.

"You haven't heard the news?"

When I didn't know how to respond and was too frightened to mouth a word, she said softly, "I'm so sorry, but he died."

My throat tightened, and all I could choke up was one word: "How?"

"He was skiing and had a massive heart attack on the slopes."

Thoughts and emotions tumbled through my mind and heart—he's gone; no way to talk to him ever again; his daughter, she's probably in high school; he was forty-three, just forty-three; John Denver strumming his guitar and singing *Take Me Home, Country Roads*; piercing sadness.

Some memories live with the same clarity as when they happened. It is that way with Ryan.

CHAPTER 17

Coming "Home"

1974

For the umpteenth time in two years, I made the six-hour drive from Philadelphia to Boston. But this trip was different from the others—I was coming to stay. For a while.

It was not what I had planned, but that didn't discourage me. I was feeling empowered—strong, energized, and immensely grateful for all I'd learned—and I was leaving the firm with no hard feelings— far from it.

Wending my way north along Route 95 through the Mid-Atlantic states into New England, I dwelled on how close I'd become to my parents—how close all five of us children now were to them. We were a family without rancor, thanks in large part to the effort of each of us to forgive and to move on.

I reminisced how just a year earlier, after endless sinus and throat infections, I had faced the reality of a tonsillectomy at the age of twenty-four and had chosen to have it in Cambridge so that I could recuperate at my parents' house.

What should have been a week's recovery had turned into a painful three weeks of confinement, the result of a viral infection in my throat. Throughout that time, my mother had attended to my every need, bringing me homemade broths in bed, brushing my hair, or running to the pharmacy for prescriptions.

One afternoon, I had awakened to see her standing over me. "You have the most delicate hands, dahling," she said. It was a touching moment, seeing my mother hovering over me, something she had been denied for most of my childhood. In that moment, the Sister Elizabeth Ann of the past had evaporated, and I had felt an immense maternal love emanating from her to me.

As my recovery progressed, the two of us had watched the Watergate hearings, which were better than any daytime soap opera, and we'd regale my dad when he came home for dinner. We were sitting side by side during the spellbinding interrogation of John Dean when he spilled the beans on the coverup.

I had returned to Philadelphia with a renewed appreciation for my parents. A few years earlier, I had fled the house when my family left the Center, foregoing the opportunity to experience day-to-day living with them. Now, as a mature twenty-four-year-old, I relished their company, and it was with a pang in my heart that I had driven back to Philadelphia.

With Father's Day approaching, I had been excited about getting my father a present that would wow him. On my salary of nearly $11,000, I had felt rich—well, kind of rich, despite being well aware that everyone to whom I reported made multiples of my compensation.

At lunchtime, I had entered Saks Fifth Avenue with a mission. My dad enjoyed fashion and style to an extent that surprised me—after two decades during which his daily garb was a black cassock, he hadn't lost his flair for the worldly.

Something he can wear in the summer, I had thought, as I perused the men's clothing aisles. *Something comfortable and stylish.* Then I had found it—a short-sleeved knit shirt with a navy blue collar and variegated vertical stripes in two shades of blue and white. It was a size large.

Perfect, I thought. *Just beautiful.* The price was $46 (almost exactly $320 today), and I was happy to pay for it with cash and have it wrapped and tied with a bow.

One of my father's favorite words was "beautiful," which he pronounced "beeeeyouteeful," extending the "beeeeee" before putting joyful emphasis on the "you" part. That's what he had exclaimed when he opened his Father's Day present. He wore that shirt summer after summer, for more than thirty years, and it never lost its quality, it never snagged, it never wore thin.

* * *

Now, as I neared the four-bedroom, white-shingled, cottage-style house, with its manicured gardens—the handiwork of my mother—it wasn't lost on me that it was my parents who now had security and I who was jobless. This reversal in fortune felt bizarre.

Always the gentleman, my father was holding the door open as I emerged from my car and awaited his greeting, "How's my little princess?" Each word was spoken with precision and perfect diction. The familiar salutation, from as far back as I could remember, brought intense pleasure and a feeling of warmth and security. I hugged him hard.

"I'm great," I replied, and I meant it. I might have been without a job, but I didn't lack confidence, excitement, or optimism. Most of all, I had my family. I was one with George Gershwin's "I Got Rhythm." Who could ask for anything more?

Barely had I unpacked the car when my father, using his typically philosophical approach, threw me a question, the words still clear in my mind. "How," he asked, "would you like a challenge?" The faint whisp of a smile on his face told me that he had something up his sleeve. *A challenge*, I thought. *Could it be some mathematical problem?* Math, or better said numbers, occupied much of his free time, combined with chess, reading, and of course tennis—in particular, ladies' tennis.

So, I was caught off guard when he then asked, "Have you ever heard of Brenda Frazier?" Without giving me a chance to respond, he went on. "She was named the 'Debutante of the Century' in 1938. She was so beautiful," he said, almost wistfully.

I did quick arithmetic and figured that my father would have been twenty-one years of age at the time of her coming out. It was a little peek into what interested him in his life before the Center. The name meant nothing to me—how could it really?

Daddy went on. "I sold her a Volvo the other day. She said that she needed it to get to her daily appointment with her psychiatrist, who's in Newton."

I was still in the dark. "And she needs someone to drive her there each day. Would you be willing to do that?"

What? What's he thinking? Is he crazy?

"Daddy, what are you talking about? I'm here to look for a job in the investment business, not drive some old lady to her shrink." I used the slang term deliberately, wondering if my father knew what it meant.

He was unruffled by my hysteria. "It's just for a brief time," he said, "while you're looking for a job, princess." As I was shaking my head, unable to drum up a comeback, he said softly, "I told her you would call her this evening."

I was silent, appreciative of his thoughtfulness, both for me and for his customer. It was impossible to refuse him, much less to be upset with him. Daddy was doing what he seemed to thrive on—helping others. His actions were never vainglorious; rather he was a giver, a helper, and an inveterate problem-solver. In this case, he was killing two birds with one stone. His customer, the once-beautiful debutante, had walked into his life in the most ordinary of fashions, and by solving the crisis she had thrown into his lap, he could vicariously relive his fascination with her in a time gone by. His solution had the benefit of allowing his daughter to enter that world of his past and to earn some much-needed money while looking for the job she really wanted.

At the appointed time, I called Brenda Diana Duff Frazier Chatfield-Taylor, whom I addressed as Mrs. Taylor, explaining that my call had been prearranged by my father, Jim Walsh. "Yes," she replied in a soft voice.

"My father said that you need someone to drive you to the doctor," I said, almost in question-like form. "Yes," again from her. Lest she get the idea that I might have been looking for such a position, I explained my situation—that I was in the world of finance, and this would be a temporary situation. "Yes," again.

"And how much will you charge?" I'd already given serious thought to that sure-to-come question. My recent salary of $10,800 had been the equivalent of a little over a five-dollar hourly rate. *That will be my rate*, I thought. *She can take it or leave it.*

"Five dollars per hour, Mrs. Taylor," I replied.

"That's awfully high," she responded, and for a moment I hoped it might kill the deal. But deep down, I wanted to please my dad. Mrs. Taylor relented, and I told her I was looking forward to meeting her the next morning.

My father's obvious pleasure when I told him that I'd accepted Mrs. Taylor's offer allowed me to see his role in the matter in a new light. He, who for so many years had been denied the opportunity to play the role of father, and who had needed advice and counsel from his eldest daughter only a few short years in the past, was now in the position to provide an opportunity, however temporary, to that daughter. It was in the spirit of gratitude to my father, whose love I'd always felt despite years of silence, that I embraced (well, almost embraced) the role of chauffeur for Mrs. Taylor.

It was the start of one of the most unusual, yet fascinating, three months of my life.

CHAPTER 18

Tongue on Rye at the Ritz

FROM MAY TO SEPTEMBER 1974

I slipped into the driver's seat of Mrs. Taylor's new Volvo. "She's on her way down," said the doorman, who had brought the polished black station wagon to the front of Mrs. Taylor's townhouse at 81 Beacon Street.

With the windows down, I embraced the summer air and took in my surroundings. Across the street was the familiar Public Garden, Boston's lush Victorian park that I knew well—both from my earliest childhood when I rode with my mother on the swan boat and then as a young adult when I lived but a few blocks away. The park was the playground for the children who lived on Beacon Street and its environs, Boston's poshest neighborhood.

My mind came back to the job at hand, and I wondered why Mrs. Taylor, who I presumed to be a wealthy lady, had chosen to buy a Volvo, at the time a practical, but hardly luxurious, vehicle.

And where is she? It had been more than half an hour since the doorman said she was on her way. What could have happened? At that moment, the front door opened and into the sunlight emerged a wraith-like figure, dressed in crisp white linen trousers and a boucle knit jacket, also white.

Whatever notion of beauty I had conjured up in my mind's eye about the seventeen-year-old who, some thirty-six years earlier, had been dubbed Debutante of the Century evaporated, and I held my breath as Mrs. Taylor, gently guided by the doorman, took the several steps up to the sidewalk. She appeared ancient, far older than her fifty-two years. Too frail to open the car door, she allowed herself to be aided into the passenger seat. The doorman nodded to me as he fastened her seatbelt.

Her powdered face, almost Kabuki-like, contrasted sharply with the perfect symmetry of her bold ruby red lipstick, and both were framed with shoulder-length black hair that met in a widow's peak and matched to perfection her black eyebrows.

"Good morning, Mrs. Taylor," I said, as our eyes met, and she replied the same softly.

It was up to Mrs. Taylor to direct me from the heart of Boston to the house in Newton (an upscale suburb about twelve miles west of the city) where her psychiatrist had his office. For reasons that would become obvious within a few days, navigation was not her strong suit at 11:30 in the morning, or perhaps at any time of the day.

We had no sooner started on our way, when I reached to turn on the air conditioner, as the day was becoming warm. Mrs. Taylor became hysterical. "Turn that off!" she shrieked, her voice shrill with agitation. Before the air had a chance to emerge from the vent, I snapped the dial off, concluding that Mrs. Taylor, with barely any flesh on her bones, probably couldn't manage the cold. But I was flummoxed when she added a seeming non sequitur. "You'll ruin the engine of the car!"

"So sorry, Mrs. Taylor," I responded, trying to comprehend the logic (or lack thereof) behind her statement. For the next ten minutes—which felt like forty—I drove in silence as Mrs. Taylor assumed the role of navigator but hardly with a sense of confidence. Each instruction came with a somewhat timorous "I think" as an addendum.

As the temperature in the car became increasingly uncomfortable, I began to second-guess my willingness to take on this part-time position. *What have I gotten myself into?* I thought. *Thanks a lot, Daddy.*

We were no more than ten minutes away from our destination when my new boss ordered me to turn on the frigid air. "Of course, Mrs. Taylor," I said with appreciation, but not daring to ask for an explanation. I didn't want to go home at the end of day one and have to admit to my father that I'd been fired.

It was close to one o'clock when we arrived for what Mrs. Taylor had told me would be a noon appointment with her psychiatrist. He took her anyway. *How nice of him,* I thought. (It would be years before I would come to discover the truth—that Dr. Chase, aware that his patient would be an hour late, kept a second appointment for her and charged her for a full two hours.)

An hour and a half later, I was delivering Mrs. Taylor back to the front door of 81 Beacon Street. As the doorman provided her a strong arm and a gentle hand, she turned to me and said softly, "Tomorrow morning, why don't you come upstairs at ten o'clock and wait for me in the foyer."

"Yes, Mrs. Taylor," I said as I wished her a good afternoon. If only I could have seen what lay ahead.

In quick succession over the next several days, Mrs. Taylor made use of my presence in the foyer to aid her in her morning ablutions. On the first day, it was to help her get her Chanel jacket on, and a day later, it included assisting her emaciated body into an A-line white linen dress and zipping it up.

Each incremental bit of help she requested seemed small on its own. That is, until my second week on the job. As I was reading the newspaper in the foyer, she called out to me in a plaintive voice, "Can you help me out of the tub?"

Get her out of the tub? What's going on? Rushing through the living room and then her bedroom, I slowed down at the open bathroom door.

"Mrs. Taylor?" I called out.

"I'm stuck," was all she said, through grunting noises, so I bounded in. The poor lady was trying to hoist herself over the side of the tub, only to slide back into the water slippery with the remnants of fragrant bath bubbles. I grabbed her extended, emaciated arm, fearing for a second that I might break it off. As she held on to me, I took tiny steps backwards and, as gently as possible, I hauled her over the edge of the bathtub—a bald, naked, cadaverous lady.

"Thank you," was her soft reply as I wrapped a towel around her.

The impeccably dressed, coiffed, manicured and made-up woman who emerged from her apartment each morning was a transfiguration that resulted from a full two hours of ritualistic theatre. Emerging from her pillow-laden bed each morning, the anorexic, drug-addicted, alcoholic, and emotionally fragile Mrs. Taylor would set upon the task of gearing up for the day, by soaking in a foaming bubble bath. When the bubbles were no more, she needed strong arms to extricate her safely from the slippery surface. If that call to action was my test, I must have passed it, because I became those strong arms five days each week.

Nothing in my life before that summer of 1974 prepared me for the role in which I now found myself—intimate personal assistant, dresser, chauffeur, confidante, and lunch companion. As a child and living within the confines of my religious community, I was taught to practice the Catholic virtue of modesty—dressing and undressing behind a closed curtain. When, at seventeen, I was thrust out into the world, I found myself relaxing those puritan strictures. But the sight of a nearly sixty-year-old woman's decrepit, naked body was, for me at the age of twenty-four, a shock.

Once seated—barely clothed—at her frilly, pink vanity, a three-way mirror no more than a few inches in front of her, Mrs. Taylor would embark on her daily ritual of metamorphosis. A small receptacle contained her "vitamins," as she referred to them, which she downed with "water"—one large gulp that caused her to wince. If I was fooled by her references on that first day, I soon caught on. It took those uppers and vodka to sustain her until lunch time.

Fortified by her "breakfast," she began the beautification process. Between puffs on her cigarette, she would apply layers of makeup over her desiccated face. Additional sips of "water" did nothing to diminish her ability to perform magic on her visage. With a steady hand, she applied microthin black eyeliner and a set of long lashes to her eyelids, and then painted a widow's peak to replicate the hair she once had. The black-haired wig that Alexander, her beloved hairdresser, set and teased in his salon around the corner completed her transformation.

Mrs. Taylor tended to forget how many "vitamins" she had swallowed and how much "water" she had imbibed, which could wreak havoc as she tried to put on her clothes. A piercing "Eeeee" was her frequent cry, a response to pain in one of her limbs as she strove to get her spindle-thin legs into her white trousers. Sometimes it was all for naught, and she'd hurl the piece of clothing onto the floor and demand a dress—one of her many identically cut linen A-lines in a variety of colors.

Dressed, but not quite ready to face the world, Mrs. Taylor turned to the selection of jewelry that suited her mood, a task that could add as much as half an hour to the ritual. The necklace was easy—a double strand of pearls that looked to be at least twelve millimeters in diameter—and a matching pair of earrings, but the search for the desired brooch or ring required a trip to the safe in another room in the apartment. Some days, it was the sapphire that had been a present from some old boyfriend. Other days, she wanted her favorite diamond ring—a gargantuan emerald cut whose sheer size made it look like a child's piece of costume jewelry that might have been picked up for twenty-five cents at the five and dime store. She would sometimes recount which of the men in her past life was associated with a particular piece of jewelry. I was all ears—the image of Mrs. Taylor enjoying dalliances when she was my age was mesmerizing.

In a perverse way, the later we were running, the more adamant she was to demand additional jewelry, and it fell to me to open the safe—armed with the combination that Mrs. Taylor inevitably bungled. That meant I had to wait for the gentle knock on the door, the signal that the police were responding to an alarm. They were invariably understanding—it struck me that they had been on this beat for years.

The best way to manage a morning's crisis, I learned, was to treat it with humor. Despite the multitude of ailments that Mrs. Taylor had accumulated over time, she kept alive both a sharp mind and a quick wit. This most often was on display when, after an hour-long session with her psychiatrist in Newton, we'd stop for lunch at the Ritz-Carlton Hotel, a stone's throw from her Beacon Street home.

The waiter greeted her the same way each day. "Good afternoon, Mrs. Taylor. Will you have your regular lunch today?"

"Yes, please," she'd reply. She could put on the best show of manners, conversation, and humor, which drew me to her in a way that I may never fully comprehend. Within a few minutes, our lunch appeared—the same every day: a tongue on rye with mustard for each of us and a double vodka on the rocks for her. I was taken aback when she first ordered that sandwich. I had never seen Mrs. Taylor consume anything but pills, vodka, and in the afternoon, a few sips of consommé. Not knowing exactly what to order, I simply followed her lead, and was soon a tongue-on-rye fan.

We'd chat softly during lunch, and on her good days, Mrs. Taylor enjoyed sharing tales from her long-gone glamorous youth. In almost cryptic fashion, and with a cigarette-induced raspy voice, she'd toss out names, some of which were familiar—Howard Hughes, Joan Crawford, Peter Arno, the Stork Club—and others that meant nothing to me—in particular a debutante named Cobina Wright Jr., a contemporary socialite whom, it was clear, Mrs. Taylor considered a competitor. Her face would contort into a frown of almost disgust when she mentioned her nemesis's name, without ever offering details to rationalize her distaste. It was almost as though I was her confidante, a friend in whom she could confide, or perhaps more likely, with whom she could share bits of nostalgia. By the end of the meal, however, when the second vodka glass was empty, and most of her tongue sandwich remained untouched on the plate, it was time to shepherd her back to 81 Beacon Street.

There was a day at the Ritz, as we nibbled and she drank, that Mrs. Taylor became animated. "'Ship' is coming for my birthday," she said, referring to her first husband, "Shipwreck" Kelly, the father of her daughter, Victoria. Despite having been divorced for nearly thirty years, she spoke of him often in endearing terms. Her abiding fondness for him was evident in the array of silver-framed photos of their life together that filled the apartment—their wedding and honeymoon, arm in arm on shopping sprees and with their daughter, Victoria.

"And he's got a surprise for me," she said, raising her shoulders as a child might when talking about something exciting. "He'll be staying a few days, so you'll get to meet him."

Her expressive black eyes lit up as she regaled me with stories of their life together during the war. He was in the FBI, she said, and together the two of them went to South America—Chile, Peru, and Argentina—where he was a spy. The life she described seemed almost fictional—flying on tiny airplanes, through the Andes mountains, attending cocktail parties, as well as her husband's feats of derring-do. Reliving, and perhaps embellishing, those memories made her gleeful and brought out her wicked sense of humor, as when she told in detail her horror at discovering that that she had to share the soap bar and the shower, in one of those far-flung countries, with the housekeeper. "Can you believe it?" she squealed with a glee she was experiencing only in retrospect.

I suddenly felt as though I was family, as though Mrs. Taylor wanted me to celebrate with her and Ship, and it dawned on me that she had no family, no one with whom to share the joys of life. She was a lonely, abandoned woman, with a daughter who lived far away, two ex-husbands, a gay hairdresser (for her wigs) who was her escort on the very few occasions she attended an evening event, a psychoanalyst who was double billing her, and a coterie of staff who lived in fear of her.

The day Shipwreck was scheduled to arrive, Mrs. Taylor was in great humor, but I had to leave before he made his appearance. When we met the following day, I was taken aback by the toll that thirty years had taken on him and unprepared for the man I met and whom I addressed as "Mr. Kelly." He was bigger, brawnier, and rougher looking than in his photos, all of which memorialized a time long in the past. At sixty-four, he seemed every bit his age, and his somewhat squashed nose made him appear more like a boxer than a retired football player.

Next to the delicate Mrs. Taylor, he was immense. But he was attentive to her, and she beamed from her bed as she held the Pekingese puppy he'd brought her for a birthday present. As she nodded off, the puppy nestled next to her, and I headed to the kitchen to make a cup of tea.

Suddenly I was aware of Mr. Kelly's hulk looming over me at the stove, and when I turned to greet him, he pushed me up against the wall, and thrust his tongue into my throat. Unable to speak, I pressed my hands against his chest with all my strength, unrelenting but silent. The memory of that night in Cambridge, five years earlier, flashed through my mind. Never again, and I pushed harder. He was slow to back off, and when he did, I stared at him cold-eyed.

"No," I said. Just one word with quiet force. I was angry. He didn't scare me because anger has a way of overcoming fear. There was no need for hysterics, no reason to wake Mrs. Taylor.

I turned on my heel, left the kitchen, and headed back to Mrs. Taylor's bedroom, tidying up her clothes until she awoke.

I wished her goodnight and left, feeling like a warrior woman who'd just been victorious in battle.

* * *

Mrs. Taylor came out of the psychiatrist's office and we walked together to the car. As I buckled her into the seat, she spoke in a faint voice that had a nervous overtone, "Dr. Chase wants to see you next week." I was nonplussed—what did he want from me?

And so it was that I found myself face-to-face with the man who, I would later learn, was charging Mrs. Taylor for two hours of treatment every day, when in fact he saw her for only one. He opened with a pleasantry and then asked how things were between Mrs. Taylor and me, which I found puzzling, and asked my own question. "Do you realize that Mrs. Taylor is drunk every day when she gets here?"

He was silent as I went on, trying to appear attentive, but he'd already lost my respect. I went on. "Her food consists mostly of vodka and pills. Her lunch is two glasses of vodka and two bites of a sandwich. Sometimes she has some broth in the late afternoon."

After another moment of silence, his response came in the form of a question. "Would you consider moving in with her? You're the only person in the world whom she loves," he said, in a quiet voice.

I was stunned and unable to speak as I tried to grapple with the meaning of his words. *Love me? Live with her? I barely know her. How is this possible?*

In the ensuing silence, I tried to pull my thoughts together. I also felt a twinge of flattery. Mrs. Taylor—this woman of the world (once upon a time), this member of high society (once upon a time), this lady who struck terror in her staff and seemed friendless—loved me.

Taken aback at his request, I did, at least, have the presence of mind to respond with good common sense, even as I knew it would be a disappointment. "No, Dr. Chase," I said. "I can't. I'm looking for a job in the investment business and won't be staying with her much longer." He didn't push me, nor did he indicate that Mrs. Taylor was aware of his request, so I assumed she was not part of his scheme.

That brief meeting left me overwhelmed. Mrs. Taylor loved me. I was the only person whom she loved.

And in that moment, it came to me—the feeling was mutual. I did indeed love her, too. Despite her insecurities, her inability to take charge of her own life, and her outbursts of anger, there was but a thin veneer to pierce in order to find a genuinely warm and painfully vulnerable human being, someone who needed and wanted what all of us crave— love. I didn't judge her; I didn't share the insanities of some days with anyone, not even my dad. When she and I were alone together, relaxed and enjoying lunch, the veil was lifted, and her true self emerged, as she shared the humor in her soul and the intelligence in her mind.

The incident with Dr. Chase brought home to me the need to prepare Mrs. Taylor for my eventual departure. My job interviews had been scant in the abysmal economic environment and stock market bloodbath, but by early August, I had a promising prospect. It was at one of our lunches that I shared the news with her.

"Mrs. Taylor, I've been interviewing for a job as an investment research analyst," I said, keeping it simple and hoping my tone of voice was the right combination of excitement and also concern for her. She responded thoughtfully. "I wish I knew more about stocks," she said ruefully. "I never know what the bank is talking about."

If there was a cause-and-effect response, I'll never know, but it wasn't more than a few days later when Dr. Chase committed Mrs. Taylor to Newton-Wellesley Hospital to "dry out." I visited her each afternoon—some days were good, and others found her despairful, begging me to find a way to get her out of "this prison," as she referred to her room. Holding her hand, I'd promise her that she'd be coming home soon, not knowing if I was lying to her or telling her the truth.

If her stay was meant to cure her, it didn't. She was released within a week or so, and almost immediately, she invited me to fly with her to her summer house in East Harwich at the far end of Cape Cod. It was a magical weekend—just the two of us as companions (excluding the essential regiment of staff). We took walks—noticeably short ones. We sat in lounge chairs in the shade and let the ocean breezes waft over us.

I had never stayed overnight with Mrs. Taylor and was not prepared for the discovery that she was an insomniac. It was close to ten o'clock, as I was heading off to my bedroom, when she beckoned me to sit on the end of her bed. It was the start of a long night. In a voice that often drifted off, Mrs. Taylor shared the misery of youth—how she'd begged her mother to allow her to stay at boarding school in Switzerland, how she never wanted to be a debutante.

The eastern sky was embracing the dawn when she finally closed her eyes in sleep, and I made my way to my own bed, with a greater appreciation for the woman I would soon be leaving. We were decades apart in years and with vastly different life experiences, but there was an emotional bond between us—and for good reason. Each of us had experienced an out-of-the-ordinary childhood, through decisions that were not ours to make, much less control. I sensed her desperation—intelligent and curious, she had not been allowed to set the course for her own life. The pressures of a vapid social life withered her soul and she fell into a pit of self-destruction. I was the lucky one—being kicked out of my home at the age of seventeen had the benefit of severing the confining bonds of manipulation, allowing me the freedom to chart my own future.

It was easy to love Mrs. Taylor—the intelligent and quick-witted lady who never found a way to jettison the shackles of society gone wrong—now wasting away from her inner demons under the weight of drugs and alcohol.

* * *

When we returned to Beacon Street the following week, my birthday was but a few days away, and Mrs. Taylor let me know that she had something for me. On that Friday, shortly before heading home to my parents' house for the weekend, she came out of her bedroom, and we sat together in the living room, a place I had hardly ever seen her frequent.

Giving that little "Eeeee" sound that could represent both excitement and pain, she said, "I have some birthday presents for you." It was almost as though I was her daughter, and she wanted to see my response to what she had dreamed up for me. She didn't let me down.

Two packages were wrapped in exquisite paper with a marvelously crafted bow on each. I started with the smaller of the two—it was a watercolor painting of a hummingbird that she had painted, unbeknownst to me, while she was "drying out" at Newton-Wellesley Hospital. She inscribed it, "To Pat, Happy Birthday, August 16, 1974."

I was speechless—almost moved to tears—and I hugged her feeble frame, as much as I dared without the possibility of breaking her in half.

The second present was equally thoughtful and creative—a leather briefcase in a soft gray-green with my initials PW engraved under the handle.

"For your new job," she said, with a hint of pride—the new job I had yet to clinch, but which she quite evidently expected me to get.

I have kept both presents for nearly fifty years now. The painting hangs in my kitchen, and whenever I look at it, I am brought back to those three months in the summer of 1974 when my father introduced me to a woman who had been abandoned by a fickle world that had once pretended to adore her, a woman who'd been robbed of her dignity, a woman I was blessed to come to know and respect and even love. We were our own version of the "odd couple," as different as night and day.

Over the next eight years, after I had moved to New York, I stayed in touch with Mrs. Taylor, making trips to Boston to visit her in the hospital as her emaciated body became increasingly ravaged by drugs, by alcohol, and in the end, by cancer. Ours was a friendship bonded through what we had in common—our humanity.

CHAPTER 19

Good-Bye, Boston

1974

I t was a time of seeming peril in the country—the price of oil had quadrupled from $3 to over $10 a barrel, resulting in hours-long lines at the gas pump. Unemployment was rising steadily, and the economy was in a deep recession. The Dow, which had peaked at an all-time high of 1051 in January 1973, was now, eighteen months later, hovering around 800, a drop of nearly 25 percent.

As if that weren't enough unwelcome news, the presidency was in a state of siege. The Watergate scandal had entrapped President Richard Nixon, leading to his resignation. It was with that backdrop that I celebrated my twenty-sixth birthday in August with my family, full of optimism, in the way that twentysomethings, who have yet to experience the full ups and downs of life, are eager to express.

* * *

And then a door opened, in the form of a first interview with the director of research at the small asset management company of Studley

Shupert. It was followed by a second interview with the team of stock analysts, a handful of young men, perhaps a few years older than I was. There was a camaraderie among them that gave me a good feeling about the place.

As I was getting ready to leave, the director of research followed me to the elevator. "Would you be available to come back next week?" he asked. "I'd like you to meet the chief investment officer." And that was how I came to be face-to-face with the man who occupied the corner office—Stewart Harvey. "Stew" he was called.

This was an era before hiring was conducted through elaborate human resources departments that analyzed résumés and did back-ground checks. Word-of-mouth recommendations from trusted sources was as sure a way as any to open the door to an opportunity.

The name Stew Harvey was familiar to anyone who worked in the world of finance in Boston. For years, he'd held the prestigious posi-tion of director of research at the renowned Fidelity Management. So, it was with a sense of awe that I entered his presence in an unpretentious wood-paneled corner office. While the minor details of the interview have faded from memory, what remains is a clear image of the man him-self and his intense engagement.

He was older—or so he seemed to me at the age of twenty-six—and was wearing a three-piece tweed suit, despite the oppressive mugginess of a late August day. Coming from behind his desk, he stretched out his hand in a shake that was strong but not aggressively so. His bespectacled dark eyes engaged me with intent.

"Take a seat," he said, in a deep, gravelly voice that was close to gruff, gesturing to one of the two straight-backed chairs that formed the base of a triangle, the apex of which was a brass pedestal ashtray, a long arm's length from each of us. It was a standard piece of office equipment at a time when those who smoked cigarettes—something I had never tried—were at liberty to do so in offices, in restaurants, and on airplanes.

The interview had barely begun when Mr. Harvey leaned forward, pulled the ash tray toward himself, and making a sound like "CHTP," he spat into it, and then turned his full attention back to me. It struck me as odd that, if he had something in his mouth that he needed to get rid of, he didn't simply use a handkerchief instead of spitting. The interview continued as did the "CHTPing"—every few seconds, it seemed. Thus, I was introduced to spittoons and the art of chewing tobacco.

In some ways, the interview seemed more a stream of consciousness emanating from an oracle—he did most of the talking, almost as though I was already employed.

"It's a tough market out there," he said. And then, almost out of the blue, he switched gears. "I can pay you twelve thousand dollars as a research analyst," he said in his crisp baritone, "and I need you to cover the savings and loans companies."

I have a job! With a pay increase! (over the $10,800 I had been making in Philadelphia). *And a real title—research analyst!* It was perfect—I couldn't ask for anything more.

Before I could think of how to respond, Mr. Harvey stood up. "Come, I'll show you to your office."

Office? My own office? How could I be so lucky?

I followed him the few steps to my new quarters. Floor-to-ceiling windows ran along one wall, a large desk filled the center of the space, and there was a door for privacy—all the trappings of success, or so it seemed to me.

"My door is always open," he said, as he prepared to leave, and then with an almost shy smile, he added, "Call me Stew."

For a moment, I sat at my new desk in my new office reveling in my new role and loving my new title—research analyst. I still had one more year to go before finishing my degree in economics at Boston University, but that hadn't concerned Stew. And then reality set in.

He's assigned me to cover the savings and loans industry. I know nothing about it.

My two years as a statistician in Philadelphia had given me a solid understanding of an array of industries—airlines, railroads, trucking, insurance, and hospitality, but nothing that prepared me to take on the

S&Ls (as they were known). But this much I did know—the industry was in dire straits.

Is this a test? To prove that I can do it?

There was only one way to find out. As I plowed through stacks of annual reports and Wall Street research, I took Stew Harvey's words to heart—"My door is always open"—and made the short pilgrimage from my office to his on countless occasions. True to his word, he had a ready answer for my litany of questions concerning the state of the economy and the impact of the Federal Reserve's aggressive tightening policing on an economy already in recession. No question was unworthy of his time, and he was patient in his explanations about concepts and terms that were novel to me—disintermediation, as an example, which was a life-or-death matter for the flailing S&L industry. The more we talked, the more evident it became that the industry he assigned to me was in dire straits.

I came to enjoy the faintly sweet smell of chewed tobacco—it represented an aura of intellectual engagement, of freedom to ask and to challenge. It also represented what felt like a pathway to success.

No more than six weeks could have passed in my new role, when I overheard a conversation at the water fountain—literally as I was leaning over to sip from the small spout. There was no secrecy about it—just two people talking about a firm called Gardner & Preston Moss, a somewhat larger Boston-based asset management company, which was about to take over the company I had just come to work for.

My mind went into overdrive—*We're being acquired? That can't be good news.*

I made a beeline from the bubbler to Stew's office, sat down in front of his desk, and came to the point. "Is it true that Gardner & Preston Moss is taking us over?"

"Yes," he replied softly.

I paused, and my words, which were unpremeditated, remain with me to this day. "Does that mean it's 'last in, first out'?"

We both knew the expression—an accounting term applied to a company's inventory—but in this case I was applying the concept to me, as the most recent addition to the employee team.

He spoke gently, "I'm afraid so."

A tear rolled down my cheek, and I let it do so because I had no other response inside me.

"Don't cry," he said, his voice soft and almost caressing. "You'll make me cry."

You'll make me cry. I hadn't seen that side of Stew—the caring human being. Over the few weeks that I'd been in my new role, I'd come to appreciate him for the generosity of his time, for his advice, and for his brilliance. He was old enough to be my father, and now he was acting like one to me. I didn't want to make him cry, so I rose and walked back the dozen or so steps to my own office.

Within a few minutes, Stew was standing in front of my desk. His voice was quiet. "I can't promise you a job," he said, "but there's a research boutique in New York that's looking for a stock analyst, and I've arranged for you to have an interview there tomorrow. The rest is up to you."

* * *

Catching an early morning shuttle to LaGuardia, it was ten o'clock when I rode the elevator to the twenty-ninth floor of 666 Fifth Avenue at the corner of Fifty-Second Street and met Brad Landon, the senior partner in the six-person research boutique that carried his name. The only preparation I had made for this interview was to be as "New York" as I could, but at the age of twenty-six, I wore no makeup and had hair that came down almost to my waist. My best attempt to appear sophisticated was to put my hair up into a bun and wear the most businesslike dress in my far-from-upscale wardrobe.

The interview encompassed the entire day—including a lunch at which Brad ordered a scotch for each of us as a cocktail (I sniffed mine) and a bottle of wine during the meal, which I hardly sipped, lest I not be on my toes for my afternoon interviews.

Brad, a soft-spoken man, at least at this first interview, had a passion for researching and investing in machinery stocks, which covered a broad swath of the industrial sector of the economy: farm and construction equipment, engines and transmissions, electrical motors, oil service equipment, and any derivations.

It was quickly evident to me that for him there was no greater vocation than to spend one's time analyzing the financial data for myriad machinery companies, flying to the companies' headquarters to engage personally with the CEOs, coming to a determination about buying or selling each stock, and then, even more importantly, convincing the customers of the validity of one's research.

Shortly after five o'clock, following a full afternoon of meetings with the team, Brad invited me to dinner. The moment of truth was approaching—*Will he offer me a job?*

We sat down at a corner banquette at the elegant La Caravelle on West Fifty-Fifth Street. A cocktail first, then an exquisite bottle of red wine accompanied a dinner of French cuisine at its elegant best.

We were still on the first course when Brad said, "This is my favorite restaurant, and we're here because everyone at the firm agrees that we'd like you to join us." He paused briefly before going on, "We're a partnership, and we do things that way," adding wryly, "If I weren't going to offer you the job, we would have gone to dinner at the St. Regis."

The St. Regis, I thought. *Not too shabby a place to tell someone they aren't being hired.*

Brad went on. "We'd like you to start on January 1, with a beginning salary of seventeen thousand and five hundred dollars. But I want you to know that if it works out, you'll make far more than that.

"Think about it and call me tomorrow," Brad said, and for the rest of the dinner, he talked about the stocks he thought I should start following when I arrived—Eaton Corporation, the manufacturer of heavy-duty transmissions for on- and off-highway vehicles, which was on the top of his list; Cummins Engine, the world's largest diesel engine maker;

and Dana Corporation—all manufacturers of engines and transmissions, a far cry from the intangible world of financial intermediaries. I loved the idea—something new to master.

It was nearly eight o'clock when Brad ordered a car to take me to the airport. Catching the last shuttle back to Boston, I found myself bouncing from one emotional state to another. I'd been offered a job in New York, the center of the world, and it came with a big raise! A 50 percent raise! It was like starting a new life. Luck just fell into my lap—what had I done to deserve it?

And then a wave of nostalgia washed over me, eroding the fringes of euphoria. Accepting this position—that I was ecstatic to have been offered—meant leaving my family once again, a mere six months after coming back from Philadelphia. Just when Boston seemed like home again.

Back and forth on an emotional teeter-totter—but how could I say "no" to any job, much less this one? I couldn't afford to be unemployed. *What will my family say? I'll so miss them.*

I slept fitfully that night.

* * *

It was close to my final trip to Stew's office—at eight o'clock the next morning. No matter how early I arrived, he was always there ahead of me.

The look in his eye made me wonder if he knew what I was about to say. It had not yet dawned on me that Stew Harvey, after years as director of research at Fidelity Management, probably knew every brokerage firm and every research boutique in the country—at least those that were worth knowing. He'd been able to pay handsomely for research that was valuable, so of course, he knew the best of the best on Wall Street. On my behalf, he had reached out to one of those small gems in New York City. He had put in a good word for me and left it up to me to prove myself. It had worked. As a novice in the world of finance, I was oblivious to the power he could wield.

My statement was short, but I gave it with a smile. "They offered me the job."

"Congratulations," he said, his deep baritone softened by the genuine smile lighting up his normally serious visage.

I grew quiet, and with a little shake of my head, I spilled out the one piece of emotion I couldn't keep quiet. "I can't believe that I've just moved back to Boston, close to my family—and now this. What do I do?"

Deep down I knew the answer, but I needed to hear it from him.

Looking straight into my eyes with his own fiercely black ones, he asked, "Do you want to make it big in this world?"

The answer was easy—"Yes," I said, and I had an inkling of what might be coming next.

His response was one that countless of mentors in the financial industry have given over the years: "Then go to New York."

CHAPTER 20

"Sister Elizabeth Ann" Revisits New York

1974

My mother reacted with genuine enthusiasm when I shared with her my impending move to New York City.

"Let's go together to find an apartment for you, dahling. I've always loved New York."

I had to smile—over the prior twenty-five years, her countless trips to Old Gotham had but one purpose. Dressed in her religious habit and responding to the name of Sister Elizabeth Ann, she had pounded the pavements of Manhattan on a singular mission. For eight hours each day, from Monday through Friday, she could be seen hauling a heavy black leather bag that was crammed with softcover books. Written by Feeney and Sister Catherine, the titles were uniquely Catholic—*Our Glorious Popes, Saints to Know and Love*, and *Bread of Life*—and my mother was in search of Catholics who might buy one (for a single dollar) or, better still, make a cash donation. There was immense pressure on her, and her Sister companions, to sell hundreds of books each day, regardless of the heat, the rain, or the snow. The proceeds were the sole source of revenue for the one hundred members of our community.

Now, having left religious life and having re-embraced the life of a woman of the world (albeit a very Catholic woman), she was aching to experience New York in ways that had been denied to her in the past.

Mother and daughter, we were a mere nineteen years apart in age, and, in a way, we were more like sisters on a new adventure than a mother-daughter team. I was accustomed to her common sense and business acumen—in that way we were much alike—but she surprised me with her big-city sophistication.

We'd been given a lead on an apartment building in the Turtle Bay section of the city—midtown on the East Side, an easy ten-minute walk from where my new office would be on Fifth Avenue at Fifty-Second Street. The one-bedroom apartment seemed perfect to me, with 1,000 thousand square feet and a reasonable rent of $395/month. On my anticipated salary of $17,500, it seemed more than manageable. (In today's dollars, that was the equivalent of nearly $2,500 rent and a salary of a bit over $112,000.) No matter that it was on the second floor and overlooked the roof of the garage next door. It was spacious, with ample closet space and windows that stretched across both the living room and the adjoining bedroom. I was ready to sign the one-year lease, until my mother raised her finger in a cautionary gesture.

"Let's look around a bit more," she advised. "It's good to see what else there is." That fragment of wisdom caught me unawares and, silently, I relished the experience of learning from my mother.

For the next two days, we scoured the East Side of Manhattan, and in the evening, we treated ourselves—one day to a Broadway musical and the next to the ballet. We ate in trendy, if not elegant, restaurants and conserved our resources by staying in a modest hotel on Lexington Avenue.

On Sunday morning, after attending the High Mass at Saint Patrick's Cathedral—a first for both of us—we joined swarms of tourists in the holiday pastime of window-shopping at Bergdorf Goodman and Saks Fifth Avenue. It was a fairytale weekend.

"In a month, I'll be living here," I whispered the words like a mantra under my breath.

By early Sunday afternoon, I had signed a lease on the not-so-fancy but the right-size and right-price apartment that we had first visited. Before we headed out on the four-plus-hour drive back to Boston, my mother gave me a whispered piece of advice.

"It's close to Christmas, dahling," she said, "and it would be a good idea if you tipped the building staff."

I looked at her quizzically, and she hastened to add, "You're not paying them for what they've done for you this year; you're paying them for what they will do for you next year."

I nodded in silence and thought, *How does she know things like that?*

A warm feeling welled up inside me. It was gratifying, after years of isolation from my mother, to observe her as urbane, to reap the benefits of her worldly experience, to learn from her. There was also an accompanying wistfulness—why couldn't it have been that way for those twenty years between when I was six and now at twenty-six?

I've pondered that question over the ensuing decades and in doing so, I have come to realize and to appreciate that despite the absence of normal family life after the age of six, I *was* able to learn from *each* of my parents during those years of familial deprivation.

A few months after "the separation" (as I think of it) when I was not yet seven years of age, it was my mother—as Sister Elizabeth Ann—who was assigned to teach the eldest of the "little sisters" how to use a sewing machine, how to knit and to purl, to crochet, and to embroider. Those hour-long Saturday afternoon sessions, despite being devoid of motherly hugs, small talk, or anything that singled me out from the rest of the girls, were nonetheless heavenly. Simply to be in her presence—to listen to her soft voice as she explained how to create embroidery stitches, or to pick up a lost stich on knitting project—was blissful. When the lesson was over, it was hard to hold back tears, and I spent the next six days in countdown mode until two o'clock the following Saturday.

Once the community left the stockade-fence-enclosed compound in Cambridge and moved to the bucolic hamlet of Still River, thirty miles west, it was in the kitchen that I found the opportunity to continue to learn from my mother. A day or two each week, she played the role of pastry chef, or as we referred to it, the dessert cook.

As I became a teenager, I was frequently assigned to assist her for an hour or two in the afternoon after school. As silence was the rule, it was in whispered tones that she explained the art of baking—how to fold beaten egg whites into an angel food cake batter; how to make butter frosting both creamy and light; how to frost a cake. And her secret ingredient for every cake batter—a few drops of vanilla extract. Her lessons have lived long—to this day, when I flour a cake pan, or cut wax paper to line a baking dish, or engage in the simple act of turning on an electric eggbeater, I am brought back to that large stone-floored basement kitchen with its industrial-sized ovens, and a warm feeling engulfs me.

I never harbored a doubt that my parents adored me, nor did I, as a child, feel that they had ever abandoned me. To me the culprits—perhaps better described as the villains—were the powers that ran the Center, Father Feeney and Sister Catherine. Forcing the adult members of the community to take a vow of obedience to Feeney, and to whomever he delegated, was a calculated maneuver used to manipulate the parents into abdicating their parental rights, and in so doing, to metamorphose a religious community into a cult.

However, with the benefit of time and maturity, I have come to accept the truth—my parents could have prevented the sundering of our family by refusing the demands of Feeney and Sister Catherine to hand over their children and to take a vow of celibacy.

I've been left to wonder—why didn't my father, a man with an exceptional intellect and a strong theologically based moral code, push back? Why did he not make the case to Feeney that God ordained the structure of nature in a way that imposed upon parents the responsibility of nurturing the children they brought into the world? What was it that prevented him from defying Feeney when, through malice and deceit, he manipulated not only my parents, but other married couples at the Center as well, into forsaking their sacred marital vows for one of celibacy, a devastating change that my parents later told me they had never wanted?

Incomprehensibly, my parents—as well as the other eleven highly educated married couples—allowed those who claimed to be dedicated to God to impose a regime that peremptorily violated the God-ordained law of nature. Growing up in that world of enforced separation and imposed silence between parents and children, I was keenly aware that my mother and father missed the family life we once had. It was particularly evident on those rare Sunday mornings when Sister Catherine would announce a community meeting, when, for forty-five minutes, the children and their parents were allowed, under her watchful eye, to sit together as a family unit, to hug and kiss and talk.

It was not lost on me that the brevity of our allowed time together as a family was a calculated decision by Sister Catherine to forestall the likelihood of children sharing with their parents the details of the physical abuse that was a regular occurrence. I can speak to my own inclination to hide anything but good news from my own parents.

I've spent countless hours wondering why I have not felt indignation, or even fury, at my parents for allowing themselves to be deprived of their rightful roles as mother and father. Once my family was reunited and the pain had subsided and I queried my parents about why they allowed our family to be sundered, the question came from a place of bewilderment in my mind, rather than anger in my heart. My mother's words still haunt me when in one exchange she spoke as if in mourning: "The day my children were taken away from me was the worst day of my life." It was clear that she spoke the truth.

Some mysteries must remain unsolved for eternity.

CHAPTER 21

New York—Here I Come

1975

"Don't arrive in the office unless you've read both the *New York Times* and the *Wall Street Journal* from cover to cover. Have the papers delivered to your apartment; they will arrive between four and five in the morning."

"We have customers, not clients, and you are to be available to them at all times of the day or night, and that includes on the weekends."

"Here's three hundred dollars. You should never be without emergency cash."

Those marching orders on day one of my new job were delivered with a hint of a Southern drawl in a barely audible voice by Brad, the de facto head of the respected research boutique I was joining. In his early fifties, Brad's looks belied his formidable reputation. The gray hair, falling in long, thin wisps across his brow, begged for a vigorous shampooing. His clear-framed spectacles sat on a rotund face that was pale, almost pinkish, suggesting that he had never lain on a beach, while his portly figure was evidence of a sedentary life. A well-fitting suit that had the look of tailor-made played the leading role of camouflage. "Unimpressive" might have been a logical first reaction to the man.

What Brad lacked in physical appeal he more than made up for with his skills as a machinery analyst—that was how he referred to himself. He was unafraid to make against-the-grain recommendations as to either buying or selling stocks because he held sacrosanct an investment philosophy that was defined by a chief executive officer's focus on profitability devoid of financial shenanigans.

While Brad's perspicacity had won him accolades as one of the best machinery stock pickers on Wall Street, he shunned the limelight, preferring to develop and then nurture enduring relationships with customers who shared his approach to investing. He was brilliant, quixotic, and could have a short fuse, but he was also quick to be appreciative. He was a mentor for sure but without the ability to personally engage, unless it was on one of the two subjects that were of interest to him—machinery companies and the Chamber Music Society of Lincoln Center.

The firm he ran consisted of six employees before I joined, as the third woman. One employee was his son and another his English stepson, and apart from his original business partner, a woman who was about his age, the rest of us were in our midtwenties.

His demand that the newspapers be read before arriving in the office was hardly a chore for me. Devouring the *Wall Street Journal* was already a favorite early-morning pastime. During my two years at The Pennsylvania Group, I'd arrive at the office as early as seven o'clock, and for a full hour or so, the silence was conducive to absorbing what I was reading.

I'd developed my own method of imbibing the financial news of the day. Starting with the "Heard on the Street" column on the inside of the last page, I'd then go to the editorials, after which I'd read the paper from back to front—in those days, the newspaper had only one section. To my way of thinking, the front-page news was already pretty much digested by the markets. On the other hand, hidden in the many small—often just a square inch or two—blurbs that dotted the back half of the paper were snippets of valuable information that tended to be overlooked if one got bogged down in the columns-long head-line articles.

Brad set me up in his unpretentious office, at a desk that was crammed with small piles, each consisting of several years of annual reports for the machinery companies that he followed. My first project was to analyze the financials of Eaton Corporation, the largest US man-ufacturer of on- and off-highway truck transmissions.

"We have an appointment with the chief financial officer next week in Cleveland," he said. "I want you to come up with the questions for the meeting."

By the end of the day, I had produced my list of questions. "We'll go over them tomorrow," my new boss said. "I'd like to take you out to dinner on your first day here."

Lunches, dinners, wine, brandy—at La Caravelle—was hard to turn down, and for sure on my first day in my new job in a new city, I couldn't beg off because I had other plans. It was only my second dinner at the vaunted restaurant, but the muraled walls displayed a friendly familiarity.

It was during cocktails—his a single malt scotch and mine the same because he told me he thought I would like it—that Brad started speak-ing, his voice so soft that I had to lean in and could get the whiff of his scotch.

"The firm has an account here at Caravelle. When you take a cus-tomer out for lunch or dinner, you must never ask for the check. The maître d' knows us, and I've told him already that you are now with the company. He will always give you a corner banquette and will automat-ically handle the check. Slip him a twenty every time you come and one hundred dollars every so often. It's a business expense, and we'll reim-burse you."

The soft delivery of this missive could have been out of a scene in a *Godfather* movie in which I was receiving my marching orders from Don Corleone himself. Absorbing his words, I got the picture—the firm treated its customers to the highest standards of investment advice, as well as entertainment.

We might have sat there until midnight—Brad would have been happy to have had a second and a third single malt scotch after dinner, and I was a bit unsure how, on day one, to say that I was tired. In a lulled moment, I thanked him for dinner as a way to end the evening.

"Let me walk you home," he said as we exited the restaurant, instinctively moving to my right to be on the outside of the sidewalk. I took note of that, remembering the advice my ever-chivalrous father had given me, on a visit he paid to me while he was still at the Center, and I was on my own: "If a man doesn't walk on the outside, don't go out with him." His words mattered to me, and while I didn't always follow that advice, I have never failed to notice when it's done and when it's not done.

For a block or so we walked quietly, as Brad continued in a somewhat garbled monotone that was hard to comprehend. We fell into a silence, and then somewhere in the darkness between Park and Lexington Avenues, he abruptly lunged at me, pushing me up against the building and making a clumsy attempt at kissing. The shock didn't diminish my ability to fend him off, as I thought, *Is he drunk? Or simply crazy?*

He composed himself as he tried to justify his behavior by saying, "I think you'll like it." I figured out what "it" was.

Only two days earlier, he had invited me to his condominium on Madison Avenue to meet his wife, a delightful Scottish woman, with an exquisite accent and flawless skin. We had spent the evening together, the three of us, and she had cooked a simple but splendid meal.

I sped away. Walking the last few blocks to my apartment on my own, I was aghast. Everything had been so perfect. *What was he thinking? It's my first day—how can I go into the office tomorrow? Will he fire me? What should I do?*

Entering my apartment, I sat on my bed, feeling nauseated. A torrent of questions tumbled over each other in my head. *What if he tries it again? What should I do? Quit? No, I don't want to do that.*

After a few frantic minutes, I switched gears and reverted to my problem-solving mode. One of the research analysts in my office, a married woman about my age, lived in an apartment that was about ten stories above mine in the building. She had been the one to let me know, a couple of months earlier, that the building had a vacancy. It was eleven o'clock, and I debated with myself. *Is it too late to knock on her door? But I need to tell someone. How can I face Brad in the morning?*

I took the elevator to the twelfth floor, walked slowly to her apartment down the hallway and rang the doorbell, hoping she wouldn't be furious with me for waking her. The door opened, and she stood there in her bathrobe, as I spat out the gory details. Her response: "Oh, just grow up. He did it to me too, on a trip to Boston. We were at the Ritz, and he was so drunk that he fell over a concrete flowerpot and scraped his face. We had to see customers for the next two days with his face full of scars. But he won't try it again. I can assure you."

"Thank you," I said. "See you in the morning."

Her words were all I needed to put the incident behind me, and the next morning, when Brad entered our shared office, I acted as though nothing had happened the prior evening. I'd moved on, and so had he. She was right.

We reviewed my long list of questions, and I brought up the issue I found most worrying—Eaton had taken out a sizable loan in Swiss francs in an effort to reap the benefit of the lower interest rates in Switzerland. That debt was about to come due, and the weakness of the dollar meant that there would be a loss associated with the principal repayment. It could have a negative impact on the first-quarter earnings report. I needed to address that with the chief financial officer, and Brad agreed. Then he shared one of his edicts. "Don't bring any notepaper. It can inhibit the management's candor if they think you're taking notes.

By the time we flew to Cleveland the following week, I was prepared—my questions were memorized and I prayed that I would be able to remember the answers. Brad, who knew the management well, sat quietly as I went through the questions in the order I had memorized them, leaving the most troublesome for last—the issue of the Swiss franc debt.

"The dollar has fallen significantly relative to the Swiss franc," I said. "Have you hedged the loan?" The company had not, he told me.

"How much will it cost incrementally to repay the debt?" I shared with him what I had calculated as the amount, which was in the millions of dollars, and the significant negative impact it would have on the reported earnings per share. He did not refute my calculation.

At the end of the hour, we thanked him for his time and left.

On the flight back to New York, Brad was ecstatic. "That was splendid work and great questioning. Tomorrow I'll call the customers and explain that you're now covering Eaton, and then you share with them what you've uncovered. Don't be afraid to tell them that you think they should sell the stock." For the rest of the trip, I scribbled notes on the pad of paper I had carried in my handbag, doing my best to relive every moment of the meeting.

I was confident when I reached out to our customers—I had done my research, unaware if any other analysts on the street had made the same discovery about the company's maturing Swiss franc debt, information that was publicly available. In April, when the company announced its full-year earnings that included a reserve for the currency loss on the debt repayment, the stock fell, despite a market that was rebounding strongly off its 1974 lows.

It was a rewarding start for my career as a machinery analyst.

CHAPTER 22

The Big Apple

1975

N ew York City was now my home, a place that, to my way of
thinking, epitomized success. It was big, diverse, and bursting with energy. Most importantly, to me as a newcomer, it
begged to be explored.

In an almost childlike fashion, I crammed my first few weekends
with the enthusiasm of a first-time tourist, visiting the Statue of Liberty,
Ellis Island, Saint Patrick's Cathedral, and the Cloisters, as well as taking the three-hour Circle Line tour of the island, up the East River and
down the Hudson, memorizing the geography of the city.

Those first forays into the sightseeing attractions of the Big Apple
were soon eclipsed by the vast cultural gems I discovered in the museums, the theatres, and the music halls of the city. After a week packed
with the stress of travel, research, and number crunching, the change in
atmosphere on the weekend was an intellectual balm for the mind. All
the while, week in and week out, working or playing, the same thoughts

persisted in my head. *Why do I have such good luck? What have I done to earn the good fortune of living in this mecca?*

My journey from Boston to Philadelphia two and a half years before coming to New York had been invigorating—an opportunity for freedom and the challenge to prove myself away from my hometown. Moving to the Big Apple eclipsed those sensations. I had gone from journeying to arriving.

I thrived on the fast pace of life in the city, the long hours in the office, and the frequent trips to the Midwest to meet with the heavy equipment giants of the day—John Deere, Allis-Chalmers, Cummins Engine, International Harvester, Dana Corporation, Briggs & Stratton—a litany of who's who in the machinery world.

Having passed the first test, when Brad Landon and I met with Eaton Corporation, I was now on my own to travel as needed—"always first class," because as Brad said, "You're working all the time, so your travel should be comfortable. And if you run into customers on the airplane, it sends the message to them that that we're doing well."

If only he could have seen into the future, just a few months away.

Our small team of research analysts was focused primarily on the heavy manufacturing sectors of the market—industries that included aerospace, defense, electrical equipment, machinery, and oil services. At other firms where I'd worked, the day started with a morning meeting, a forum that allowed the investment professionals to share their research and insights with the rest of the team. But Brad had little use for formalities. In his opinion, it was our responsibility to engage with our cohorts at all times.

Except for Brad and his original business partner, Margaret, the remaining half dozen of us were in our twenties, and almost all were at their first job out of college. We created our own version of the Monday morning meeting—a half-hour rehash of the high points of the prior evening's episode of *Monty Python's Flying Circus*. It was my introduction to the infamous six from Oxbridge—comedians who wrote and acted their farcical skits. When we'd laugh ourselves silly, it was time to get to work.

Before Excel electronic spreadsheets became available in the late 1980s, the tools of a Wall Street research analyst were relatively primitive and decidedly manual. They came in the form of a raft of number two pencils, soft rubber erasers, a calculator, and pads of long, pale green ledger paper. Oh, and Scotch tape, in case one had to add an additional sheet of ledger paper. Then, of course, a briefcase in which to carry those accoutrements of the trade.

There's a saying in the world of stock analysis, "Garbage in, garbage out." In other words, if the analyst is sloppy with financial input regarding a company's revenues and earnings, the output, in terms of expected profits and growth, will be flawed. There's no faster way to lose the respect of a company's CEO than to ask questions based on sloppy analysis. And there's no faster way to lose clients than to give them bad advice on a stock's earnings prospects or valuation.

Machinery companies, along with most heavy manufacturing, require major investments in capital equipment—factories and assembly facilities, as well as machine tools and metal-bending equipment. The capital intensity of the industry makes profitability highly dependent on the volume of production.

As an analyst, it was my responsibility to estimate revenues and earnings for several years into the future on a quarter-by-quarter basis for each of the companies I was following. That required projecting the volume of manufacturing output, which itself was influenced by the economic health of countries around the world and by the levels of unsold inventory. So, I pored over prior years' annual reports to extract trends that might provide clues to the future. Trial-and-error was a good way to describe the process of estimating revenues and earnings into the future—hours of back and forth between my brain and my ledger paper, with my calculator, pencil, and eraser working overtime. The economy, in early 1975, was still in the throes of a recession, which complicated the equation.

The mental gymnastics might go something like this. *No, that net income number's way too high. Cut the volume by 6 percent. No, by 3 percent. That looks better.* And on and on until I was convinced that my estimate for earnings could withstand anyone's challenge.

* * *

For a full week, Deere & Company, the largest global manufacturer of agricultural equipment, was my preoccupation, as I prepared for a meeting with the chairman, Bill Hewitt.

In the dead of winter, my plane landed well after dark in Chicago. A thirty-minute puddle jumper brought me to the windswept northwest tip of Illinois and the town of Moline. In the sub-zero cold, I drove to a one-story motel, to discover that the heating system was not functioning, nor was there any response from repeated calls to the reception desk. Fully dressed, and swaddled in my winter coat, with my feet wrapped in a bath towel and my face buried between two pillows, I made the best of the situation. It was a long night.

Wearing the same clothes and still trying to thaw out at ten o'clock the next morning, I arrived at the impressive headquarters of John Deere & Company, designed by the renowned architect, Eero Saarinen. In the spacious and sunlit corner office, I pulled from memory the questions I had crammed into my brain and had repeated and repeated. For more than an hour, I questioned both Bill Hewitt and his hand-picked successor, Bob Hanson.

Was Europe's agricultural business in as deep a recession as the US? It was. Was the high price of fertilizer continuing to put a damper on large agricultural sales? The pressure was bad. We discussed inventories at all stages of production, inflation, and commodities prices. There was little to find exciting. What about the small equipment market? (Deere made equipment for the housing market, an important leading indicator of economic activity.) Has it started to pick up?

"Not yet, but inventories are low, so we're starting to increase production." The answer I wanted to hear. One big plus from that meeting.

It was close to noon when I got to the end of my questions, and my head was crammed with answers I was dying to write down. But first,

Bill Hewitt took me on a guided tour of the building and the grounds, the latter, fortunately, from inside the seventh-floor glassed-in offices that ran along the periphery of the building. Then came lunch in the company's private dining room, where he recommended the fried catfish, with the encouragement, "It's right from the river."

What? The Mississippi River? People eat the fish from that river?

All the rivers that I knew were polluted—from the Nashua River in Still River, where I had grown up, to the Charles River in Cambridge, the Schuylkill River in Philadelphia, and both of New York City's rivers. There was no possibility of my eating fish from any of them. However, I was the guest, and Bill was the host. I ordered my first and last fried catfish meal, took the puddle jumper back to O'Hare, spent the two-hour trip from Chicago to New York jotting down notes from the morning's meeting, and got back to my apartment around midnight, with instructions to myself to visit Moline, Illinois, anytime except in winter.

I shared with Brad the one bright tidbit of information regarding the small equipment market—much to his delight.

"Call all our customers," he said, and I did.

* * *

Energy and optimism best described this honeymoon phase of my new professional life. On the other hand, I was puzzled by the daily headlines in the newspapers and on television that blared the impending bankruptcy of New York City. How could it be so, I wondered, when the streets of Manhattan exhibited all the signs of a flourishing metropolis? The retail stores on Fifth and Madison Avenues bustled with shoppers speaking myriad languages, an indication that tourism was healthy and pocketbooks open. The theatre scene was lively, and restaurants, from the grand to the mundane, were crowded.

However, by April 1975, New York City was close to insolvency. When the bankers turned to President Gerald Ford in the hope of a bailout, he refused, and the next day, the front pages of the three New York City daily newspapers told the story.

It fell to Lazard Frères investment banker Felix Rohatyn to devise a bailout plan in the form of what became known as Municipal Assistance Corporation (MAC) bonds. In genius fashion, and within a matter of weeks, Rohatyn formed a public-private partnership, and working with Arthur Burns, then head of the Federal Reserve, he oversaw the issuance of $10 billion (the equivalent of $57 billion today) in bailout bonds that yielded 14 percent. To pull that deal together, he negotiated major job cuts with the unions, ultimately winning over the federal government—the key to finding support among private investors.

While New York City's financial crisis was being resolved, there was another deadline approaching. It may not have risen to the level of a New York City bankruptcy, but it was, nonetheless, a matter crucial to the viability of countless small brokerage firms on Wall Street—ours among them. The history bears understanding.

Starting in the late 1960s, a tug-of-war emerged between the New York Stock Exchange (NYSE) and the Securities and Exchange Commission (SEC) over the commission rates that brokerage firms charged for stock transactions made on the floor of the Exchange.

While the NYSE was technically a not-for-profit organization, its owners—the 1,365 members who owned seats on the Exchange—wielded immense power and generated vast profits for themselves and the firms for which they traded. The SEC, an agency of the federal government, was established by President Franklin Roosevelt in the early years of the Great Depression for the purpose of restoring faith in the banking system. Its powers included regulating the securities industry, including the NYSE.

Since its inception in 1792, the NYSE had been guided by its founding document, known as the Buttonwood agreement, which included an iron-clad rule that commissions on stock trades must be quoted as a fixed dollar amount.

As stock trading exploded in the late 1960s, there was concern by both the SEC and some members of Congress that exorbitant commissions were becoming an embarrassment of riches to the disadvantage of investors. By the early 1970s, the tide began to turn in favor of abolishing the highly profitable fixed commission rates in favor of negotiated ones, thus forcing the broker and the buyer/seller to haggle with each other in determining the commissions.

The most powerful names on Wall Street at the time, Merrill Lynch, the largest retail brokerage firm, and Salomon Brothers, a heavyweight in the institutional block trading business, supported negotiated rates, in large measure because they correctly saw an opportunity to grab market share, as smaller companies floundered under the pressure of falling revenue and inability to adjust costs in a nimble fashion. The majority of firms, however, opposed reduced rates, as a matter of self-preservation.

In the fall of 1973, Congress and the SEC put their combined feet down and declared May 1, 1975, to be the deadline for the elimination of fixed commission rates. It was dubbed "Mayday"—the international call for distress—by the then chairman of Morgan Stanley, a firm that had yet to reach powerhouse status. There was growing trepidation within the industry as the countdown to the first of May approached.

At my firm—a small research boutique, with fewer than ten employees—consternation was high. *How far will commission rates fall?* That was the unanswerable question. The euphoria with which I had arrived in the Big Apple just three months earlier was now tinged by the anxiety that permeated the office, but optimism being my middle name, I kept up my hopes that the impact would be manageable.

Mayday arrived, and it was a metaphorical bloodbath for small brokerage firms like ours. Commission rates dropped by 50 percent at the opening of the market. In a single day, our firm's revenue was cut in half.

What was a disaster for small brokerage firms like ours, however, was a boon for our customers—those who paid us for the proprietary research we provided them. The commissions on their trades declined, enhancing the returns on their clients' portfolios.

By the middle of May, our small firm was reeling, and we had our first defection, as one of the analysts left for a position in a larger firm that could weather the storm. Brad was furious, convinced that the worst would soon be behind us, but the math was not adding up. There was no way to make up with volume what we were losing in revenue.

Only a month later, the company was facing a cash crisis. Our fixed costs—rent, the trading desk, and travel expenses—had to be paid. We continued to advise customers and do our research, now more often by phone than in person, and we certainly were no longer flying first class. The appearance of a viable entity was in stark contrast to reality.

A second defection from within our ranks had the benefit of reducing payroll but not sufficiently to forestall the inevitable. By the end of June, there was not enough money to pay salaries.

Brad broke the news to me gently in the office we shared. "None of us is getting a paycheck this month," he said, and followed it with a reassuring, "Things should get better."

I took the news in stride. What else could I do? Brad was desperate that he not lose more of his team, and I, the newest kid on the block, felt honor-bound to stay with him. Loyalty was ingrained in me—it had been part of the fabric of my life from infancy. The adult members of the community in which I grew up had signed a pact to fight for the doctrine of "no salvation outside the Catholic Church." Father Feeney dubbed as "traitors" and "the enemy" those unwilling to defend that dogma, for there was no virtue greater than loyalty, even if it derived from fear.

My loyalty to Brad, on the other hand, derived from appreciation. On a cold call interview some eight months earlier, he had offered me a job that catapulted me into the vortex of Wall Street. In a matter of weeks, I was experiencing success and building a reputation for offering valuable insight to customers regarding the stocks I covered, as well as gaining the respect of the CEOs of giant corporations.

I had Brad to thank for having opened that door, for encouraging me to be bold when I had conviction. Now in his time of trouble, the least I could do was stay at the firm, continue to work, and hope for the best. As June turned into July, there was no improvement for small research boutiques. On the other hand, the behemoths on Wall Street—Merrill Lynch, Solomon Brothers, Goldman Sachs, Morgan Stanley—were reaping the benefits of size and deep pockets.

A second month came and went without a paycheck—a second month of crunching numbers day in and out; of poring over the footnotes in annual reports; of looking for hidden bits of news, mostly bad news, that others might not have found; and of creating financial spreadsheets on long green ledger sheets. By August, the force of worry began to play tug-of-war with the virtue of loyalty. My bank account could sustain but one more month before it was empty. My stock holdings were a backstop—from that first bonus check seven years earlier, together with the small inheritance from my great aunt, I had accumulated a total of $16,000 (the equivalent of about $91,000 today).

There was the temptation to rob that sacrosanct kitty for a few more months of hope, but I could tell that even Brad was beginning to waver. In a moment of anxiety, I reached out to my trusted mentor from my days in Philadelphia, Sherif Nada. "I don't want to leave New York. I love the city." He promised nothing but said he would put out feelers. The maxim made famous by Alexander Graham Bell—when one door closes, another one opens—came true for me. One of Sherif's clients, Columbus Circle, the pension management division of Gulf and Western, was looking for an analyst who could cover an array of industries.

Many years later, when I asked Sherif what he had said to open that door for me, he recalled the incident. "I told him, 'Give her a shot. She and I worked together, and you won't be disappointed. She's a real self-starter.'"

I hated breaking the news to Brad, but he wished me the best. Within months, he and his original partner were the only ones left at the firm. It fell to Brad, now in his early fifties, to become a sole proprietor broker, and it wouldn't be long before I was his client.

CHAPTER 23

Footloose and Fancy-Free

1975

Was I the unluckiest girl in the world, finding myself unemployed three times within the space of thirteen months? Who loses three jobs in a year? Or was I the luckiest girl in the world? Lucky that I managed to land on my feet, in large measure through the good graces of people for whom I had worked and also on account of the skills I had acquired.

Before September came to a close, I had been hired as an analyst at Columbus Circle. I was now on what's called "the buy side of the street"—the customer rather than the broker—part of a team of analysts and portfolio managers who invested pension assets. If my new position at Columbus Circle was less pressured, and certainly less fraught with risk than working in a research boutique, I nonetheless embraced it with energy, while the more measured pace of life in the office provided the opportunity to explore a more vivacious social life.

The torrid on-again, off-again romance with Josh, my old flame from Marblehead, became on-again, when we discovered that we lived within five blocks of each other. His life was as peripatetic as ever, which suited me. While he was globetrotting as a television producer, I was anything but pining.

At twenty-seven, I was footloose, fancy-free and a sponge for all that the world had to offer. Josh was a veritable nomad, a professional vagabond, whose visceral stamina could be both intoxicating and exhausting. Each of us thrived on the psychic energy derived from the intense pressures of our very different careers. Our passion for each other defied the trite notion that opposites attract; rather, it flourished because we were free from the bonds of commitment—free to charge at breakneck speed towards goals we set for ourselves in the world of business.

* * *

What had happened to dispel that romantic childhood dream of being transported by a handsome prince to his castle far away where we would have lots of children? The more I explored the worlds of finance and culture, of travel and romance, the less I felt compelled to follow a path that I feared might lead to boredom.

If a relationship was starting to become too romantic, I'd have a little talk with myself. *Do you think you will be happy with him for the rest of your life?* I could never assure myself that the answer was "yes."

But one day, that mindset almost changed. I rang the doorbell to Josh's apartment one evening and entered what could, at best, be called a bachelor pad—a two-bedroom space devoid of any semblance of creature comforts or any colors other than gray and brown. Seldom was there food in the refrigerator, but an array of liquor bottles in various stages of near empty was always within reach.

I nestled down onto the couch, anticipating that we'd be ordering a pizza that could be washed down with some alcoholic concoction. The hyperkinetic Josh sat next to me, and I sensed something was amiss. Gone was the bluster. Instead, it was a somber man who shared the news he'd received a few hours earlier—possible cancer.

"They're doing exploratory surgery next week," he said and gave the details. "I'm really scared."

What ray of optimism could I find for him? I racked my brain—this was not a man who ever spoke of religion or prayer, and I didn't want to annoy him with a suggestion of turning to God.

A couple of drinks took the edge off the anxiety, but there was nothing jovial about our conversation as we sat quietly side by side on the worn couch.

Then seemingly out of nowhere, he spoke in a quiet voice. "Will you marry me?" A brief pause, and he repeated. "I really mean it. Will you marry me?"

His plea was genuine, and I was taken aback. We both loved each other, but...

I was silent as I pondered Josh's plea. The reasons to say "yes" were abundant—we loved each other; he needed me; I wanted to support him; he might not live much longer and the least I could do was to take care of him. I tried to push out of my head the reasons to say "no"—questions with no answers. Were we ready to make a lifelong commitment; on the spur of the moment; what if he recovered; would we go back to our old ways? My head and my heart were in conflict. I had long told myself that when I did get married, it would be for the rest of my life. An unsuccessful marriage—a marriage ending in divorce—was, to my mind, the ultimate failure. Josh and I had much in common—boundless energy and immense curiosity. We also shared the same compulsion—wanderlust. I feared our similarities would eventually kill our marriage. That night was not the time to share my quandary; I needed to be alone to work it out. A few days later we had a long conversation. We both knew and agreed that marriage was not the solution to the moment's crisis.

I stayed by Josh's side during his frightening health crisis. He came through the ordeal as well as other subsequent challenges. While we did not marry, we did what was better for both of us—we remained loyal friends to this day, more than half a century later.

CHAPTER 24

Romance—A New Way of Life

1976

T he energy analyst at Columbus Circle invited me to attend lunch with one of Wall Street's most renowned oil analysts. I was game because the oil service stocks were part of my new responsibility. It was one of the fastest-growing industries in the country, the beneficiary of OPEC's oil embargo and the subsequent rise in the price of oil, which was fueling a boom in exploration and drilling.

The two-hour lunch was a brilliant tutorial on the energy business, full of the jargon of the oil industry. The analyst, Jack, explained the fast-growing technology known as fracking and how it would expand the supply of oil in the United States. His knowledge was monumental, and he responded to my myriad questions with clarity.

Beyond his encyclopedic mind, there was something about the man himself that intrigued me. Soft-spoken and erudite best described him—not the norm on Wall Street.

I returned to my office, not only more educated but also with an intense curiosity about the analyst himself. However, I pushed him to the back of my mind and spent the next few weeks analyzing the stocks in the oil service industry—names that included Halliburton, Schlumberger, Baker Industries, and Hughes Tool.

Nancy, the saleswoman from that lunch, continued to share information about both the oil and the oil service industries and within a month or two, we became well-acquainted and quite friendly. That was when I could no longer hold my tongue, and I blurted out my question, "Is Jack single?"

She knew the answer. "Yes," she replied. I left it at that. It seemed inappropriate to ask for a social introduction. But when she pushed me on the matter sometime later, I couldn't hold back my admission of interest.

And so it was that Jack and I met together for dinner—to socialize without any discussion of the world market for oil. Cultured could have been his middle name—there seemed to be no subject on which he couldn't opine with intelligence. When, in response to his question, I let slip that I grew up in Cambridge, he shared with me that he was class of '51 at Harvard. The panic button went on in my head, but I maintained my composure, while realizing that he had been living in Harvard Square when I was a stone's throw away at the Center's headquarters, next to Saint Paul's Church.

I changed the subject. When he asked me where I had gone to college, I told him the truth—Boston University—but somewhere deep inside me I wanted him to know that I'd been accepted at Vassar, a Seven Sisters school. It sounded more prestigious.

The evening ended without a plan for another rendezvous. My interest had been piqued, despite discovering that he was twenty years older than I was. But so had my anxiety, as I feared that another date might uncover the full story of my past.

However, when he did call some weeks later, I was quick to accept his invitation. After a few more evenings together, he invited me to his weekend place in East Hampton. A large shingle-style house, with views of the ocean from the third floor, it was neither grand nor ordinary, but it had good bones and grace—large open rooms with tall windows on the ground floor and mullions on those on the upper stories.

It was a blustery autumn day, and to get some warmth into the ground floor, Jack turned on the gas oven in the large kitchen stove. "Does the house have heat?" I asked, fearing the worst.

"Oh, yes," he replied, "but sometimes I use the stove to warm up quickly." This brilliant man apparently didn't seem concerned about carbon monoxide fumes. I kept quiet. This was his domain, and I was his guest.

Shabby gentility was the most apt description for him, and I found it endearing that he wore merino wool sweaters with holes in the sleeves, through which poked his shirted elbows. Nothing, it appeared, was too old to throw away.

Tiptoeing my way into this relationship gave me a warm feeling, and between rendezvous, I tempered my dreams of what the future might hold. Then, out of the blue as we walked along the unpopulated East Hampton beach and imbibed the sea air, he said, "How would you like to come to Haiti with me? Right after Thanksgiving. I've got reservations at the Oloffson Hotel."

After a speechless moment, all I could blurt out was something like, "Really?"

"I've been there before, and I'm sure you'll love the place."

He was taking the lead, and I followed and never regretted it. The Victorian gingerbread-style hotel in the center of Port-au-Prince had a quirky charm, with a hint of the haunted. Long-armed fans created an undulating pattern of warm air that alleviated the sticky, humid atmosphere. The screened veranda was ideal for the local rum drink at cocktail time. The place fostered romance.

By the end of the week, I had fallen in love with the island—its people, its art, its Creole cuisine, its colored fabrics. I had also started to fall in love with the man himself.

The age gap of twenty years between us felt like a gift. I was the eager student, and he the scholar who read me poetry by Stephen Spender and pages from E. M. Forster's *A Passage to India*, on which he had authored his senior thesis at Harvard. He loved "moving fiction," he said, referring to Forster's masterpiece and, in an effort to please him, I read the novel—a deviation from my addiction to memoir and biography—and found it both enthralling and distressing.

For Christmas, he gave me an immense volume of Skeat's Etymological Dictionary, a book I find useful to this day and keep close at hand in my writing nook. He also presented me with a pair of 18-karat gold, shell-shaped earrings from Cartier. I was astonished and touched.

Jack had an apartment on the Upper West Side, an unfancy penthouse with skylights, and it was there that I found the courage to share my past with him. It was six months after we'd met, and as we sat sipping our favorite wine in the evening light, it began with my sharing the details of my upcoming business trip to Paris.

"My mother lives outside of Paris, in a small town called Orgeval," he said. "She broke her hip in a fall and is recovering slowly. I talk to her almost every day."

"I'd love to visit her," was my immediate response.

That's when he became quiet. A tear welled up in his eye, and he reached out for my hand, which I took into mine.

"My mother is a lesbian," he said quietly.

His pain seemed to come from a place of shame. It was a moment of emotional bonding for me. This man, whom I had slowly come to love, was sharing a secret that broke his heart, one he had hidden from the world. He spoke of his parents' separation when he was a tiny child and how his mother left the family in Philadelphia to move to France.

In that moment, I found myself freed from the bondage of my own deep secret, one that I had concealed for a decade, and blurted out, "Well, I, too, have a story."

Mine took longer to tell, and there were moments when the tears rolled down my cheeks, and I had to stop and compose myself. And there were also parts that made me laugh. Through it all, he was a compassionate listener, his own pale blue eyes moist with emotion at times. Our pasts had been so divergent—he, born into privilege, and I into a religious community turned cult. But we shared the same childhood pain—parental separation. His mother ran away from an unhappy marriage; my parents sacrificed the joys of parenthood for the sake of my soul.

"You're the only person in the world with whom I've shared my story," I said at the end, as I snuggled next to him.

"I love it," he replied. "I want to meet your family and the community also."

With shared secrets came shared love, and before long, we were inseparable, although I was unprepared for his next move.

One evening, he arrived at my apartment with an armful of shirts, which he hung in my closet. I was perplexed but didn't say anything. A couple of days later, he brought his shaving kit and shoes, and then came sweaters and trousers. Without any discussion, the man had simply moved in with me. Except for my one glorious year with Susan as my roommate in Philadelphia, I had lived on my own for ten years. In the matter of a day, I was having to share—my space, my privacy, my meals—my whole life with him.

It was a few months later that he put a ring on my finger—a three-diamond ring that had been his grandmother's. Had my childhood fantasy come to fruition? That never crossed my mind. I had no idea what the future might hold, but one thing was certain—there was no way I was about to abandon my career at the age of twenty-seven. I was just hitting my stride.

Jack and I became lovers. For the next four years, we were also immensely compatible, with hardly ever a harsh word between us. All that said, he never broached the subject of marriage, and while I wore the family ring with pride, I came to accept the reality that he did not plan to marry me.

Despite that disappointment, Jack was like a member of my family. His house in East Hampton became the Walsh family Thanksgiving meeting place and at Christmas, the two of us would head to Boston. Despite his Quaker upbringing, he would accompany my parents and me to midnight Mass at Saint Paul's Church in Cambridge. He was particularly close to my father. The two of them could talk for hours on their shared interests—science and mathematics. When Jack and I took a second vacation in Haiti, he invited my father to join us, and then did so again for a trip to Mexico.

Then one day, nearly six years after I first met him, it was over. At fifty-two, he had found another woman, someone even younger than I was. It came as a shock. Despite our very different personalities—he a placid, old-school Quaker from Chestnut Hill, Pennsylvania, and I an energetic go-getter Irish Catholic from Boston—our relationship was romantic and amiable, and unscarred by even a hint of rancor. We hardly ever argued. Perhaps I should have been more attuned to signs of possible trouble—the unusually long business trips and the frequent late dinners. On the other hand, the optimist in me was predisposed to see the positive and discard the negative.

Even in our separation, we remained cordial—for the most part. I returned the three-diamond ring that had been his grandmother's—I treated it as a loan, given that we were not married.

But I pushed back hard when he suggested I move out. "I'm not sure you can afford this place," he said. "I think you should find another apartment, and I'll stay here."

He was referring to the airy and spacious 1,400-square-foot, two-bedroom apartment we had bought together a couple of years earlier.

"Don't start worrying about my financial straits," I retorted. "I'll manage fine on my own. You chose to leave, and now you can find your own apartment."

That settled it, and quietly we negotiated how we would split the rest of our joint belongings.

Two weeks into singlehood and still in a state of disbelief and grief, I visited my next-door neighbor in East Hampton. Some thirty years my senior, she treated me as both a confidante and the daughter she never had. Through tears and vodka—lots of both—and overlooking the wintry Atlantic Ocean, we talked long into the night.

The next morning, when I was giving her my tearful farewell, she broke it to me coldly. "You can tell the story once, but after that, no one is interested. This happens a million times a day. You're not unique."

I took her words to heart. While it would take some months before the sorrow subsided, by the time summer rolled around, I was embracing my new status as a single woman with the same energy I was investing in my professional life.

A couple of years later, Jack reached out to me. I had heard from friends that he was once again single. I had moved on but was pleased when he called. We had lunch and, for the next fifteen years, remained friends, dining together every few months. Sadly, he died of Parkinson's disease at the age of seventy-two. I remain in touch with his children to this day.

CHAPTER 25

The Maven of Wall Street

1970S AND 1980S

My accumulated experience as a statistician in Boston and Philadelphia, followed by a tortuous baptism of fire in the analysis of the savings and loan industry, was an asset in the small research department at Columbus Circle, where each analyst covered a large array of industries and an even greater number of stocks. In addition to the machinery industry, I was responsible for stocks in the oil service, transportation, chemicals, and insurance industries.

I was grateful to be employed, but—and it was a major but—I longed to be back following the heavy equipment stocks in the market. The eight months with Brad's firm had instilled in me a passion for any company that manufactured machinery or its component parts—engines, motors, freight cars, transmissions, ball bearings, fly wheels. The gratification was twofold—cerebral and experiential. While comparing and contrasting the financial strengths and weaknesses of companies in competition with one another was essential, so too was touring the companies' facilities. Donning helmet and goggles, I learned through observing and questioning—molten steel being poured into casings for engines, aluminum being hammered into components for trucks, transmissions being assembled on endlessly long production lines. The smell of grease on the concrete floor, the clanging of metal on metal, the long, slowly moving assembly lines—all were part of the learning experience.

In the 1970s, men comprised the majority of machinery analysts. Women tended to be assigned industries that included cosmetics, food, retail, and pharmaceuticals, which I was sure would have bored me. If being a machinery analyst made me "one of the boys," that was fine with me.

Both the corporate and the investment worlds were male-centric—there was not a single woman in the C-suite of the companies I followed. Wall Street was also devoid of women in places of power. There was only one woman in the decade of the 1970s who might be considered a powerhouse on Wall Street—Muriel Siebert (whom everyone called "Mickie").

A generation older than I was—she and my mother were born within a couple of months of each other—she was a trailblazer. The daughter of a dentist in Cleveland, with nothing in her background that might have inspired her to go into the world of finance, she set her sights on Wall Street when she was about twenty after a visit to the New York Stock Exchange.

Reading her story many years later, I was struck by how similar certain parts of our lives had been. Like me, she moved to New York at the age of twenty-six, without having yet received her college degree. In her own words, she arrived "with $500, a Studebaker, and a dream."

Her rise was meteoric. From a bottom-rung position in the research department at Bache & Company, she was soon a successful broker. In the mid-1960s, she had the temerity, in the opinion of many, to attempt to buy her own seat on the floor of the New York Stock Exchange. At the time, every one of the 1,366 seats that constituted ownership of the Exchange was owned by a man, and the application had to be sponsored by a fellow member. Her first nine such requests were denied, and it wasn't until 1968 that she became an owner. With that event, the ratio of men to women owners became 1,365 to 1, and it would be almost ten years before another woman was allowed to buy a seat.

My first visit to the floor of the New York Stock Exchange had been back in 1972, when I moved to New York from Philadelphia. The vast trading floor was virtually swarming with men—from pagers, to runners, to clerks, specialists, and brokers. I was literally the only skirt on the floor, and that made me a spectacle. The gawking was palpable.

By the time I moved to New York three years later, Mickie Siebert's name was legendary. Much as I wanted to meet her, there was little reason to believe our paths would cross—she was a broker downtown, and I was an uptown analyst.

A decade later when we finally came together, the setting was far from what I could have imagined. It was dusk as I was walking home to my apartment on the East Side when the soft light from a garden-level nail salon lured me to treat myself to a manicure. Entering the cozy space, I was greeted by a courteous young woman who settled me into a chair, and the day's tensions melted away as the pampering began. In moments, I had nodded off, my reliable response to a manicure.

I came to my senses by a startling noise—not fifteen feet from me was a woman, oblivious to the world around her, spread-eagle, her skirt hiked up around her thighs to allow for a leg massage. She was snoring deeply, as two young ladies attended to her, one on her hands and the other on her legs and feet. She was Mickie Siebert.

I couldn't help but stare at her—the most powerful woman on Wall Street, a millionaire many times over. Thoughts tripped through my head.

Is this my opportunity to meet her? Should I ask to have a pedicure, so that I'll still be here when her treatments are done?

The idea was tempting, but I came to my proper senses.

No! She came here to relax, to get away from work. Leave her alone.

One more temptation. *But what if I never see her again?*

The good angel inside me won. I left Mickie to enjoy her well-earned relaxation in solitude. I never saw her again in person.

Within a decade, the ranks of successful and increasingly powerful women in the world of investing swelled, and I would come to know many of them. Yet, Muriel Siebert holds a unique place in the dog-eat-dog world of Wall Street. Much like Joan of Arc, she led by example an army of women who would come behind her on the battlefield called Wall Street.

CHAPTER 26

Machinery Woman

1976–1980

I t was December—nearly twelve months since I'd left Boston for New York. Despite the ups and downs—several months without an income, the demise of the company that gave me my first job in New York, and the financial challenges facing the city—there was almost nothing I would have changed about my life as the new year arrived. Except that I longed to concentrate solely on machinery stocks.

A week or so before Christmas, I was being dined—and since it was the holiday season, I allowed myself to be wined as well—at the pre-eminent New York restaurant, Lutèce. My host was John Sullivan, the institutional salesman who covered Columbus Circle for Merrill Lynch. In the matter of a couple of months he'd introduced me to every analyst at his firm who covered any of the stocks I was responsible for.

On this occasion, he came alone and was quick to explain why. "The Ford Foundation is looking for a machinery analyst, and I think you'd be perfect for the position. It's a wonderful place to work, and you can analyze whatever stocks you want in the sector."

He went on. "The firm is my client and I know the director of research well. If you're interested, I'll speak to him."

The Ford Foundation managed an endowment of more than $2 billion (the equivalent of $11.5 billion today), and the firm was held in great regard, not only for its "dedication to the public well-being on a global basis" as it stated in its annual report, but also as a powerhouse investment management firm. Its team of research analysts was well-respected on the Street.

My initial instinct was to jump at what sounded like the perfect position. At the same time, my responsible self was shouting in my head—*You can't leave Columbus Circle after only three months! Three jobs in the space of fifteen months—that's too many!*

Then I thought—*But it's the perfect job! And a great place to work. Why not interview for it?*

Was it the holiday spirit, or the advent of a new year? I responded aloud, "Yes, I'm interested. Thank you for giving them my name."

It seemed as though a Christmas present had dropped into my lap.

The highly desired position drew thirty-seven applicants, and a string of interviews that culminated in an offer of $27,500 (about $154,000 today) and a start date of February 1, 1976. Excitedly, I shared the news with my family, who quickly dubbed me "twenty-seven-five," celebrating both my salary and my precise age of twenty-seven years and six months when I started in the position. In the span of a year and a quarter, my salary had catapulted from $12,000 to $27,500.

After the first wave of exhilaration, my thoughts turned to the mentors who had paved the way for me to achieve this new step up on the ladder of success. There were George and Ed in Boston, Sherif in Philadelphia, and then Stew and Brad.

The Ford Foundation hadn't been my new home for more than a week when the phone rang—it was Brad calling to congratulate me. His barely audible Southern drawl was almost vivacious, and I could well understand why. "I'd like to take you to La Caravelle and update you on the stocks you're now following." It was the start of a rewarding professional relationship that would go on for a couple of decades. I was now

Brad's customer and felt pleased that I could, in a literal way, pay him back for what he had taught me.

In short order, I was traveling not only to the great Midwest but also overseas, where global machinery companies had significant manufacturing operations—Mannheim in Germany, Lincoln in England, Grenoble in France, and Belgium—often as part of an entourage of fifty or more analysts on what some might refer to as a "boondoggle." But those multi-day trips had a way of three-dimensionalizing the manufacturing of heavy equipment.

On one occasion, Eaton Corporation, the manufacturer of transmissions for Class VIII on-highway trucks as well as off-highway vehicles, added a special event to its annual gathering by including a trip to the proving grounds where each of us was allowed to get the feel of driving the cab of an eighteen-wheeler—without the trailer, of course.

I was ill-dressed for the surprise event, in heels and a dress, but no one could dissuade me from hiking up my skirt to climb into the cab. Once in the driver's seat, I plowed through ten of the thirteen gears. For half an hour, the pleasures of speeding like a race car driver overtook the daily challenges and rewards of analyzing the company's financial statements.

Another time, Joy Manufacturing invited machinery analysts to a mine in western Pennsylvania to witness its newest equipment for extracting coal from narrow seams in low-ceiling underground mines. Goggles, a mask, and a safety helmet were essential to keep from breathing fine coal dust but observing the machinery in action brought home the value of the new extraction technology, which, in time, came into high demand.

A group trip to a Pullman passenger railcar assemble facility in the Midwest brought to light the primitive state of amenities in manufacturing plants. We were a group of close to fifty analysts, and it was a raw November day. When I asked to be directed to the ladies' room, I was informed that there was no such accommodation in the plant, but he took me to what they had—a lavatory, with one hanging light bulb but neither heat nor hot water, much less a single product that could be useful to a woman. I leave the rest to the imagination.

When I expanded my research coverage to include some of the aerospace companies, Bob dePalma, the bigger-than-life CFO of Rockwell International, invited me to tour the company's space shuttle assembly facility outside of Los Angeles. Sitting in the not-quite-finished shuttle cockpit was one experience I wish had been captured on camera—it was a tight squeeze even for someone less than five and a half feet tall. I came away impressed on several levels—the almost antiseptic environment in which the capsule was being assembled, how small the shuttle actually was, and the engineers involved in the project who took great pains to answer my endless questions.

I flew to Morgan City, Louisiana, and took a pontoon plane that landed on the bayou outside the local office of J. Ray McDermott, the country's premier oil rig construction company. Abandoning my normal business attire—high-heeled shoes, a suit, and a fashionable handbag—I dressed for the role of "roughneck for a day," in jeans, a cowboy jacket, and sneakers.

We took a helicopter several miles over the Gulf of Mexico and landed on a deepwater oil rig. For the next several hours, I observed daily life on the rolling seas of the gulf—a dirty, dangerous, and derring-do way to make a living, but a great way for an analyst to three-dimensionalize J. Ray McDermott's business.

The mid-to-late 1970s was a time of buoyant oil prices and even stronger stock prices for companies that explored, produced, and refined oil and gas, and I took on coverage of Houston-based Cooper Industries, the premier manufacturer of gas turbines and other energy-production-related components. My yellow legal pad was crammed with questions—having discarded Brad's rule prohibiting pens or paper—as I sat down to interview the CEO, Bob Cizik. My mission—to determine if the Ford Foundation endowment should make a first investment in the stock.

I was there to impress, but so was Bob. What normally would have been a forty-five-to-sixty-minute session lasted nearly two hours. Unlike many a CEO whose tendency was to answer only the question that was asked, Bob's responses were more like tutorials, brimming with examples and offering the rationale for his explanation.

When I queried him about the possibility of a strike at one of the firm's plants, Bob's stark blue eyes became animated, and his gesticulations accentuated the point he wanted to get across. I paraphrase his comments:

> Any time we have a strike, even if it's in a small part of our business, I lay the blame solely on myself. It's my responsibility, as CEO, to bring the two negotiating parties to a successful agreement. A strike serves no purpose. It deprives workers of pay, customers of products, vendors of business, and it harms shareholders. It is the result of a flaw of management.

I hadn't witnessed that level of honesty and willing self-criticism among the myriad CEOs I had met. At a time long before it was accepted wisdom to consider the impact of corporate decisions on a broad cast of stakeholders rather than solely on shareholders, Bob was a leader in that thought process. It didn't take me long to realize that he stood hands above legions of other corporate leaders. The Ford Foundation made a significant investment in Cooper Industries and was well-served.

The hours were long, but time was my friend. Unfettered by the obligations of marriage and children, all my energy was directed to my career—one that I loved with a passion. The appeal was multifaceted—part sleuthing, part interrogating, part number crunching. I had the best job in the world.

CHAPTER 27

A Funny Thing Happened on the Way to Harvard

1977-1978

I t was the fall of 1977 when, on an impulse, I applied to the Harvard Business School. I told no one about the application—no one.

What if I don't get in? Maybe I'm not smart enough. To encourage myself, I made a list of what I could call my accomplishments in my short life. Then I found a way to knock each one down.

As a junior in high school, I had aced the National Achievement Test for Latin, ranking in the ninety-ninth percentile. My retort to myself was, *How many students in the country had been studying the subject since the seventh grade? You'd have to have been a dummy not to shine.*

I graduated at the top of my class as a senior in high school. *So what? It was a class of just five people, far from the competition you might have faced in a large public or private school.*

I'd been accepted at Bates College. *Was it only because you noted on the application that it was your father's alma mater?*

And Vassar accepted me, too. *But what if you'd been interviewed on campus, as the admissions team had suggested? Would that have been a tougher process than having tea with two alumnae—spinster sisters in their eighties? Did they just like you because you seemed as old-fashioned as they were?*

After nine years of going to college in the evening, I had at last earned my degree from Boston University, graduating summa cum laude. My retort to myself was another put-down: *Maybe those evening school classes were easier than the daytime coursework taken by full-time students.*

Not even laudatory notes from professors—which I hoarded and have to this day—convinced me that I was an above-average student. Such was the imposter syndrome that overwhelmed me at the age of twenty-nine. Despite having achieved a reputation as a respected machinery analyst in the dog-eat-dog world of Wall Street, I failed to see my accomplishments as anything but ordinary.

If I don't get in, I'll accept the reality—I wasn't good enough. No one will need to know. If I do get accepted, of this much I'm sure—people don't flunk out of the Harvard Business School.

* * *

It was late May when the package arrived at my apartment. The envelope was fat—the universal indicator of good news. Opening the letter, the first word that caught my eye was "pleasure."

I'd done it—gone for the hardest challenge I could imagine and achieved it. Letter in hand, I strode into the office of the vice president of investments at the Ford Foundation, Jon Hagler— himself a graduate of the school—to share the news and to let him know that I would be leaving the firm in three months. His congratulations were genuine.

When I called Bob Cizik—who, I'd discovered in one of our many conversations, had also been an HBS graduate—he sounded ecstatic. "You'll never regret it," were his words of encouragement.

Within a day or two of my head swooning with elation, a certain reality began to creep in. I reviewed the financial application forms that

At Ladenburg Thalmann, with Ed Taff (left) and Phil Kaminski (right), 1969.

A very expensive chocolate. Vienna, Austria, 1971.

St. Stephen's Cathedral. Vienna, Austria, 1971.

With our landlord in Dubrovnik, Croatia, 1971.

With Susan on the Acropolis, 1971.

In the market in Athens buying a fur coat, 1971.

On the Island of Spetses, Greece, 1971.

Dancing at three in the morning. Island of Spetses, Greece, 1971.

In front of the Parthenon, 1971.

Christmas at my parents' new home, 1971. It was our first family Christmas in seventeen years.

Brenda Diana Duff Frazier with her first husband, John Simms ("Shipwreck") Kelly. Photo by Bert Morgan/Getty Images.

Watercolor by Brenda Frazier Chatfield-Taylor for my 26th birthday, 1974.

East Hampton, 1976.

With my dad at the Hotel Oloffson in Haiti, 1977.

With my dad at the Hotel Oloffson in Haiti, 1977.

With Betsy Sullivan, visiting the Grand Canyon after a Machinery Analysts' Conference in Arizona, 1978.

The offshore rig that I visited in the Gulf of Mexico, 1979.

Doing research on offshore drilling in the Gulf of Mexico, 1979.

Dinner at the Rainbow Room with John Sullivan of Merrill Lynch and Maureen Sullivan, 1982.

Lunch in Venice, where everyone thought we would get married, 1984.

Wedding day, March 9, 1985.

My parents, celebrating my 40th birthday, 1988.

Bigger than a basketball—with my sister, Peggy. Thanksgiving, 1993.

A few hours out of surgery. February 13, 1994.

Abbot Gabriel with Caroline and Jim. February 1994.

Seminarians from the Center. February 1994.

Caroline and Jim. First day of school, 2000.

The stay-at-home mom with the children, Okemo the Chow Chow, and Happy the Bichon Frisé, 2000.

Croissants for breakfast. Paris, 2000.

In front of the Louvre with my children. June 2000.

With a bobby in London, awaiting the arrival of the Queen, 2000.

My mentees at Our Lady Queen of Angels School in East Harlem, 2017.

came with the packet of information from the school. The tuition was somewhere around $5,000 per annum, excluding the cost of room and board, which I estimated would be a similar amount. My salary was $32,000, so quick arithmetic left me chewing on the fact that the two-year package, including the opportunity cost of my income, would be at least $80,000.

I was still paying off college loans from my undergraduate degree, and I couldn't fathom what it would be like to be without a source of income. *What if my family suddenly needs money? If I'm not working, how can I help them?*

After several sleepless nights, I turned for advice to the one person I trusted to help me through my dilemma—Jay Light. A Harvard Business School professor, he'd been hired by Jon Hagler as a consultant to the investment department at the Ford Foundation. Three days a week, he traveled from Boston to our office in midtown Manhattan. In the manner of a great professor, he had an open-door policy and I took full advantage of the generosity of his time. An obvious believer in the merits of the most prestigious business degree in the world, he seemed the best resource for an honest opinion.

As he was passing my office, I asked him to come in, and I closed the door.

"I need your help. I'm having second thoughts about going to the Harvard Business School," I said and explained the financial predicament. For close to an hour we talked, and when it came to summarizing it all, Jay made it seem so logical.

"You're at a fork in the road," he said. Those were his precise words. "If you are interested in changing careers—if you want to go into investment banking or become a consultant or run one of those manufacturing companies you follow—the Harvard Business School will be immensely helpful. If, however, you want to continue your career as an analyst and perhaps move on to portfolio management, you don't need the Harvard Business School. You're already a success, and you have a great future ahead of you."

He needed to catch his plane back to Boston. I thanked him for his time. I took to heart his thoughtful and measured advice.

A week or so later, a call to Bob Cizik went very differently. "You're making a mistake," he said bluntly.

I appreciated his honesty and found myself in a quandary—two people, each of whom had my best interest at heart, were offering me contradictory advice. It was now up to me to make a decision.

I had no interest in running a company like Cooper Industries or in changing careers. Life in the corporate world was of little appeal—I feared that its structure would be stultifying. Much of what stimulated me as an investment analyst was the intensity of the work, the opportunity to forge ahead in my own way. It was empowering to be granted autonomy in my professional life—something denied to me throughout my upbringing. Each new day offered the opportunity to learn, to satisfy my innate curiosity, to explore the world, and to get paid for it—there was no better job in the world.

As I entered my thirties, Jay Light's words became my mantra. "You have a great future ahead of you." Twenty-five years later, Jay was appointed dean of the Harvard Business School. To this day, our late afternoon conversation on a sunny June day fills me with gratitude for his guidance and his wisdom.

CHAPTER 28

Time for a Giant Step

1980

T he consequence of having walked away from the Harvard
Business School was not lost on me. I would forever be minus
one monumental credential—that badge of honor in the world
of business and finance called an MBA. And one from Harvard meant I
could hold my head high as one in a league of the brightest.

However, my upbringing and my own natural instincts had hewn
me to discard remorse or second-guessing (for long). That sage dictum
of the Victorian era—"Don't cry over spilt milk"—suited my case. So
did the words my father was wont to repeat. "Don't waste time regret-
ting the past. Look to the future and find happiness there."

* * *

It was around my fourth anniversary at the Ford Foundation, when John
Sullivan called from Merrill Lynch, "There's an opening at Citibank for
a job. Peter Vermilye's growing the business there, and he's looking for

someone to head the capital goods sector in the research department. Would you think of leaving the Ford Foundation and going to Citibank? It's a great opportunity."

Forty years ago, before the world of search firms became a major force in recruiting, it was often by word of mouth that opportunities became available. On Wall Street, well-connected research analysts, portfolio managers, and salespeople were often the entrée into an opening.

For more than a year, various asset management firms in the city had reached out to me in the hope that I might leave the Ford Foundation and join them. While I was willing to interview, I was not tempted by the notion that "the grass was greener" elsewhere. However, this time was different.

Peter Vermilye—his name was legion in the world of investment management. Following a twenty-five-year stint at J. P. Morgan, he moved to Boston as vice chair of research and management for State Street Research. Returning to New York, he became the president of the renowned Alliance Capital Management in 1970. Seven years later, he departed for Citibank. Wall Street was abuzz with what he had wrought in just a couple of years, but Peter wasn't through. He was looking to build a powerhouse investment management team that would raise both the profile and the assets of the bank.

I leapt at the invitation from Citibank to interview for the position. The meeting with the director of research went very much by the book, until he excused himself, saying he'd be back. When he returned, he said, "Peter would like to meet with you."

I smiled to myself—I'd passed the first hurdle. As I entered Peter's office, he gripped the arm of the wing-backed chair that formed part of a conversational nook of sorts. Pushing himself up, he leaned forward with an outstretched hand. "Hi, have a seat."

It was just the two of us, and he was direct. "Tell me about yourself. What's going on in your industry?" An open question that turned into a conversation. "What are your favorite stocks?" "Why are they attractive investments?" "What's happening overseas?"

I was sure he had his own convictions, but I called it as I saw it—the global recession was wreaking havoc on the earnings of machinery companies, but they'd been through the oil crisis recession and come through. For every answer I gave, he had another pointed question.

Then, in a sudden shift, he changed the subject. "What do you do for fun?" "Where have you traveled?" I shared the highlights of my vacation behind the Iron Curtain, and his dark eyes opened wide. I got the feeling that he was a cosmopolitan man.

I lobbed in a question of my own. "What's your vision here at Citibank?"

He was direct, and I paraphrase: "I want to have the best research department and the best investment business in the world."

I wasn't prepared for what came next. "And I want you to be part of the team," he said straight out. "I want you to head the capital goods research group here and hire whatever people you need."

My response was genuine. "I'd love to work here."

"Work it out with Charley," Peter responded, referring to the director of research.

The interview was over, and I stood to leave. The slightly crooked smile that I'd soon recognize as signature Peter when he was pleased with himself was all the message I needed. "Thank you," I said. "I'm really looking forward to coming."

It was left to me to inform Charley that I had accepted Peter's offer.

Professional and polite, he let me know that he needed to speak to the Personnel Department. But I could sense that Peter ruled.

"And we haven't discussed your salary."

I'd come prepared with what I knew was a bold—and almost outrageous—salary request.

"I was thinking about seventy thousand dollars." Only I knew that it was a whopping 80 percent increase over what I was then making.

"We can't pay you that much," he said, almost apologetically. "But we can do sixty-two thousand dollars and make up the difference with stock options. And you'll have the title of vice president."

I agreed, and on Monday, June 2, 1980, I moved into a corner office on the twenty-third floor of Citicorp Center—recently completed, sleek, postmodern, with state-of-the art glass and aluminum features and its trademark feature, a triangular roof. I was fired up to make the most of what felt like a giant step forward in my career.

Six months later, almost to the day, Charley walked into my office. "Happy New Year," he said. "Peter wanted me to let you know that he has just approved a ten thousand dollar raise for you. Congratulations."

I was on top of the world.

CHAPTER 29

Peter Vermilye

1981

I looked up from my desk and was surprised to see Peter standing in front of me. Looking over the top of his spectacles, he came to the point.

"Japan seems to be taking the lead globally in a number of industries. I want you to go over there and see what's happening in the capital goods area."

That was Peter—sharing what was on his mind with a paucity of words that belied the depth of thought behind the statement. His longevity in the world of investing, combined with his monumental success in making money for his clients, had honed his faculty for discarding the informational noise that confused many a less-sophisticated denizen of the world of Wall Street.

Peter was both leader and teacher. At Citicorp, he was famous for the personalized notes that he might simply drop off on one's desk. We called them "Petergrams"—pithy commentary that was uniquely his.

"That was an awesome presentation this morning," might be one—nothing more than that.

"Remember, stocks don't go to the sky."

"If you're on a pedestal, there's no place to go but down."

There were pieces of advice he never tired of offering. "You want to buy straw hats in January," was one. In stock market parlance, it meant to buy stocks when they were out of favor.

"Buy saucers and sell umbrellas," was another maxim of his, with a respectful nod to technical analysis. A saucer was the depiction of the chart of a stock price that had been languishing and was just starting to pick up momentum, usually the result of an improvement in its earnings outlook. An umbrella, on the other hand, was the chart of a stock whose price had peaked and was rolling over, an indication that there were more sellers than buyers.

"Go to Japan and come back with the scoop on Japan's secret sauce."

That was the task—hardly a trivial assignment. I reached out to the biggest and the best of Japan's brokerage firms, Nomura Securities, to work out the details of a trip to visit with the giant machinery companies—names that included Komatsu, Hitachi, Kubota, and Mitsubishi Heavy. Without the heft of an investment superpower in the world of Japanese finance, there was little to no chance for an American, much less an American businesswoman, to get to the inner sanctum of corporate Japan.

Nomura invited me to join a one-week trip that would include a day with the head of the firm's investment team and the chair of its board, as well as a series of meetings with government officials and senior members of the Bank of Japan. That came with the guarantee that they would arrange a second week solely for me, during which I would meet with the CEOs of the major machinery companies. They promised an interpreter.

Forty years ago, Japanese companies offered far less in the way of financial information than did their American counterparts. Nonetheless, I pored over the annual reports of each of the companies I would be meeting in Tokyo and discovered a universal issue that was confounding—the profitability of Japanese heavy manufacturing companies was unimpressive and far beneath the level achieved by their American counterparts. That would be my challenge on this trip—to uncover why, or perhaps more importantly, to determine how they looked at the entire issue of profitability.

I had a certain skepticism about how successful the trip might be when I couldn't speak a word of Japanese. But the mission was clear—come back with a deeper understanding of the workings of Japanese companies. What were their goals? Was there a secret sauce? What did leadership look like at a giant Japanese machinery company? What about the workplace culture?

Over a couple of months, I compiled my questions for each company, and hoped I'd have a reliable translator.

* * *

Sometime in the weeks leading up to my trip to Japan, I participated in a machinery conference in New York, together with analysts from around the country. Not surprisingly, the ratio of men to women was at least ten to one. At the end of the day, I joined a small group of out-of-town analysts for dinner.

It must have been close to ten o'clock as we were concluding our meal, when one of the guys asked me, "Where do you go dancing in this town?"

I was caught flat-footed. My social life did not include the likes of Studio 54—I had little interest in the media frenzy it created, and cocaine was of no interest to me. I was more a Café Carlyle or Bemelmans Bar kind of girl, often tripping from one to the other in the Carlyle Hotel to hear the best of Bobby Short and Marian McPartland. A bit too tame for the cadre of analysts I was trying to impress.

Embarrassed by the reality that I was out of touch with the night-club scene, I wracked my brain for a moment and then it hit me.

"I know a place. Let's go to Doubles." The words spilled out of my mouth before I could process the insanity of my idea.

As we headed up Fifth Avenue to the Sherry-Netherland Hotel, I wondered if machinery analysts from places like Cincinnati, Detroit, Milwaukee, and St. Louis were sophisticated enough to know that they were about to enter the holy of holies in the world of posh nightclubs. One thing I was sure they did not know—I, a non-member, was crashing Doubles.

Walking into the lobby of the hotel, I opened the hidden door that led to what almost had the feel of a modern-day speakeasy. The narrow landing was swathed in red velvet, as were the walls and stairs that led down to the underground club. None of my associates had an inkling that I, like them, was visiting the place for the first time. The rich crimson decor extended throughout the club's dining room and cocktail nooks, supplemented with framed photographs of the social world's rich and famous.

Approaching the desk, I smiled at the receptionist, gave my name, and then signed it: "Mrs. Peter Vermilye." At least, I had the decency to refrain from signing in with her first name, Lucy. My "guests" were none the wiser, and when we sat down, I ordered what they requested—champagne.

The late evening became early morning by the time we had imbibed a second bottle of champagne and had taken to the dance floor. As we parted ways, I walked the mile to my apartment building, stopping at a late-night Irish pub in my neighborhood for a trusted "final final," an Irish coffee—the whiskey to help me fall off to sleep and the coffee to ward off what I should expect might be a nasty headache in the morning.

By two o'clock, I was in the land of nod but not for long. Before there was a fragment of dawn, I awoke, and in the darkness, I pieced together the appalling reality of what I had done. The facts were immutable—in a moment of lunacy, I had impersonated Lucy Vermilye, a woman I'd never met. The sooner I made my confession to Peter the better.

I stood in the doorway of Peter's office at seven thirty and watched in silence for a moment—only his trousered legs were visible beneath his fully opened *Wall Street Journal*.

"Good morning, Peter." The response was a grunt of sorts, as though I was interrupting his solitude.

I opened my mouth to speak and forgot what I had practiced on the walk from my apartment, so I just winged it. "Everything's going to be OK," I started. The newspaper barely budged, and I went on. "I'll pay the bill. Just let me know when it comes in."

Peter's soulful eyes were now peering at me over the top of his paper. I tried to recapture how I wanted to tell the story, but then just blurted it out.

"Last night after the machinery conference, I went out to dinner with a few analysts, and then they wanted to go dancing. I couldn't think of anywhere, so I took them to Doubles."

Peter lowered his newspaper, and I could gauge his countenance as curious but calm.

"I'm not a member there, so I signed in as Mrs. Vermilye."

The ensuing momentary silence was broken as Peter threw back his head and let out a hearty laugh.

"Now," he said, "they'll never know who the real Mrs. Vermilye is."

A couple of weeks later, I reminded Peter that I wanted to pay the bill for my misspent evening. He mumbled something and changed the subject. When another few weeks went by, and I brought the subject up again, he looked at me as though he had no idea what I was talking about.

I changed the subject to my upcoming trip to Japan, and Peter came alive.

"Stop off in Hong Kong first and see the Citibank office there. They know what's happening in Japan."

And so, my two-week sojourn turned into three weeks.

CHAPTER 30

Machinery—Japan vs. USA

1981

S itting in a first-class window seat of a 747, I looked down and scanned the unfolding city that lay smothered in a sultry haze on an early morning in June. Dozing off for what seemed like mere seconds, I awoke to a terrifying vision, as the plane was barreling its way through a maze of high-rise apartment dwellings, so close that the tip of the plane's extended wing seemed ready to pierce the building frames.

Holding my breath and squeezing the arms of my seat, I was horrified to see into people's kitchens and bedrooms.

Why are we gathering momentum as we're descending? Why doesn't the pilot say something?

But not a word. I closed my eyes to shut out the frightening scene and then opened them—I couldn't watch, and I had to watch. Then the plane banked sharply to the left and the landing field opened up, barely a few feet beneath us, or so it felt.

"Welcome to Hong Kong," came the voice of the TWA pilot. No explanation, no apology, and certainly no advance preparation. I later learned that was how planes had to land at Hong Kong's postage-stamp airport. That was the start of a week in British-ruled Hong Kong that might aptly have been described as an eye-opener.

The short taxi ride from the airport to my hotel was accompanied by a cacophony of vehicle horns—a harbinger of the hectic life in the island city. It took but an hour or two to absorb Hong Kong's vibrancy and to observe its raw capitalism, which flourished despite oppressive humidity and seemingly little air conditioning outside of newly constructed office buildings and fashionable hotels.

The tangled web of black wires that covered the steep hillsides leading up to the posh neighborhood known as The Peak was evidence of the ingenuity and prolific work ethic of the impoverished neighbors who lived below. With seeming impunity, they tapped into the electric grid paid for by their wealthy neighbors. That free electricity transformed the quality of life for millions of the poor, offering entertainment in the form of a small color television, often the only "luxury" in a one-room tin shack that had a plywood plank for a bed and no toilet facilities.

The mélange of Hong Kong's population was itself mirrored in Citicorp's investment team—an assortment of Americans, Brits, and Japanese who were hardworking, while living life to the fullest. I arrived in the office midafternoon and was greeted by a memorably friendly lot, including one Chris Murphy, a Brit with a very Irish name and an even bigger Irish sense of humor. We'd hardly finished introductions when Chris, in the style of Captain Corcoran of HMS *Pinafore*, announced that it was time for a sail in the harbor.

The bank had its own junk, a three-sail pleasure boat used for entertaining clients, and by five o'clock, the team had migrated from the office to the boat—from work to play. The marina was dotted with junks much like ours. The cocktail hour—better described as the cocktail evening—was followed by dinner at an unfancy seafood restaurant with stunningly delicious food. An early night might end at midnight, and it took some pots of coffee to kick the brain into action by nine o'clock the next morning.

Welcome to Hong Kong. Evenings of food and drink belied the intensity of work during the day—in 1980, the workweek included a half day on Saturday. The investment team was a serious group that focused its research exclusively on Japanese stocks, and I honed the preparation for my upcoming trip to Japan with their analysts. Interestingly, mainland China, the behemoth to the north of Hong Kong, with a population that exceeded one billion, was an investment wasteland.

* * *

The vibe of Hong Kong, a city of five million, had been energizing, and I was geared to experience an even more lively environment in Tokyo. Why shouldn't I? With nearly thirty million people, the city was twice the size of New York and six times that of Hong Kong.

First impressions have a way of lasting. The forty-mile-long taxi ride from Narita International Airport into the center of Tokyo had the feeling of a funeral procession—painfully long and entirely silent. As I spoke not a word of Japanese—except for the obligatory "*arigatou*" (thank you)—I felt like a prisoner. The inability to communicate left me to stare out the taxi window at what seemed like interminable miles of monotonous gray slabs of concrete—buildings, walls, sidewalks—that added to the sense of melancholy.

However, once I arrived at my hotel—the elegant Imperial Palace Hotel, overlooking the Imperial Gardens that housed the Imperial Palace and the Japanese royal family—the drab evaporated, and a new vision of Tokyo began to unfold. Full of grace was the best way to define the staff at the hotel, and the simplicity of the ikebana arrangement in the lobby added an aura of elegance.

I must have been easy to pick out in a crowd, because hardly had I reached the check-in desk, when two gentlemen from Nomura introduced themselves.

The company had put together for us—for the first week, I was part of a group of three American investment professionals—a series of meetings with officials of the Bank of Japan and other government agencies, a valuable preamble to what would be, for me, a long follow-on week of meetings with machinery companies.

Evenings were inevitably at an upscale restaurant in the Ginza— Tokyo's fashion hub and nightlife mecca. The meals were memorable and beyond expensive, but we were the clients and Nomura the host.

On the last night of the group tour, we were treated to dinner at the home of Nomura's chairman. There were eight of us, including senior officials of Nomura, as well as three clients—seven men and me.

The chairman, assisted by a translator, guided us through what seemed like a museum of gardens, each an exquisite masterpiece. There was a waterfall garden and a cactus garden. There were peaceful places with stones and sand. Doing my best to balance a cocktail in one hand while meandering in a pair of five-inch stilettos was a challenge none of the other guests had to tackle.

The dinner was held in a softly lit, bamboo-screen-paneled room. I was seated next to the chairman, and kneeling between us and just slightly back from the low table was a young woman who functioned as the translator for our conversation. Fearful of making a social faux pas, I let the chairman take the lead and was startled by his first question.

"Are you married?"

"Not yet," came out instinctively. *What a question*, I thought, and wondered if perhaps he had never sat next to a woman during a business dinner. In an attempt to tilt the conversation toward business, I asked him about his world travels.

Conversation was curtailed, for which I was grateful, when three young women, in formal Japanese attire, provided musical entertainment while we ate in silence. The translator, wearing her own kimono, remained poised between the chairman and me, replenishing our sake cups after each sip. The incongruity was not lost on me—in Tokyo, the capital of what the world believed was the most technologically advanced country in the world, tradition remained sacrosanct.

* * *

With my first week in Japan behind me—the easy week, as I thought of it, because others did most of the talking—I was ready for the tough week ahead, when I'd be visiting the machinery management teams on my own—Komatsu, Kubota, and others—with the aid of a translator, of course, and a Nomura broker.

But first there was the weekend, when I set out to explore Japan outside of Tokyo on my own. I'd planned the trip weeks in advance— two nights in Kyoto and one in Nara—towns to the south and west of Tokyo, which were easily accessible by train. The allure of Kyoto harked back to my teenage years within my community. Forbidden to read newspapers, listen to the radio, or ever go off the premises to see a movie, I was a ready audience when on Sunday evenings, we were allowed to watch travelogues of countries around the world. Despite their being highly edited—no beach scenes, no young lovers holding hands, no dancing—I was mesmerized by the world beyond my confining borders. There was something exotic, it seemed to me, about Kyoto, and my one free weekend in Japan gave me the opportunity to explore that ancient town.

Arriving by train in the center of the city around noon, I settled into a miniature boutique hotel, the name of which has now faded from memory. What does remain forever is the ambience of the thousand-year-old historical district of the city where I chose to stay. Gone was the unending sensory overload of the Ginza, and in its place, an aura of tranquil silence along the narrow streets and in the tiny shops.

The quietude brought me back to my childhood, to a time when I bristled against silence—more specifically, the imposition of the rule of perpetual holy silence—a mandate enforceable by punishment, and thus devoid of peace. Some fifteen years later and in my early thirties, I was finding the hushed environment of Kyoto to be therapeutic—an opportunity to observe the townsfolk and to admire the gardens and ancient temples. Artists and craftsmen plied their trades; kimono-clad women gathered in small clusters; an elderly couple held hands as they walked in slow motion in a garden—all a welcome reprieve from the sensory overload of Hong Kong and Tokyo.

An artist caught my eye—an ancient man, his desiccated skin sagging from his face and arms. He was making paper cutouts, using what looked to be an X-Acto knife rather than scissors. He looked up at me and offered a toothless smile. We engaged minimally, given our language barrier, but each of us went away happy—I with two of his delicate cutouts, and he with a hassle-free transaction. The artwork hangs in my house to this day.

The monastic vibe in Kyoto was addictive and, were it not for the train ticket I had purchased to Nara, I might have spent a third night there. But Nara had its own appeal, with the Great Buddha that dated to the ninth century and was said to be the world's largest bronze statue of Buddha.

It was early evening when I checked into the Nara Hotel, itself an early twentieth-century historic gem. The rain was coming down hard as I set out for the temple armed only with an umbrella, a map drawn by the concierge, and my sense of direction (which was a problem). It wasn't long before I was lost, as the day grew darker and the rain fell harder.

The streets were nearly empty and, fearful that the temple might close, I approached a two-story building with an inviting light on the outside, in my hope that it might be a restaurant and I could get further directions to the temple. I walked up the four or five stone steps and opened the door. The front room was arranged with pillows on the floor surrounding low-set tables, but no one to be seen. In the background was the sound of a television program, and I was embarrassed that I had entered a private home. Mortified, I started backing out of the front door, when a woman, dressed in blue jeans and a sweater came rushing up to me. Not sure what to do or say, I blurted out a one-word question: "Restaurant?" Smiling, she nodded her head, and I felt brave enough to ask the only question that I needed answered: "Buddha?"

The woman looked intently as I showed her the makeshift map that was barely legible from the rain that spilled from the rim of my umbrella. A moment later, we were in business. Grabbing her own umbrella, she took my arm, and together we walked through the now dark streets. I did my best to memorize the several turns we made and it wasn't more than three or four minutes before we were standing in front of the wooden temple. Her bow told me she was delivering me to my destination. "Arigatou" was all I was equipped to say, as I bowed back. She disappeared into the darkness.

The temple, the Great Buddha, the silence of the crowd, the reverence, and the sense of awe were inspiring. I joined the single line that moved a baby step at a time and crossed the threshold into the Great Buddha Hall and into the presence of the massive, seated bronze Buddha, fifty feet tall and weighing more than one hundred tons. The silence was broken only by the staccato clicks of cameras. Like nearly every visitor, I took out my Kodak Instamatic, the layperson's high-tech camera of the day. Looking through the viewfinder, I could make out nothing. I looked again and realized that my camera could focus only on a minute part of the statue—a knee, the tip of the nose, the lips— hardly material for a scrapbook. It didn't matter. I put my camera away and lingered in the hall, staring at the Buddha and examining the gifts of flowers, fruits, and incense brought by grateful visitors.

By the time I exited the temple, it was well past seven o'clock. The rain was still coming down in sheets, but I knew where I was going— back to that tiny restaurant just a few corners away. Up the short set of steps, I cautiously opened the door to see the lady, who less than an hour earlier had been clad in a sweater and jeans, now dressed in a pale blue kimono. Greeting me with a smile and a low bow, she beckoned me to sit on one of the pillows. The small room felt like part of the home, and I wondered whether, in fact, it might be the family dining room when it wasn't a restaurant.

My hostess knelt next to me, less than a few inches away. It was my turn to speak, to order my meal, and I resorted to two of the small handful of words in my Japanese lexicon, each with a vocal question mark. "Sashimi? Sake?" Not sure what selection of fish she might have, I chose to leave that decision to her, and I was not disappointed.

Nodding and then bowing, my host disappeared to return with an exquisitely displayed array of sashimi on a rectangular, white porcelain plate, accompanied by seaweed salad and a sizable carafe of warm sake that was a treat after the driving rain. As I ate, my hostess stayed by my side, and after each sip of sake, she would replenish what I consumed, much like the dinner at the home of the chairman of Nomura Securities.

There wasn't another customer in the minuscule restaurant, no one to take her attention from me. Wanting to break the silence and wracking my brain to find a way to communicate, I was stunned when my kimonoed companion blurted out one word, in the form of a question: "BEEZNUS?"

Elated, I nodded my head as I slowly enunciated the name of each of the cities through which I had traveled before arriving at Nara: New York (pause), London (pause), Dubai (a stop-off on the way to Hong Kong), Hong Kong, Tokyo, Kyoto, Nara. Then I added Tokyo and New York to indicate that I was heading home. At that moment, we migrated from strangers to friends. There was little that I could explain about the nature of my trip, but sharing my itinerary with her felt like a conversation.

When she brought the bill, I stared at it, incredulous. *This must be an error*, I thought. The total came to ¥2,800. The Japanese yen, at the time, was worth a little over 200 to the dollar, bringing my blissfully delicious meal to less than $14. Speechless, I paid my bill, and said my many "arigatous" and then pressed an additional ¥2,000 into my hostess's hand. She accompanied me outside and walked alongside me until she could point out the Nara Hotel. "Thank you, thank you," were her parting words.

* * *

The early morning high-speed train brought me back to Tokyo in a little over two hours, in time for my first interview—with the CEO of Komatsu. Armed with my trusty yellow pad of questions and accompanied by a Nomura Securities analyst, as well as a translator, I was prepared to ask questions and looked forward to answers that would unveil the secrets of Japanese prowess.

The headquarters of the major machinery companies were located in the modern glass and steel high rises that dotted the heart of Tokyo, and the offices of the CEOs were sleek, evidence of the status to which Japan had risen. But I found one thing lacking, at least compared to senior management offices in the US. There was not a single picture on either the desk or the walls—nothing representative of a personal life, a family, a trip to somewhere, nothing to humanize the man I was about to interview, to give me a hint of the person behind the corporate face.

I spoke slowly, enunciating each word for the interpreter, and posed my question something like this: "I'd like to talk about profitability. Given Nomura's low profit margin and low return on equity, how can you generate the capital required to grow your business?" That question could not have taken more than twenty seconds, or thirty at the most, to ask.

The translator's interpretation to the CEO lasted at least a minute (or two, it seemed). The CEO, in turn, engaged in a conversation in Japanese that was far longer than any response I would have expected. Poised with pen and paper, for what seemed like an eternity, I watched the two men intently, wondering if my question had been fully understood. Then came the answer, in the form of a single sentence: "We think our profits are good."

Hmmm, I thought. *Better try another tack.* Throwing away my original scripted questions, I decided on a softball approach, something that might give the CEO an opportunity to answer in a way that shed light on his views and his mission. "What are the greatest challenges and opportunities that you face in trying to grow market share?"

I could have had a cup of green tea and a biscuit in the time it took to get the response. *What's taking so long? Does the translator understand the question?* The longer I waited, the more absurd my thinking became. *Are they talking about me? Are they saying they've never seen a businesswoman before?*

Eventually the answer came—something that simply acknowledged that the opportunities were great and that market share growth was most important to them. And then one additional snippet of real value—they were looking at the long term, not the short term.

That last tidbit—they were focused, not on short-term profits but on long-term market share—spoke volumes and provided an instantaneous answer to the company's low profitability. Price, not profitability, was management's key strategy—focusing on volume and sales at the expense of profitability, the polar opposite of how US machinery companies managed their businesses.

At a meeting later that day with a second machinery company, I framed my questions around the issue of market share and got almost identical responses to those from Komatsu. A picture began to emerge of a Japanese business ethic distinctly unlike that in America. Good work for day one.

By seven o'clock, I'd earned my dinner in the heart of the Ginza—sushi beyond anything New York could dream of offering, accompanied by the perfect sake, in a setting that could best be defined as hip and energetic. Thankfully, my Nomura Securities host picked up the tab, as a quick glance showed it to be over ¥200,000 yen, or almost $900, for three people. I thought back to my meal in Nara and wondered what Tokyo real estate must cost.

Several days into the week, I awoke with a serious case of laryngitis for no explainable reason. Nomura Securities arranged for me to see a doctor, and the experience was a revelation. The doctor, who seemed barely older than I was, spoke almost flawless English, a delightful surprise after having spent the better part of ten days doing my best to make myself understood. In the course of my examination, he mentioned that he had gone to medical school at the University of Pennsylvania, and we bonded instantly, when I shared with him, in a barely audible whisper, that I had attended the same university and its Wharton School of Business. We reminisced about Philadelphia, he by asking me yes-or-no questions and me by nodding or shaking my head.

When the visit ended, he gave me, instead of a prescription, a plastic container of small white pills, instructing me to take as many as ten or twelve up to three times a day. He promised me that I would be better in a day. There was no charge, and I thanked him as I left with my booty. *Could they just be placebos?* I wondered. I'll never know the truth, but within twelve hours, I was once again in perfect health and full voice. I have enduring respect for the little I know of Japan's health care system.

I had requested the opportunity to visit a machinery company's manufacturing facility, something apart from the plush office headquarters and arrived at eight o'clock the following morning to witness an outdoor calisthenic exercise program in action on the grounds of the facility. For fifteen minutes, the employees and the plant management, dressed in identical work uniforms, engaged in a team-building exercise that included jumping jacks and running, and was interspersed with syncopated shouts. When it was over, the men walked single file into the open-air assembly plant.

At a meeting with the plant manager, when I asked a question about the volume of output, trying to elicit from him a sense of the revenues generated by the plant, he produced an abacus from the side of his desk. As his fingers manipulated the small wooden beads along the metal rods, my brain was spinning—this is the country of Sony and Panasonic and Toshiba, but he doesn't have a calculator?

Scenes like that were part of the conundrum that was Japan. Tokyo represented the forefront of modernism with its skyscrapers, its Ginza, and its high-fashion stores. Yet, within that thriving metropolis, its residents remained tradition-bound.

The long flight home gave me time to ponder the two weeks in Japan. I had gleaned much from meetings and observations, from questions asked but not answered, from personally experiencing both the business and the cultural life of the country. Capitalism was the basis for both the American and the Japanese economic systems, but with distinct differences in how it was viewed.

American-style capitalism was impatient—short-term profitability was its god—and success was measured on a quarterly tied to stringent metrics, often ignoring the long-term nature of capital investment. Individualism and self-reliance, integral to the fabric of American life, were essential for success.

In Japan, however, success seemed to be defined differently and to be measured over a far longer time span. The virtues of conformity and collaboration, ingrained in the culture of the country, were themselves measures of success, as was employment for life, which was both the expectation of workers and the obligation of management. Autonomy was frowned upon, as was self-promotion. A company's sights were set far into the future—long-term share of market, rather than short-term measures of profitability, was what defined Japanese capitalism.

I tossed questions over in my head. *Could both approaches to capitalism be successful? Could one trounce the other? Or was this long-term strategy by Japanese companies the result of the weakness of the yen, which allowed them to undercut their competitors in the US? What might happen when, or if, the dollar weakened and the shoe was on the other foot? Would the Japanese loss of market share force them to reverse their strategy?*

Questions without clear answers but observations that brought insights—all part of the process of researching and analyzing—and Peter was attentive as I spoke, particularly the part about trading off market share for profitability. That resonated with him.

None of what concerned me about the Japanese business strategy of sacrificing profitability for long-term market share gains seemed to put a damper on the price of the Nikkei (Japan's stock index). Six years later, in 1987, their stock index reached an all-time high of 38,957. In the subsequent thirty-five years, it has never returned to that level. The Japanese machinery companies certainly made market-share strides on a global scale, yet today Caterpillar Tractor's revenue is more than twice that of Komatsu, its closest Japanese competitor. In the farm equipment industry, Deere & Company has more than double the revenue of Kubota.

CHAPTER 31

For the Greater Good

1981

It was Peter on the phone. "I want to see you," he said.

"I'll be right down."

It was unusual for Peter to request a visit to his office. Most often, it was he who made the journey up the internal staircase to the twenty-third floor, despite his uneven gait, the evidence of his victory over polio some half century earlier. At times, he might simply "walk the floor," less a "homeroom monitor" and more someone looking to discuss what was on his mind. Or his goal might be to deliver a Petergram—those brief, handwritten missives intended to advise, or on a rare occasion congratulate—generally deposited when one was away from the office.

What does he want? What challenge is he going to throw at me?

Peter was sitting in the tall wing-back chair that he preferred to the rolling chair behind his desk. It was where he read his newspapers and held his meetings—a less formal mode of engagement than from behind a desk. I took a seat on the couch next to his chair. Silence for a moment, and then he spoke.

"I want you to join the portfolio management team." He did not elaborate.

I was taken aback. At the same time, I knew the business well enough to be flattered, yet I was entirely unprepared to respond. I was grappling with what to say.

He's promoting me, but, but, but…

In the world of investing at that time, there was a perceived, but not fully defined, hierarchy among the professionals that made up an investment team. It was generally considered a promotion to migrate from research analyst to portfolio manager.

The role of analysts could best be described as narrow and deep. It was their responsibility to be a highly knowledgeable and reliable resource on stocks within a particular industry. In my case, it was the full spectrum of the capital goods sector of the economy.

A portfolio manager was responsible for selecting which stocks, covered by the firm's team of analysts, were best suited as investments in a client's portfolio. That position required a broad understanding of a wide range of companies and how they responded to anticipated changes in the economy. Most portfolio managers rose through the ranks of the research department, having cut their teeth as analysts on one or more industries. They understood the value of the research process.

After a few moments of silence, I spoke quietly. "Peter, you've given me the best job I've ever had. I love what I do—meeting with the CEOs of some of the most powerful companies in the world. I get to challenge them, to compare the strengths and weaknesses of companies globally. I know I do it well. How do you know that I'll be a good portfolio manager?"

Peter listened without interrupting and responded in a subdued voice, "I need you, and I have confidence in you."

"Will you give me some time to think about this?" I asked. I was loath to turn him down. At the same time, I feared losing the intellectual challenge and the immense satisfaction that was the very essence of being a research analyst.

Peter consented to my request, and I returned to my office, pondering what had just occurred. He had offered me a promotion, one at which most people would have leapt in a heartbeat. He had, in essence, told me, although not in so many words, that he believed I was ready for the next step. Instead of thanking him for his confidence in me and accepting his offer, I had begged off, putting my own interest ahead of his need.

I did not feel good about my response. Over the next few weeks, I gave more thought to my reaction. Peter had played the noble role, yielding to my request to remain an analyst. I was keenly aware that I had let him down, something he had never done with me. *Am I afraid of what I don't know? Afraid of losing my reputation as a tough-minded machinery analyst? Afraid of failure? Am I stuck in my ways at the age of thirty-three?*

I wasn't sure of the answers and tried to put the issue behind me. But it wouldn't go away. Peter made no mention of our meeting again, nor did I discuss it with anyone.

A few weeks later, three Citibank portfolio managers announced that they were leaving to form their own company. Three out of a team of twelve was a significant loss of talent.

Within seconds of hearing the news, I left my office, took the stairs down to the twenty-second floor and walked into Peter's office.

"Peter, I know you need me. I'll join the portfolio management team."

CHAPTER 32

The Year of Living Dangerously

1982

I t was Monday, January 4, 1982. Over the long holiday weekend, my office had been moved from the grand window-lined corner in the research department to a small office next to the bank's most respected portfolio manager, the thoughtful, experienced Dwight Hyde, some twenty years my senior. Peter had assigned me to work with him in my new role.

Dwight gave me full responsibilities for a single portfolio with assets of about $16 million (the equivalent of about $54 million today), with the agreement that I could invest it as I chose, and we would discuss my thoughts and rationale for my decisions every few days.

The economy and the markets were anything but friendly in the early months of 1982. The stock market rally at the beginning of the prior year had fizzled by summer, as the economy rolled over into a second recession in as many years. Inflation reached 13 percent, and mortgage rates were even higher.

Uneasy about investing in a market that made new lows day after day, I held a large cash position in the account—as high as 30 percent, which felt like a security blanket.

For a fledgling portfolio manager, the first six months of 1982 were a baptism of fire. There was no place to hide as, month after month, stock prices crumbled. My conversations with Dwight Hyde increased in frequency, if only so I could be comforted by his calm demeanor.

Selecting stocks to buy was a case of trying to decipher which were the least vulnerable. The safest recourse was to hold cash. I had yet to develop the ability, as Peter would often advise, "to buy straw hats in January." At this point in the market malaise, every stock seemed to fit that bill—cheaper than it had been the prior month and the month before that.

I watched, listened, queried, read—did everything but pray. It seemed to me that God had more important things on his mind than the Dow Jones Industrial Average. I was being paid well—far more than I had imagined I'd ever make—and it was up to me to learn from those who had lived through bear markets before and were more experienced than I was.

But there seemed to be no bottom to the market. By August, S&P 500, the best broad index of stock prices at the time, reached 102.77, down from a high of 140.52 in November 1980, a drop of 27 percent in under two years.

However, despite the disquieting economic news, the Federal Reserve had started to ease monetary policy as the trend in inflation began to subside. But how long, I wondered, would it take before their action would have a positive impact on the economy? Peter, however, with decades' more experience than I, saw green shoots in the Fed's action.

It was Thursday, August 12, around noon, when Peter exploded onto the twenty-third floor, striding from one office to another and barking orders. I could hear him coming down the hallway.

"Put your cash to work."

I looked up to see him standing in the doorway of my office, his dark eyes squarely on me.

"Now," he said. "Right now."

"OK, I hear you." This was not a moment to ask "why."

"I mean now. I want all your cash invested by the end of the day. Today!" I could hear the exclamation point in his voice.

He moved to the next office and the one after that, his stentorian voice booming the same words. No time for a thoughtful Petergram. Peter was on a mission.

He was back in my doorway. "Where's Fran?" He was referring to Francine Bovich, one of the portfolio managers.

"She's on vacation," I responded, deliberately neglecting to tell him that she was in Paris with her husband.

"Put the cash to work in her portfolio. Now."

"But, Peter, I don't manage her accounts. I don't know what she would do."

"I don't care what she would do. I want all her cash put to work. This is the time to buy. The market has bottomed. This opportunity won't come again. We're going to have the biggest bull market you have ever seen. Buy right now."

Peter would track Fran down an hour later at the Ritz in Paris and give her the same order. By the close of the market, every portfolio in Citibank's institutional investment department was fully invested, and not a day too soon.

The normally placid and judicious Peter was for one day on an uncharacteristic and brilliantly correct rampage. He called the absolute bottom on the stock market to the day. Within twelve months, both the Dow Jones average and the S&P 500 had soared by more than 50 percent from their August lows.

The cash that had sheltered my one portfolio through the first half of the year turned to gold by the end of the year. In what I will forever consider the best case of "beginner's luck," I had outperformed the market by a full 10 percentage points—one thousand basis points!

Peter's words came to my mind. "When you're on a pedestal, there's no place to go but down." It was applicable to stocks and to company managements, and I saw it apply to me as a brand-new portfolio manager.

CHAPTER 33

No Stopping Me

1983–1984

The Petergram was on my chair when I returned from lunch early in 1983. It was short and to the point. I paraphrase it: "Nice performance. Keep your eye on the ball."

Peter's missives had purpose—this one was both congratulatory and admonitory. *You're doing a fine job* [it said], *but don't let it go to your head.*

With that as a backdrop, I was unprepared for what he was about to throw at me—an additional seven portfolios of pension fund assets, with a market value of close to $2 billion. Within a year, as the stock market continued to rebound, it had become $3 billion, equivalent to about $9 billion in 2023.

The apprehension I had felt when Peter first asked me to forsake my vocation as an analyst and take on the mantle of portfolio manager had dissipated. It was true that I missed the challenge of engaging with corporate decision-makers and the ability to create my own mosaic from those intense interviews. That said, it didn't take me long to relish the new world into which Peter had thrust me.

There's a saying in the investment community, "You're only as good as yesterday's performance." That was a humbling thought, and I soon found myself feeling grateful when I had stocks in my portfolios that were lagging the market because I saw them as the fuel for when my winners would run out of steam. Peter enjoyed the competitive energy derived from portfolio managers competing for first place. I may have been a neophyte, but I was in the same marathon as my more experienced associates.

It was invigorating to spend a day where breakfast, lunch, and dinner were business affairs and the telephone was a blunt instrument with which to grill Wall Street research analysts, institutional salespeople, and investment strategists—almost all of whom were men. For me, information was power, and the more I had, the better the decisions I could make. Investing was akin to a blood sport. As I gained experience in the cutthroat world of portfolio management, I became increasingly demanding of those on whom I relied for information.

What I neglected to appreciate was the often intimidating ferocity of my passion. Subliminally, I suppose, I expected everyone to share my zeal. Question after question, until I was satisfied and my counterpart—a Wall Street analyst, or a salesperson—was worn out. That's the way, with the benefit of hindsight, I now picture my interrogations. What I saw as the virtue of diligence neglected what could be interpreted by others as the vice of tyranny.

What I expected of myself, as my career was barreling ahead—perfection—I also expected of others, be they my assistants, junior folks who reported to me, or the array of analysts and institutional salespeople on Wall Street whose responsibility it was to share with me the best thinking of their firms' research.

One colleague, in particular, seemed to take offense at my approach, and I learned from a fellow portfolio manager that he had been heard to say, "I hope her plane crashes," when he found out I was on a business trip. She and I laughed it off, but I was convinced he meant what he said. Many of us on the investment team attributed his bizarre behavior to his thirteen-month tour of duty in Vietnam. "Too much Agent

Orange," was the universal jocular comment, particularly after he once stated, "There are two things in life I can do well—pick stocks and kill people." The world of money management comprised a strange set of bedfellows.

But he had it wrong when, at a group research lunch—an almost daily event—he snapped at me. "It's obvious you were born with a silver spoon in your mouth." At first I laughed it off—so typical of him. Then I thought, *If only he knew my story.* A few moments later, it occurred to me to be flattered.

Without realizing it, I was falling into a bad habit; namely, failing to consider that others might do their best work at a different speed than mine. Armed with the advantage of a research background, I attacked the portfolio management side of the business with the same drive and attention to detail. Those less well trained—most often the institutional salespeople who covered the firm—were generally unable to answer my probing questions and found themselves having to go back to their research departments.

Even within my own office, I was getting a reputation as a perfectionist. "She'd better not find any mistakes in your work," was the general attitude. I couldn't understand why assistant after assistant lasted at most a year with me. It never occurred to me that the nonstop dynamics of the stock market that were my career adrenaline might not have the same appeal to those who worked for me.

Endless energy, a passion for perfection, and a willingness to fight for every eighth on a stock trade were attributes that could backfire if not tempered. In my case, they justly earned me the moniker—Witch of Wall Street.

* * *

Peter, nearly thirty years my senior, was facing mandatory retirement at sixty-five, just a year or two away. In anticipation of that day, he added to my responsibilities that of liaison with Citibank's European investment team, which had offices in London, as well as on the Continent—mostly centered in Geneva and Zurich. As a member of Citibank's European Investment Policy Committee, I found myself flying to one or more of those cities every six weeks.

A seven-hour flight would land me in Geneva or Zurich by nine in the morning, in time to bolt by taxi to the office and slip into the conference room, shrouded in the heavy haze of cigarette and cigar smoke. For a woman who had never had a puff on a cigarette, I accepted the obnoxious fumes as a fact of life in the world of business in Europe.

The pace of the investment business in Europe, most particularly in Geneva, was more measured and less hectic than in New York. Lunch was hardly ever a sandwich affair in the office. Rather, it took the better part of two hours in one of the small but elegant local restaurants that were within walking distance of the office. The meal inevitably included a bottle of a simple but fine wine.

While I refrained from alcohol at lunchtime in New York, it would have been considered rude to do so in Europe. Imbibing had a way of moderating the tempo of business, allowing the opportunity to develop social relationships. Upon returning to the office, I would observe what seemed to be the aura of siesta, particularly in Geneva, as people closed their office doors and communication with associates all but died. That was fine with me because the markets back in New York were just opening. As the workday seemed nearly over in Europe, I'd spend the next six hours immersed in managing my clients' portfolios until it was time for dinner—another opportunity for social engagement.

It was a peripatetic life, but one that I found challenging, exhilarating, and fulfilling. I'd been on this European circuit for more than a year, and in a quiet moment when I was sharing my thoughts with Peter, he asked me out of the blue, "Where do you stay in London?"

I responded, "At Claridge's."

He tossed his head back, gave a hearty "Haah!" and said, "You *are* a Claridge's girl." I knew what he meant and was flattered.

"And do you stay at The Connaught?" I presumed to ask him.

His black eyes opened wide and then he gave a little "Huh" before asking, "How did you know?" I just smiled back.

Peter was "old money," like The Connaught, with its gilt-mirrored elevators, warm-toned carpeting, and overstuffed furniture. In my early thirties, I found the place too old-fashioned for my taste. I preferred the sleekness of Claridge's. Its art deco features created an elegant 1920s ambience, while the tasteful black-and-white photographs of the royal family, as well as Hollywood's royalty, lent an air of coziness. There was something endearing about the modest-sized photo of Queen Elizabeth II, taken some decades before I ever set foot in the hotel, that was placed in such a way that she appeared to be overseeing the check-in process.

The staff was as much a part of the ambience as was the decor. I was taken aback, and then touched, when Paddy, the diminutive and engaging Irish porter, greeted me with, "Welcome home, milady," as I stepped out of the taxi.

I had my favorite room, and seldom was I disappointed. On one occasion, the gentleman at the reception desk shared confidential information with me, speaking in close to a whisper.

"Ma'am, don't be alarmed by the armed guards in the hallway on your floor. There's a special guest staying here, but we know you well and have informed security."

"Who is the guest?" I queried back, sotto voce.

The fellow paused, looked right and then left, and whispered back, "I'm not supposed to say, but…it's the king of Jordan." I nodded my head as if to say this was our secret, and he added with a twinkle, "You will be very safe, ma'am."

I thought it best not to ask further questions, but my curiosity was piqued. *Is Queen Noor with him?* I wondered to myself. She was the elegant, Princeton-educated American, Lisa Halaby, whom King Hussein had married a few years earlier. There was no sign of her, but I did enjoy the "celebrity moment" of exiting the elevator as the king was entering it.

Claridge's was my "home away from home," and London felt like my home city in ways that New York City—which better represented the frenetic pace of my career—didn't. At the end of my stay in London, I would tack on a full weekend in which I found time to shop—for art, for clothes, and, of course, for shoes. I'd scour the antique jewelry shops on Bond Street and at Grays Antique Market.

* * *

Peter was a sage who thrived on play as much as work. Hardly had he arrived at Citibank in the role of chief financial officer in 1977 than he established the tradition of an annual outing in late June for all investment professionals as a way to build camaraderie and team spirit. By the time I arrived in 1980, the event was finely honed—a day of sports activities, followed by cocktails, a barbeque dinner, and some raucous entertainment. I was happy to become a member of the "entertainment committee," a team of eight to ten research analysts, portfolio managers, and traders who spent tens of hours writing skits, rehearsing songs, and putting together the after-dinner program.

The 1984 outing would be Peter's last, and we put together a jovial tribute to the man. Earlier that year, Ed Koch, the beloved mayor of New York City, had come out with his autobiography, *MAYOR*, the front cover of which showed a smiling Ed Koch, with his arms high in the air, holding a sign with his title, MAYOR. That best-selling memoir was the prop on which we created the evening's entertainment, by putting Peter's face in place of Koch's with the word MENTOR across the top.

Peter retired from Citibank at the end of 1984, a couple of weeks before his birthday. To anyone who knew him well, it was evident that the word "retirement" was not part of his lexicon. Upon leaving the bank, he assumed the position of chair of Baring American Asset Management. Peter would be investing his clients' money until his last day.

For the next twenty-five years, he and I stayed in touch, mostly by phone and always in January around his birthday. It was usually he who made the call.

"Darling, how are you?" in a booming voice. We'd share bits of family news until he'd say, "What are you investing in now?" and we'd talk stocks. "What do you think of…" and he'd list some stocks. We'd discuss the economy and then politics. Peter was a moderate Democrat and had a balanced and thoughtful view of how the world should work. The conversation wasn't over until he queried, "What shows have you seen lately?" We were both Tom Stoppard fans.

Who knows how long we talked, but I could almost hear Lucy in the background saying, "Petey, come get your lunch." I'd wish him a happy birthday, which was always around the corner on the seventeenth of January, and we'd then say, "Goodbye," knowing that we'd be talking again.

It was January 2009, four months after Lehman Brothers' bankruptcy threw the stock market into a turmoil that cost it 30 percent of its value by year-end. The phone rang, and it was Peter.

"Darling," was his joyous greeting.

"This market's going to rally soon and big," he said. "And in June, I'm going to hang up my spurs. I want to write a book. Will you come visit me and tell me stories?"

"Of course, I will."

For years, even before he left Citibank, I'd been urging Peter to write a memoir—to share with the world the story of his fabled life and career, his insights, and his contrarian approach to investing. I couldn't wait for June.

Sadly, our meeting would not come to pass. Peter never did get to see his prediction come true. He died of a stroke on March 9, the very bottom—to the day—of the Great Market Crash of 2008–2009.

Peter—perpetually curious, sometimes crusty, always thinking—a man who lived life to the fullest, who seemed invincible, despite his physical ailments, whose mind was as sharp at the age of eighty-nine as it was when I first met him thirty years earlier. Now fifteen years since his demise, I still miss him.

CHAPTER 34

I Do

1985

George Gershwin's fifty-year-old song, "I Got Rhythm," epitomized my life as 1984 drew to a close. I was in my rhythm—that was for sure, and I loved it. But now there were a few other reasons the song encapsulated my life. I had sweet dreams. I had my man. Who could ask for anything more?.

I was in love once again, and this time I was heading to the altar.

* * *

John Chadwick and I had worked together for nearly two years before there was any spark. We had arrived at Citibank within weeks of each other during Peter Vermilye's hiring binge in 1980—he as a portfolio manager, and I as the capital goods analyst. He was engaging and a team player, but when it came to the matter of managing his clients' money, he was all business.

Some months after I arrived at the bank, I recommended Ingersoll Rand, a global manufacturer of compressors for both industry and energy production. Like many machinery companies, Ingersoll Rand's revenues and income could be highly variable, particularly in the economic turmoil caused by inflation and rising interest rates that epitomized 1980 and early 1981.

When the company's earnings fell short of my expectations, John was an unhappy portfolio manager and he let me know it. My response was to give myself some advice: *Distance yourself from him.* I did, and John was well aware of it.

When, a year later, I acquiesced to Peter Vermilye's request that I join the team of portfolio managers, I realized that meant working side by side with John on a daily basis. I gave myself a pep talk: *Go into his office and tell him that you're looking forward to working with him.* I knew it was the right thing to do.

As I was getting up my gumption to go into his office, I paid a visit to the trading desk—an active, boisterous center of activity—and there was John chatting with the traders. I gulped, but before I could leave the room, he came up to me and said, "Congratulations on becoming a portfolio manager. I'm looking forward to working with you." He had taken the words right out of my mouth.

From then on, we were partners—in business. The spark of romance wasn't spawned until more than a year later. It was in the spring of 1982, a few months after Jack and I had broken up and we were grabbing a quick hamburger at a pub a couple of blocks from the office—a common occurrence among portfolio managers.

"You're not wearing your ring," he said softly, halfway through the meal.

I was silent for a moment. "Jack left me," was all I said, and thought we'd move on. Instead, he let me in on his own personal angst.

"I'm in the middle of a divorce."

For two hours, we shared stories and emotions. By the time we returned to the office, we knew we wanted to see each other again.

Romance ensued. Despite our best efforts to be discreet, and despite the lack of any impropriety on our parts, our romance soon became the topic of gossip. We laughed it off—what else was there to do?

Six months later, we traveled on vacation to Europe for three weeks, and by the end of the year, we were sharing residences, meeting each other's families, and doing our best to keep our relationship private.

In the fall of 1984, we took a romantic two-week vacation to Italy, followed by a few days in London. Upon returning to the office, my secretary greeted me with a surprised question.

"Where's the ring?" she asked. I looked at her quizzically, and she said, "Everyone in the office expected you to get married on your vacation."

In truth, she was on to something. On the last evening of our vacation, when we were about to head out to dinner in London, John had quietly asked me to marry him. Mind you, it was not during our blissful stay at the Splendido in Portofino or on the balcony of the Londra Palace, overlooking the Grand Canal. It was without fanfare—no ring, no getting down on his knee—not that I wanted any of that. I simply was unprepared, but isn't that the way engagements are supposed to be?

So unprepared was I that I gave a pathetic response about something to do with taxes and maybe it wasn't the right time. It's almost embarrassing to share that reaction, but that was the truth. John was good enough to accept my rebuttal without a further response.

A month later, we invited John's parents from Washington, DC, to Connecticut for Thanksgiving. It was a small family dinner for four that came with all the trimmings, including sweet potato pie, as homage to my Southern "not-yet-mother-in-law." On Sunday afternoon, after we'd dropped them off at the airport and were back home sharing an evening cocktail and reflecting on the enjoyment of the long weekend, the conversation somehow gravitated toward the subject of marriage—this time without any pushback on my part. It seemed like the perfect idea and the perfect time.

I laughed. "Honey, your parents are going to think we're nuts. They were here for a full four days, and we said nothing about getting married. Now that they're back home, you're going to call them with the news?" But in his low-keyed way, John carried it off.

We looked at our calendars, and the first open Saturday was January 12. When a few days later, we received an invitation to a party for that evening, we revamped our wedding plans and selected the next available Saturday, which was March 9.

At the age of thirty-six, I wanted a simple affair. We agreed to have immediate family only, which included my maternal grandmother, my parents and siblings, and John's parents, his sister, and his three children. Only later would we realize how many friends and relatives we disappointed. Given that my husband was divorced, the church ceremony could not be Catholic, but my parents expressed no reservations. I wasn't the first of their children to marry outside the church, and I've wondered if they were unwilling to let the matter of religion be a wedge between them and their children, after the years of emotional pain it had brought to all of us years earlier.

Saturday March 9 blossomed with brilliant sunlight, and by early afternoon, the temperature reached a balmy sixty-four degrees.

In lieu of a grand ballroom, an orchestra, and 200 people, we splurged on the reception that was held at the house we were renting in Connecticut. Caviar and foie gras; lobster and oysters; filet mignon with bearnaise sauce—accompanied by champagne. It was a meal that still makes my mouth water.

Three months later, we honeymooned for ten glorious, sun-filled days in the English Lake District.

Life after marriage was more perfect than before.

CHAPTER 35

Daughter, Mother, Grandmother

1986

My mother called. "I want to buy a house on the ocean," she said with an air of confidence, as though she'd already made up her mind. "Will you go in on it with me?"

It was 1986, and Mother was on top of the world.

Her journey from nun to businesswoman had been nothing short of spectacular. A woman with a brilliant vocabulary and an immense knowledge of literature and history, she left the Center to be with me and then did what was necessary to make a living, at first cleaning houses for those who could afford her services. Perhaps having lived the life of servitude for twenty years as an obedient nun, she had the grace to accept that lowly position without complaint.

It was her nature to view the world as full of opportunity. From housekeeper, she took on the role of nanny for the infant daughter of a brilliant couple getting their PhDs at Harvard. Then, after a stint in the world of real estate, she became the manager of a branch of Cambridge Savings Bank, with responsibility for approving, or not, all personal loans. She had a sixth sense and was proud to highlight that no loan she ever made went bad.

It was some time in the late 1970s, or perhaps the early 1980s, that she became the secretary to the owner of a small manufacturing company—a firm that made wooden pallets, a forklift-ready stock item for every warehouse that needed to move cartons of products. Within a couple of years, she was handling the day-to-day affairs of the business, from negotiating leases to hiring employees and managing sales.

Her boss rewarded her handsomely, and by the time she was in her late fifties, she was making more than $100,000 annually, which in today's terms would be in excess of a quarter of a million dollars.

I knew that she was proud of me, and I was equally proud of her and honored to have inherited her business acumen, which she, in turn, credited to her own mother, Laura Miller.

Laura's pregnant mother had succumbed to the 1918 flu epidemic, leaving behind a husband and four daughters in Leondardtown, Maryland, a small town on the Potomac River. Laura, the eldest of the four children, and twelve years of age at the time of her mother's death, left school in the sixth grade to raise her siblings, the youngest of whom was just two years old.

Eight years later, she married Bill McKinley, a World War I veteran, and moved north to his home in Cambridge, Massachusetts, bringing her youngest sister, then ten years old, to live with them. Bill had been stationed in France during the last year of the war and was active in the local VFW. Laura, in turn, joined the "8 and 40" the women's auxiliary group, and soon began her public speaking career.

She became the organization's parliamentarian, and in that role, she committed to memory *Robert's Rules of Order*. Over the next fifty years, she traveled to each of the lower forty-eight states, as the lead speaker at the organization's annual conference.

Her speaking voice was strong, her diction perfect, and her vocabulary sophisticated. Even in her eighties, she never lost her poise or faltered over a word. I understood why my mother was so proud of her.

* * *

Mother had two vacation loves—one was her annual trip to Europe with Daddy, the focus of which was twofold. Ostensibly, they were visiting, over and over again, the great Catholic cathedrals of Italy, France, Germany, and England. Almost as importantly, they traveled to explore the small towns on the outskirts of those cathedral cities. Seldom making either accommodations or restaurant reservations in advance, they would drive until they came to a village that appealed to them, and they were rarely disappointed. John and I curated our own vacations around many of the sites they loved most.

When not traveling, Mother was happiest by the sea. She would reminisce about her childhood summers with her grandmother in Cohasset, a seaside town on the south shore of Massachusetts, while her own mother remained back in Cambridge.

Now, in her late fifties, she wanted her own place. "I love Maine," she said. "I want to see the ocean from my bed. I have a place in mind." She had done her homework, and together with a couple of my sisters, we headed north one Saturday morning to Wells Beach on the southern coastline of Maine to look at a particular four-unit condominium building that had been recommended to her by a real estate agent whom she trusted.

It was love at first sight, so to speak, for Mother, as she stood on the balcony of the two- bedroom apartment and scanned the Atlantic Ocean in front of her. By the end of the day, it was ours.

CHAPTER 36

And Then It Crashed

1987

From the market bottom in August 1982, which Peter Vermilye had called in brilliant fashion, the trajectory of the stock market had been in one direction, namely straight upward. Five years later, in August 1987, it had increased threefold, from 808 to just over 2700 points, an all-time high. Similarly, the S&P 500 had risen two-and-a-half-fold, without so much as a single 10 percent correction.

By 1985, the major industrial nations known as the G5—the US, the UK, West Germany, France, and Japan—agreed on a program whereby the US would reduce its interest rates in an attempt to weaken the strong dollar and thus bring some relief to the country's trade deficit. The plan proved too successful, and the tumbling dollar required the Federal Reserve to reverse course. With that spike in rates, the US stock market came under selling pressure.

By early October, 1987, market prognosticators varied widely in their predictions for the outlook for stocks. But it was a brash thirtysomething woman—Elaine Garzarelli—an analyst and portfolio manager at Shearson Lehman who stood out from the crowd. For a full month ahead of the October volatility, she'd been calling for a bear market. Her prediction was based on quantitative analysis that was grounded in the fundamentals of corporate earnings.

The week of October 12 was a choppy one for stocks, and by Friday, there was an aura of market capitulation on Wall Street. I had made a four o'clock appointment for a manicure—yes, a manicure—in Connecticut, where John and I spent the weekends. I caught the 2:30 p.m. train for the hourlong ride from the city. Smartphones were still in an imaginary state, so ninety minutes later I called the office to get the closing price on the Dow Jones; it had fallen 108 points, nearly 5 percent.

Over the weekend, two friends from Citibank's Geneva office visited John and me in Connecticut. As we were proudly showing off our dream house that was in the final stages of completion, I was wondering silently if we might come to regret having put so much capital into a weekend place. I was almost as concerned about the wisdom of buying a brand-new red Volvo—ordered three months earlier and delivered that Friday—and jokingly asked my guests if they would like to take it off my hands.

Our conversations that weekend were dominated by the stock market. Monday was going to be bad—really bad. That we knew. But how bad? None of us dared to hazard a guess.

On Sunday my husband, who had recently joined Kidder Peabody as the equity portfolio manager for the firm's mutual funds, flew to Seattle on business. His plan was to arrive in San Francisco on Thursday, where we planned to meet up for a long weekend at the Ahwahnee Hotel in Yosemite National Park, a place we were excited to visit for the first time.

October 19, 1987—"Black Monday," as it came to be called—started out badly, with massive sell orders preventing many stocks from opening. As the day wore on, the downward pressure on stock prices intensified, exacerbated by the implementation of what was called "portfolio insurance" programs, the recent brainchild of quantitative "geniuses" who created a rules-based strategy that was intended to mitigate losses in corporate pension plans in a falling stock market. That new product that had yet to be tested in a highly volatile market, and the algorithms embedded in the strategy neglected to take into consideration that the derivatives market was far more liquid than the stock market itself. As those derivatives—stock options and futures—plummeted, they created a vortex of sorts that sucked the stocks down at an ever-increasing speed.

By the time the market closed at four o'clock, the Dow Jones Industrial Index had fallen 508 points, a decline in value of 22.6 percent, the largest one-day percentage drop in its history. The S&P 500 nearly matched it with a collapse of 20.4 percent. A state of exhaustion permeated the office. Not a single portfolio manager, regardless of how long he or she had been in the business, had experienced a day like that.

Moments after the market closed, I called my husband, and the words tumbled out of my mouth with a whimper of a laugh: "Well," I said, "four more days of down five hundred points, and there'll be no market, and we know *that's* not going to happen."

It was a brief moment of levity before we attempted to analyze the behavior of the market. That was when I learned from John that, over the prior week, he had hedged 80 percent of all the money he managed. In other words, he bet big that the market would decline, and he was right. On the worst day in market history, when most portfolios fell by more than 20 percent, his funds declined by less than 5 percent. I was in awe of his investment savvy.

The next couple of days in the market were rocky, and we discussed cancelling our trip—brief though it would be. Would it be a dereliction of duty, I wondered, to take time off when clients were anxious? How long could this volatility continue? There was one person whose counsel I sought—Peter Vermilye.

"Think long term," were his words. "It's going to be rough for a bit, but there's a lot of value in stocks. Don't panic out; stay the course."

When I shared with him my anxiety about taking time off, he was quick to respond. "Go. Enjoy yourself at Yosemite. The market will be here when you return."

Peter was right.

The bloodbath of Black Monday was short-lived, and the stock market bottomed out at the end of November, ending the year with a positive return. The bullish vibe in equites couldn't be squashed.

The "market crash," while shocking and viscerally alarming as it unfolded, was in the long run an invaluable experience for a portfolio manager. Living through it, minute by minute, provided a basis of comparison for the many stock market turbulences that lay ahead in my career. However, it was unable to insure against other types of investment misfortunes.

In the mid-1980s, an electronics retailer—Crazy Eddie—went public at around $8 per share. It was a hot stock with an even hotter advertising campaign that seemed to legitimize the company's explosive growth but that, in essence, was acting as camouflage for the fraudulent activities of the family-run business. Within about eighteen months, the stock had increased almost tenfold to the midseventies and it was a larger-than-life holding in my portfolios.

Unbeknownst to shareholders, including this author, who owned a large position in client accounts, Eddie Antar, the CEO who had run the business since its inception, was skimming the profits and wiring them into an Israeli bank, then laundering them through a series of Panamanian banks and back into the company as "new" sales and "growing" inventories. If that sounds crazy, it was—criminally so. But the company's audited financial statements—the primary source of information for investors in a publicly held company—gave no indication of any financial improprieties, much less shenanigans. When the fraud became difficult to keep on recreating and earnings began to falter, the stock price came under pressure, exacerbated by short sellers who smelled blood. When the Securities and Exchange Commission finally entered the picture, Eddie Antar fled to Israel.

The vagaries of the stock market can hit a portfolio at any time and that's part of the psychic challenge of managing money. One learns from one's inevitable mistakes and moves on. But to have fallen for a windbag of a salesman who was able to produce entirely fictitious financials and get away with it for two years—that was a monumental embarrassment, and it stung for at least a decade. On the other hand, it was on account of that humbling experience that I became a more circumspect, and a wiser, investor.

It was around that time that Citibank sold its institutional investment division—the one that Peter Vermilye had brought to great heights—to the Baltimore-based insurance company USF&G. It was a seamless transaction—we remained as a team with the same assets and the same clients, in the same building. All that changed was our name— we were now known as Chancellor Capital Management.

CHAPTER 37

Facing the Truth

1988

My mother was on the line when I answered the ring. "Hi, dahling," she said and came to the point. "How would you like to celebrate your fortieth birthday?"

"I want something simple that includes the whole family—cousins and all," was my reply.

"Wonderful, dahling."

I had to smile, as I could sense my mother's mind at work. She was fifty-nine and wouldn't turn sixty until three months after I had my fortieth birthday. I was thrilled to give her the pleasure of throwing a party for her daughter who loved celebrating birthdays. She fulfilled my every wish—the extended family was fully represented as we had cocktails and dinner aboard a yacht that sailed through the placid waters of Boston Harbor on a gorgeous August evening.

I was nearing what people still referred to as "middle age," and feeling full of life and energy. Happily married, and managing more than

$6 billion, I felt on top of the world. But…there was something missing, and I knew it.

When John and I had married three years earlier, I had accepted what I knew. He had three teenage children and was intensely involved in their daily lives and was not looking to start a new family. It was part of the unspoken compromise I seemed to have made as part of our life together. To put a good spin on it, I rationalized that it would be difficult to keep up with the stresses of my career, maintain a wonderful marriage, be a caring stepmother, and also raise my own children.

Now on the verge of turning forty, I was increasingly drawn to motherhood, even as I faced the reality that time was not on my side. I was unable to push the thought out of my mind—the intense yearning for my own family would not recede.

Some days after the family birthday celebration, John and I were celebrating my birthday in a quieter fashion—in a corner banquette at La Côte Basque, one of my favorite New York restaurants.

The meal was coming to an end, when almost inspirationally, I blurted out, "We need to talk about something." I paused, and John put down his knife and fork.

"I've been thinking about this for a long time. You need to know that I really want to have children of my own. I have to bring this up now, because if I wait ten years, it will be too late to do anything about it and I'll be an angry woman."

John was silent, a tendency of his when confronted with an unexpected dilemma. I was sympathetic to his plight—his life was full. He loved telling me how perfect our marriage was. I understood that he had put childrearing into his past and was looking forward to enjoying his children, now all in college. The notion of round-tripping fatherhood from the very beginning at the age of fifty had not been on his radar.

He breathed deeply and then spoke quietly. "I wasn't expecting this." I appreciated that he didn't flatly say "No."

We talked long into the evening over wine and dessert soufflé and then over and over again for the next few days and weeks.

CHAPTER 38

Chasing Two Dreams

1989–1994

The air turbulence made for a rocky flight, and the seat belt sign had been on for more than an hour. For me, there is something calming, even soporific, about an airplane bouncing on air currents. And under normal conditions, I would have dozed off, my neck pillow offering support for my always cranky neck, and I'd likely have come back to my senses as the wheels hit the tarmac and we screeched to a halt. But not on this flight.

Forgotten now are other facts about the trip—from where and to where I was flying. All that mattered was that I kept an eye on my watch—seven-thirty was the witching hour, at which moment, and in defiance of the overhead seat belt sign that was clearly indicating the need to remain seated, I rose and made my way forward to the lavatory. Anticipating that the flight attendant might interfere with my mission, I was armed with a spiel—one I hoped would engender sympathy from her.

"I've got a special situation," I planned to say and then just blurt out the truth, "I'm trying to get pregnant, and I have to give myself a shot at exactly seven thirty."

The attendant, however, looked up and said softly, "Be careful, honey, it's bumpy."

All those silent practice sessions for nought. I thanked my guardian angel.

Locking the door behind me, I withdrew a syringe and a small vial of liquid from my handbag. With my back against the wall to brace myself, and with my feet stretched across the width of the tiny space, I inserted the needle into the vial and slowly withdrew the fluid. That was the easy part. Using an alcohol wipe, I swabbed a small spot on my right lower hip as I'd done what seemed like hundreds of times over countless months. But never before on an airplane.

I jabbed the needle into my flesh just as the airplane lurched, and my reaction was to put all my pressure on the syringe. *Don't let it fall out, don't waste a drop.*

OUCH! It didn't matter. Mission accomplished.

An onlooker would have had good reason to believe I was a heroin junkie, and Wall Street, unfortunately, had its share of them. My mission, however, was nobler than the ephemeral kick of a drug—I was in a race against time, in the hope of starting a family with my husband. He was as emotionally invested in the outcome as I was. Having jettisoned his initial cautious response at my birthday dinner, he was now a constant support in our journey together.

That endeavor would be long and arduous with what felt like an unfair share of emotionally crippling failures, but the journey was also bolstered by the optimism and wisdom of the third person in this partnership—the brilliant Dr. James Grifo, a pioneer in the world of fertility at New York's Weill Cornell Center. I was a newcomer at this, and in much the same way that I needed and thrived on mentors throughout the early years of my career on Wall Street, once again, under the care of my physician and his team, I was grateful for his expertise and his advice.

* * *

While I put myself in the hands of the doctor, I continued to run full speed in the office. The pace of business at Chancellor was robust, and we took that opportunity to buy back a majority interest in our company from our parent, USF&G.

Wall Street was, and still is, very much a man's domain. But at Chancellor, we seemed to break the mold. As our assets under management grew, so did the ranks of our senior management, comprising mostly women. On more than a few occasions, the male-dominated world of Wall Street would jocularly refer to us as the "Wall Street gams." Rather than express outrage at what some might have considered a demeaning slur, I chose to take it as a compliment, to view it as an acknowledgment of our success.

Stories of bad office behavior on Wall Street were legion—mostly tales of men taking advantage of their female counterparts or subordinates. My nightmare experience at the hands of a broker when I was twenty years old was all I had needed to put myself on the offensive for the rest of my life. Had anyone dared to pinch my behind or rub up against me, he would have felt the strong, flat palm of my open hand on his face. The Witch of Wall Street would tolerate no funny business.

By 1990, Chancellor had become a highly coveted account on Wall Street, managing billions of dollars in assets and generating a profitable stream of commission revenue for the major investment banking firms on the street.

That year, Morgan Stanley invited me to its annual investment conference at the plush Lyford Cay Club in the Bahamas. Only fifty clients were asked, and few, if any, were women. For the next decade, I was part of that four-day event, run by the famed duo of Barton Biggs, who oversaw the asset management division of Morgan Stanley, and Byron Wien, the firm's investment strategist.

Attendees at the Lyford Cay conference included an array of some of the biggest egos on Wall Street. Fifty fund managers from around the world took their seats at the long oval table that dominated the conference room. No one was shy about offering an opinion—but I often wondered whether the loudest hedge fund voices were throwing the rest of us curve balls by actually buying stocks they claimed to be shorting. Hedge fund management was not my cup of tea. For me the challenge and the intellectual appeal of investing lay in searching for companies that had the potential for significant price appreciation. I had no stomach for the potentially unlimited loss associated with shorting a stock, and anyway I was too much of an optimist to find thrill in corporate events that often led to the destruction of people's livelihoods. Such an approach to investing felt unsavory and I was happy to leave it to others.

One faithful annual attendee was Julian Robertson, the renowned founder of Tiger Management hedge fund. At a conference that was virtually oozing with testosterone, Julian seemed cut from a different cloth. His height and girth belied his gracious demeanor, which had Southern gentility embossed on it. I came to covet a seat next to him for the enjoyment of his personal engagement. A tribute to his business savvy was evident when "tiger cubs"—the products of his former employees whose nascent businesses he funded—showed up at the conference.

While Barton and Byron took turns at the head of the table, Dick Fisher, the president and chairman of Morgan Stanley, was happy to sit among his colleagues on the back bench—the ring of seats that lined the periphery of the conference room. A quiet visionary, it was under his leadership that Morgan Stanley soared to the heights of global investment banking. Despite his prominence, his ego needed no stroking, and the best part of the conference for me was sitting with him well after dinner, each of us enjoying a Cuban cigar, as he shared his views on endless topics, from global politics to collecting art.

* * *

The limelight associated with the Lyford Cay Club was ephemeral and once back home, I found myself running hard and fast on two parallel fast tracks—the never-ending treadmill of managing a growing base of investment assets while pursuing the state-of-the art science in an endeavor to become pregnant. There was no conflict in my mind—I loved my career, and I was determined to have my family. I didn't allow myself to think it couldn't or wouldn't happen. It was just a matter of when.

We had recently hired a new head of marketing, sales, and client service, a dynamic woman ten years my junior—Nina Lesavoy. The two of us traversed the country, from Texas to Nevada, from Illinois to Oregon, in pursuit of acquiring more pension and endowment assets. Late into the night before an upcoming final presentation—whether sitting in a grungy motel room in Carson City, Nevada, or at the posh Ritz Hotel in Chicago—we'd rehearse one more time. The competition was stiff. Often we were pitted against the best of the best—most notably Alliance Capital and its renowned portfolio manager, Al Harrison.

Nina was the expert coach, and it fell to me to execute flawlessly because the outcome of those twenty minutes before the trustees would be binary—success or failure. We seemed to be the perfect team, and we surprised even ourselves with win after win.

Returning from a whirlwind trip with Nina, it was back to Weill Cornell Center at six o'clock the next morning in my unending quest for motherhood. The somber silence that hung over a waiting room crammed with women was reflective of the gravity of our individual, yet identical, missions.

In an eerie way, the pursuit of that goal was not unlike my business life—there was success or failure and nothing in between. I had no intention of failing.

CHAPTER 39

The Best Birthday Present Ever

1993

Alexandra Trower was my closest friend and also a coworker—vice president in charge of corporate communications—at Chancellor. She was fifteen years my junior, and our friendship grew in little steps over a decade. A trusted confidante, she offered endless moral support in my often-emotional journey to motherhood. She was married and herself keen to start her own family.

For my forty-third birthday, she gave me a present in the form of a gift certificate to a psychic reader.

"You must visit her. She's amazing," were her words as I opened the envelope and read the name Verushka. The image that instinctively came to mind was of an elderly Russian woman in a shroud, hunched over an orb and speaking with a heavy accent.

"I will," I responded, trying not to sound half-hearted. I was a skeptic when it came to psychics and palm readers, and I thought tarot cards were a hoax. My mistrust harkened back to my childhood when Father Feeney would lambast what he called "sorcerers."

However, I kept the gift card, and each time I opened my desk drawer, the name Verushka stared up at me, but I couldn't drum up any interest in making contact with her. *Why should I go to some charlatan who's going to pry me with questions and then give me answers couched in gibberish? I'll just be wasting my time.*

In December, my hopes for motherhood were dashed once again, when the nurse from the hospital called to let me know that the pregnancy test had come back negative. The report was emotionally crushing, in particular because the signs of pregnancy had been so prominent. In the privacy of my apartment and before John came home from work, I sobbed.

At the age of forty-three, I was beginning to fear the worst, despite the continued optimism on the part of my doctor. This was not like me—failure was not part of my lexicon. I was used to putting my shoulder to the wheel and effecting the results I wanted.

My only New Year's resolution was to stay optimistic and believe in miracles. A few days later, when I opened my desk drawer, the Verushka gift certificate came alive, and unexplainably I found myself eager to visit her. I dialed her number—the voice at the other end of the line was as American as mine. I explained my purpose and settled on a time a couple of days away.

Inviting was the best description of the curtained-off space in Verushka's apartment that was dedicated to her profession, with a soft-cushioned couch and a warm glow emanating from the colored lights in the small lamps. There was nothing exotic about the woman herself, and in short order, she shared with me that her real name was Ann Johnson and that she'd been married to an oil executive.

As she turned over the tarot cards that were in small piles, she spoke in terms of "seeing things." I did my best to keep an open mind, but was finding it difficult not to harbor a significant dose of skepticism. *What kinds of things is she seeing? Just looks like pictures of weird people.* I was an obvious neophyte in realm of symbolism.

Then came a question. "Do you have children?"

"No," I responded, doing my best to put no emotion into the statement, lest she be swayed in her thinking.

Then examining my hand, she said, "You have the longest lifeline I've ever seen."

I smiled. Who wouldn't be appreciative of a long life? The analyst in me wanted to ask, "And will it be a healthy long life?" but I didn't want her to be distracted from the important matter at hand.

She returned to the small piles of cards, and spoke of family as she made her way through them, but she drew no response from me. If she was a genuine psychic, why did she need me to answer questions.

Then taking my right hand again, she turned it sideways and stared with intensity at the outside edge. After a brief silence she said, softly, "I see two children. Once again, the skeptic in me came to the fore. *Two children? Are they mine?* Externally, I remained calm, but inside I was all aflutter. More questions, more cards, more internal angst.

The session was coming to a close, and my skepticism had turned to curiosity. *What did she mean when she said, "I see two children."*

As I opened my mouth to speak, she looked up at me and said, "You will become pregnant in May." It was around January 10.

I stared at her, speechless. She offered nothing more, and I, unfamiliar with the appropriate etiquette for a psychic meeting, thanked her and left, carrying with me a secret that I shared with only two people—my husband and Alex Trower, who'd given me the gift card and who had recently shared with me the news that she was pregnant.

CHAPTER 40

The Countdown

1993–1994

A thousand times I repeated Verushka's words. "You will become pregnant in May." It was my new mantra.

I called my mother. "Mother, I need your prayers more than ever." She knew what I was talking about. She'd been on prayer patrol for me since I told her that John and I were trying to have a child.

"Dahling, I pray every day to Saint Margaret of Scotland and Saint Gerard Majella for you," was her response. We both knew, from our years at the Center, that they were the two patron saints for mothers.

I chose not to divulge the story of my meeting with Verushka nor to share the seer's fateful words. My mother would likely have been dismissive of my visiting what she would have called "a fortune teller," and I wanted nothing to diminish the fervor of her prayers.

As March turned into April and that May deadline was approaching, my anxiety was heightened. For more than three years, I'd been plodding the tortured road of self-administered hormone injections and predawn visits to the hospital for blood tests, often before racing to the airport and a far-flung city. There had been repeated failures—disappointments at first and then near despair—as attempt after attempt at pregnancy proved unsuccessful, and my dream of having children began to feel unattainable.

Throughout that painful purgatory, my husband offered unfailing support. Behind the scenes, however, even he was challenged. One weekend evening as we were enjoying a candlelight dinner at our home in the suburbs, John made a confession. "This morning," he said, "after dropping you off at the doctor's, I just sat in the car and cried. I feel so helpless."

I had to smile. "Don't worry, honey," I reassured him, "you're doing your part."

But most of the time, it was he who was bucking me up. After one long session with Dr. Grifo that sent me into despondency, John offered an optimistic interpretation. "But he was really encouraging. He's talking about a fifty-fifty chance. So maybe we're just two more tries away."

I saw the truth in his words but retorted, "Well, you and I would be looking for new jobs if all we could achieve was a fifty-fifty track record of outperformance in the stock market." But his words allowed the innate optimist inside me to come alive again.

One incident brought both tears and laughter at the same time. It was a Monday evening, which meant that we were greeted by Christine, our housekeeper, when we arrived at the apartment after work. The middle-aged French woman, with whom I conversed almost entirely in her own language, seemed happiest when armed with an iron, which she applied to any and every piece of fabric she laundered—tea towels, knee socks, boxer shorts, pajamas, nightgowns, and even ladies' lingerie.

Behind the closed doors of our bedroom, John offered to administer my daily evening injection, before we headed out to our favorite bistro for dinner. He had become quite adept at the process, but on this occasion, he managed to hit a blood vessel, and as he withdrew the needle, a red geyser soared into the air and landed, in pointillist fashion, across the front of his white button-down shirt and his khaki trousers. I shrieked at the sight, and, putting all the pressure I could muster on the injection spot, I burst into tears.

"She's going to think I tried to murder you," I whispered through sobs, referring to our faithful housekeeper, who most likely had heard some sort of yell. As John deftly applied a bandage to the tiny puncture site, I calmed down, and he started to laugh at my outlandish fear. Within a couple of minutes, I'd regained my composure and did my best to explain to the housekeeper, in French, "le petit accident."

I was sitting at my desk in the office when the phone rang. As I reached for the receiver, a voice in my head told me it would be the hospital. The person on the line identified herself as a nurse at Weill Cornell Hospital and was scheduling me for my next treatment on May 27.

Verushka's words—"You will become pregnant in May"—were starting to take on the feeling of an impending miracle.

On the Thursday before Memorial Day, I had yet another treatment and headed home to enjoy the annual family holiday gathering at our house. It tended to be a raucous affair, with four siblings, their spouses, and an array of children ranging from teenagers to six-year-olds.

While they swam in the pool, played ball in the backyard, barbequed steaks, and steamed lobsters, I took to my bed, in true Victorian style, enjoying visitations but refraining from any exertion, lest it act as a detriment to a successful pregnancy.

The two-week waiting period was as tortuous as it had been time and again over the prior three years. The telltale signs of pregnancy made their debut, but I no longer trusted them because they'd proven heartbreakingly wrong too often. Yet they were there, loud and clear.

Then came the call, and I braced myself for bad news once again.

"Hi." It was the nurse from the hospital. She sounded upbeat, but I held my breath. "Is this Mrs. Chadwick?"

"Yes," I said, trying to sound calm.

"I've got great news for you. The results are positive," she said.

"Really?" I asked in disbelief, not knowing what else to say. Then I got to reality. "But it's been positive before and then not." I didn't know how else to say it.

She spoke again, "Your HG levels are very high."

Like a child, I asked, "And that's good news?"

"Yes, very," she replied.

"Thank you," I said, and we then scheduled another blood test appointment for later in the month.

Within moments, my husband, my parents, my siblings, and my two closest friends were in the know, and for the next two weeks, I tiptoed through life like a ballerina, as though normal activity might endanger what was, at last, a real pregnancy.

The good news continued, and six weeks later, an ultrasound brought even better news—I was having twins. I had known that was a possibility but had put little anticipation into such an outcome. One child was the miracle I wanted, but two was twice the blessing and twice the joy. Now my prayers, and my mother's, were for the health of the little ones growing inside me.

My instinct—one I'd honed over a quarter of a century of working—was to separate, in iron curtain fashion, my business life from my personal one. In this case, however, that was an impossibility because, within a few weeks, I was bursting out of every tailored business dress and suit that I owned. I was also bursting with energy and keeping up the hectic pace of travel, bringing in new business and visiting existing clients.

Perhaps most surprising to me was the evaporation of any trace of anxiety that the responsibility of raising children might impinge on my ability to carry on my career or interfere with a wonderful marriage. I was euphoric in the anticipation of how my new life would unfold. In mid-August, when I celebrated my forty-fifth birthday, we learned that we were having a boy and a girl. We'd chosen their names long before they were even conceived.

"I've always wanted a boy named Jim," my husband had told me. I had to smile because he already had two sons, but I was delighted, as that was my father's name.

"And I think Caroline is the most beautiful name in the world," I had responded. "It's a bit old-fashioned, but I like that it's no longer a common name."

That was true when I spoke, but there must have been something in the water—two and a half years later, when our children arrived for their first day of nursery school, Caroline had three classmates with the same name.

* * *

My next-door neighbor in Connecticut, an English woman, came to the front door one day when I was about six months along in my pregnancy. I have no recollection of the purpose of the visit, but what remains with me was her statement as she turned to leave.

"I certainly hope that you're planning to stay home and raise the children." There was an air of authority as she spoke and then awaited my answer.

Oh dear, this is the downside of suburban life, I thought, racing to come up with an appropriate response. I smiled and replied politely.

"That's my decision to make, and I fully anticipate returning to work."

I could see by her reaction that I had fallen measurably in her esteem. I didn't care.

By late November, the doctor was advising me to stop traveling, which meant that I wouldn't be sharing that day with my family in the Boston area. As a consolation Christmas present, I sent my parents a caricature drawing of me by the well-known cartoonist, Sam Norkin, done the day before at the firm's holiday party.

During my late January visit to my doctor, he shared news with me.

"You're only two weeks from your delivery, and there's no sign the babies want to come out. We're going to have to do a caesarean. Your due date is February 16, so what day around that time would you like to have the operation?"

"Valentine's Day," I said, without hesitation.

"That's my day off," he replied.

"OK," I answered, "let's do the thirteenth, and the children can be my first Valentine's present."

Some decisions were easy to make. I lived with no superstitions—no fear of black cats or ladders, no throwing salt over my shoulder, and no anxiety about Friday the thirteenth.

What I hadn't anticipated was the blizzard that fell on Manhattan in the wee hours of Thursday morning, February 10. We awoke to behold the city blanketed in more than a foot of snow.

Drats, I thought, as I looked fourteen stories below at the mounds of whiteness with peaks like well-beaten egg whites on their way into an angel food cake. John and I agreed that there was no sense in taking unnecessary risks, and for the first time in my pregnancy—just four days before my scheduled delivery—I missed a day in the office. Only then, when I was confined to my apartment, did I become aware of aches in my back. Somehow, racing around the office was an antidote to the weariness that came from carrying an extra forty pounds.

I called my husband at work. "Honey, I know why it's called delivery. I need to be delivered of these two. Sunday can't come fast enough."

CHAPTER 41

The Present from Saint Valentine

1994

In the silent, white Manhattan predawn, John walked out onto Second Avenue and hailed a taxi, directing the driver to stop at a ten-foot, shoveled-out space in front of our apartment building. Taking my arm, he guided me, a baby step at a time, into the vehicle. Then the two of us—or better said, the four of us—made our way slowly up First Avenue to New York Hospital.

En route, and bursting with excitement, I called my mother, "We're in the taxi and almost at the hospital. I'm feeling fabulous."

"That's wonderful, dahling," she responded. "I'll be praying for you all the way down on the train. Don't worry about a thing, sweetheart, and I'll see you at the hospital by around six o'clock this evening. Love you, dahling."

"Love you too, Mother."

Her excitement was palpable, and in my mind's eye, I pictured her on the other end of our call—beautifully coiffed and dressed as elegantly as was practicable for a four-hour train ride from Boston to New York

City, her handbag a perfect match for whatever outfit she had selected. At sixty-five, she was the picture of health, and a take-charge woman who reveled in her growing clan of grandchildren.

Despite my good fortune to have had no complications throughout my pregnancy, the team of doctors on my case had designated it as "high risk," both on account of my age—forty-five—and because I was carrying twins. But having New York's most renowned high-risk obstetrician, Milton Hutson, as my doctor was reassuring.

In short order we were in the labor ward. While I was being hooked up to an array of electronic devices, John began dealing out cards on my enormous midsection, setting us up for a few hours of gin rummy as we watched the first day of the Winter Olympics in Lillehammer, Norway. Not a bad way to kick back on a lazy winter Sunday morning.

There were no private rooms in the labor ward, just curtains on metal rings, much like in a shower stall—the standard type of accommodation for a large teaching hospital in New York. While the flimsy screens offered a modicum of privacy, they did nothing to diminish the sound of wailing mothers in labor. Inside our cubicle, the primary sign of unborn life was the undulating pattern of bumps on my stomach that I knew well to be elbows or knees—four of each—that gave the impression of porpoises in the ocean and caused the playing cards to be a bit unsteady.

A swishing sound, and the curtain was pulled open. "We need to take your blood," said the friendly voice. The action was quick, and we went back to our gin rummy, mixed with some bizarre Nordic Olympic sport. An hour later, the doctor arrived.

"We've got a problem," he said, and I remember his words verbatim, as the subject was completely Greek to me. "Your platelets are falling, but I think it's a mistake in the test. We'll do it again."

Platelets—I'd heard of them. They had to do with blood, but beyond that, I had no idea their role or function. A couple of hours went by. The blood routine again. By now it was well into the afternoon, but still no labor cramps and no indication that the babies were entertaining any thoughts of exiting their pleasure garden. I was getting antsy.

"When's something going to happen?" I asked my husband. We'd grown weary watching hours of the Nordic version of nearly every winter sport, and in my usual fashion, I had been losing badly at gin rummy.

The babies inside me settled down for a nap, and I did the same, until the curtain rustle awoke me, and the doctor was looking down at me.

"There's a problem." His voice was soft but serious, without a shred of hysteria. "Your platelets are falling rapidly, and we need to operate immediately."

His answers to our questions were curt but polite. "No," he said to John when he asked if he might be allowed in the operating room. "There will be twenty-one staff, which is all the room can handle. We'll have two pediatricians, two nurses, anesthesiologists, as well as residents. But I promise to bring the babies out to you as soon as they are delivered."

"Will I be able to see them born?" I asked, as a cloud of nervousness enveloped me.

No, again. "You will need to be asleep because we have to move quickly."

With barely time to kiss my husband, I was whisked away, down a long corridor and through giant metal doors that opened automatically. The trip was short, but it still gave me time to reflect on a conversation I'd had with my mother many years earlier. It went something like this.

"Mother, I know this is weird, but ever since I was a child, I've had the fear that I might die in childbirth." I offered a partial explanation. "Maybe it's because in so many of stories of the saints, they died when they were very young."

Mother was silent for a moment before saying, "Dahling, if that happens, it will be because it was God's will."

Not exactly the answer I was hoping to elicit from her—my mother who had given birth to five healthy children before her twenty-sixth birthday and who liked to brag that she had delivered her own son in the few minutes between the time my father had called for Dr. Grant and when he arrived at the house.

As I was wheeled into the operating room, it was a sea of faces housed in blue surgical scrubs and caps that greeted me amidst bright, glaring lights. The scene vanished almost immediately.

I awoke some four hours later to see my mother standing next to me, and it took a few moments to come to my senses. "Where are the babies?" was all I could get out in a hoarse whisper.

"Right here, dahling. They're adorable, and they're beautiful."

The events of the afternoon drifted slowly into reality—the problem with my blood, the doctor, the operating room. I had a panic. "Are they OK?"

"They're perfect," she said as she laid one next to me in the crook of my arm, and then the other one. She was right. They were perfect, asleep and tightly swaddled.

"Take some pictures," I said, as I lay with Caroline in the crook of one arm and Jim in the other. "I want to breastfeed them—now." The spirit was willing, but the flesh was weak—it was, however, a valiant first try, and it was close to midnight when John and my mother left, with the promise to return early the next morning.

The sun poured into the large private room nestled at the far end of the corridor—a quiet spot away from the bustle of the nurses' station. It was Valentine's Day and the only presents I wanted were lying asleep in the bed with me. My marching orders included "no walking," which was an impossibility anyway, given that I was hooked up to a slew of both informational and life-sustaining devices.

Within an hour or two, a veritable tsunami of flower arrangements began to arrive. By noon, the nearly two-foot-wide shelf in front of the giant plate glass window was a sea of pink and blue, interspersed with red—it was Valentine's Day. With each new delivery, Mother read me the name of the sender—there were family and friends, of course, but how did tens of brokerage firms get the news? And customers whose money I managed from as far away as Nevada?

"How will we ever get them home?" I laughed. "We'll need another car."

Little did I know that I wasn't going to be making that journey home any time soon. It was four o'clock when the doctor gave me the news.

"I'm so sorry. You have preeclampsia, and we have to take you back to the labor ward right away. We suspected yesterday that might happen, which was why we rushed to do the caesarean."

I felt fine—except for the pain of the incision. How could there be anything wrong? In a moment of panic, I asked her one question.

"Can the babies stay here with me? You won't send them home without me?"

"Of course," she replied. "They will be here as long as you are."

I chose not to ask the second burning question. "How long will I have to be here?" The first one was all that mattered. It took a week to recover, a week during which I spent quiet time with my babies, my husband, and my mother, and rejoiced in my new role—that of mother.

It was a balmy and sunny Saturday morning when we made the trip to our home in Connecticut and were greeted by a covey of children— my nephews and nieces—as well as my siblings. The house was brimming with flowers, from more friends around the world, who assumed that I had arrived home days earlier.

I'd been given strict orders to remain in bed for another week, which was easy to obey, given the army of family that was now encamped in our house for the February school holiday week.

Barely had I settled into bed when the front doorbell rang. "More flowers?" I asked laughingly of one of my sisters and turned back to gazing at the tiny infants in my arms. A moment later, through my bedroom door came Abbot Gabriel Gibbs, now the head of Saint Benedict Abbey, my childhood home in Still River, which had been converted to a Benedictine monastery when Leonard Feeney became reconciled with the Catholic Church in the mid-1970s. With the abbot were two young members of the community, Brother James and Brother Andrew, both of whom I'd known for years, and who were studying for the priesthood.

"Abbot Gabriel," I nearly shouted—loud enough to get a startled reaction from the babies. "I can't believe you've come all this way to see me. Will you please bless all three of us?"

"Of course, my dear." From the time I was a small child, he always addressed me that way. He had been part of my intimate prayer group throughout my years of trying to conceive.

"I remember when *you* were this small," he said, as he held Jim and then Caroline. I knew he was right. He'd been a part of the Center since the mid-1940s when he attended Harvard as a navy veteran.

He took his time with the blessing, cupping his hands around each infant's face and making the sign of the cross on their heads and their chests. Then he gave me a more grown-up blessing. Once pictures were taken, the abbot and the two seminarians said their goodbyes and drove the three hours back to their monastery in Still River.

CHAPTER 42

Sabbatical and Then...

1994–1999

Whoever invented the three-month maternity leave should be canonized. That sabbatical from Wall Street was enlightening, educating, and ultimately reenergizing, as sabbaticals are meant to be.

In a matter of a day, life slowed down. With deliberation and delight, I forsook reading the *Wall Street Journal* at six o'clock each morning. I had a better way to spend my time—nursing my children and changing and dressing them.

During the daytime hours, when the house was quiet and the little ones were sleeping, the atmosphere was as though I was on a retreat. Silence, uninterrupted by the sound of television or even soft music, was a respite from the life that had been sustaining and stimulating me for twenty-five years.

Quietude allowed me to put my life—my new life as a mother—into perspective. First smile, first rollover, first push-up—times two, of course—were the events that made my day. My camera replaced my keyboard as the tool of my new trade. I was blissfully oblivious to the daily meanderings of the stock market. That was now—at least for the next three months—someone else's problem, not mine.

As the days rolled into weeks, and the first signs of spring brought an end to a winter with record snowfall, I bundled the children up and brought them into the office in midtown New York. For an hour or more, I happily shared my two-month-olds with my work family.

Walking into my empty office, I was surprised to find it inviting. There was something appealing about walking into that space, sitting at my desk, taking in the view, and breathing in the energy associated with it.

"Hi." The voice was familiar and I swiveled to see the head of human resources standing in the doorway. "I need to talk to you. Do you have a minute?" Her soft voice had a tone of urgency to it, and she closed my office door.

"Sure," I responded, wondering what could be so pressing.

"We need you to come back. When are you returning?"

I breathed a sigh of relief that the crisis was manageable. "I'll be back on May 16," I said. "That's only a month from now."

Her smile broadened. She looked as though I had just given her a surprise present, and she relaxed.

I was taken aback.

I was also flattered.

I was also torn.

That brief exchange flipped a switch in my mind, one that brought me back to reality. Three months of a maternity leave sabbatical had not killed the warrior spirit in the Witch of Wall Street, but she had undergone a metamorphosis. Success now came with an added dimension.

During those last few weeks of maternity leave, as I wrote thank-you notes for the more than a hundred baby presents that arrived from every corner of the earth, I engaged in an ongoing conversation with myself.

It's time to slow down on the business front. You have other priorities now, and they're of greater importance.

I thought about highly successful women—both those in the intensely charged world of finance and those in the C-suite of corporations—and I deduced a certain pattern that seemed to emerge among many of those who had crashed through the glass ceiling.

Women at the very top of the corporate pyramid—admittedly there were not that many of them in the early 1990s—were often devoid of the responsibilities of raising children. Wall Street legend Mickie Siebert came to mind, as did the rising star Carly Fiorina, the CEO of Lucent, who at the time was on her way to taking over the helm at Hewlett Packard. Admittedly, she had stepchildren, as did I, but that entailed—and in fact mandated—less parental engagement. It was hard to think of powerful women without including Oprah Winfrey, also without children, and the ubiquitous Martha Stewart, whose one child seemed to be the exception that proved the rule.

I was happy to differentiate my path from their journey to success. They had chosen to invest the full measure of their energy and brilliance into their careers. I had now made a different choice. The time spent on my career would henceforth have to play a secondary role to raising my children. It was without fear or anxiety that I took on that challenge, knowing it would require compromises.

So, I returned to work with every intention of slowing down, of doing my best to manage my time in a way that let me harness the kinetic energy of a career in the world of investing while adapting to the patience required of motherhood. It wasn't long before two full-time roles seemed normal, and I'd wonder what I had done with all my free time in days gone by.

The irony of that double goal was to, in fact, speed up the pace of my life. Those every-six-week trips to Europe were now crammed into four days, as though I could trick my children into thinking I had hardly left.

Gone were the days of tacking on a self-indulgent weekend of shopping in London or Paris, but that didn't obliterate the temptation to window-shop on my way to the office in Berkeley Square. A lingerie boutique caught my eye one afternoon, and I paused to look at an elegant nightgown in the window. I could almost feel the silky texture through the imperceptible glass. Instinctively, I reached for the door handle, and I caught the eye of the smiling shopkeeper inside. But something made me stop and a voice inside my head spoke to me. *Just because you can afford it doesn't mean you need to have it.* I was frozen in place for a moment and then let my hand drop, took a step away from the door, turned around, and headed for my hotel. In that moment, I saw worldly possessions in a new light. They seemed ephemeral, unnecessary, and a distraction from what really mattered—my children.

CHAPTER 43

Time for a Change

1996–1999

In early 1996, I assumed the position of chief investment strategist at Chancellor, without giving up any of my other duties—managing billions in assets, meeting with clients across the country, and continuing to travel to Europe.

Had I forgotten the resolution I had made just two years earlier—to slow down the breakneck speed of my career? Or was it that I felt comfortable assuming new responsibilities, having digested the career-mother balance, particularly by setting up an office at home where I worked a day or two each week. At a time before Zoom meetings and remote working, the opportunity to save three hours of commuting was a gift.

An invitation by Goldman Sachs to attend the festivities surrounding the handover of Hong Kong to China in late June 1997 was an opportunity to witness history, and in the process to meet Tung Chee-hwa, the first chief executive of Hong Kong after the handover. Sitting at his table at a luncheon for hundreds of investment professionals, I was impressed. A billionaire shipping tycoon who was fluent in English, he spoke like a Westerner, like a capitalist, like a man confident in Hong Kong's future. He also spoke like the politician he now was—someone who was serving a new master—the Communist party in China. By the end of the trip, I convinced myself that he was the perfect leader in a new era. I wasn't the only optimist.

The role of investment strategist suited my perpetual curiosity about world economics and politics and also gave me the opportunity to pick some of the best brains in the worlds of finance and industry—people like Morgan Stanley's Dick Fisher; Ken Langone, a cofounder of Home Depot; and Jack Welch, the CEO of General Electric. For years, Jack had been a regular visitor to our offices, sharing his approach to management. While his star may have faded in the aftermath of his successors, he was exquisitely versed in the skills needed to run a global company.

I made the trip to his Fairfield, Connecticut, office on more than a few occasions to discuss global issues that impacted corporate profits. There was no one more honest—with me, at least—about his failures and what he learned from them. He'd pick my brain as well, but I always thought I came out the winner.

Jack's insights were invaluable, but I wasn't sure it was a two-way street until one weekend when John and I brought our three-year-old children to Nantucket for a "Christmas Stroll" weekend. At a cocktail party, someone introduced the two of us.

"Jack, do you know my friend Patricia Chadwick?"

"Of course, I do," he replied. "She's the smartest woman on Wall Street."

* * *

It was flattering for sure to be respected and praised by someone as renowned as Jack Welch. I felt like a winner. However, back in the office, I was feeling more like a loser. One of my favorite clients—a large public pension plan in the West—was unhappy with the performance of their account with us. The flagship product at Chancellor—a growth equity strategy—was out of favor and had been underperforming for several years. Our conservative approach to growth investment eliminated seemingly overvalued companies with no earnings—companies that were part of the emerging dot-com bubble of the mid-1990s.

I was anxious as we entered the conference room to meet with the board of trustees. We put on our best face, but I knew we were on slippery ground. When the board chair asked for a voice vote on a change in manager, it was unanimous. The vote of no confidence was crushing. For ten years, the account had been more than a work assignment—it had been a labor of love.

As I exited the conference room with my associates, I went straight to the ladies' room where I couldn't stop the tears—I was devastated and humiliated. My associates and the plan's chief investment officer, a woman with whom I had become very friendly, had left the room with me and were waiting for me to come out. I looked in the mirror and said to myself: *Patricia, you did your best; this wasn't personal. Now move on.*

Splashing cold water on my face, I pulled myself together with my signature bright pink lipstick and rejoined the group. The CIO gave me a warm hug, and I returned to New York deflated but ready to put it behind me. I'd picked myself up before, and this setback was part of the ups and downs of business. Like disappointments in the past, this one would help me be stronger in the future.

* * *

It was around that time that we, the majority owners of Chancellor Capital Management, sold ourselves to Lichtenstein Global Trust, or LGT, as the world knew it. It was an odd but seemingly logical marriage. With its business headquarters in Europe, the firm gave Chancellor a valuable global presence.

The transaction provided me with a financial windfall. For a woman who had earned every penny in her bank account, I felt the need to pinch myself to believe it was real, and then had the good sense to entrust its management to my husband, who had recently been hired by Bessemer Trust to manage the equities of its high-net-worth clients.

The corporate marriage, as is often the case, led to some challenging moments, and a year or two after the acquisition, there was a defection by several of the most senior members of Chancellor LGT, as we were now called.

I saw an opportunity for a giant step up in the management of the firm, and I threw my hat into the ring, knowing there was no one else internally who had the experience I did. When LGT approached me to take on additional responsibility, they offered me a significant part of the position but not the entire role. Well aware that there was not a second candidate, I demanded more.

"I want responsibility for the entire New York–based institutional investment division. You have no one else who can do it."

At a tense meeting in my office, the LGT executive tried again to cajole me into accepting only part of the responsibility.

Looking straight at him, I asked, "And who will manage the rest?" He was unable to answer.

"What makes you think I can't do this job?" I asked.

"I think you can do it, but…"

I squashed the rest of the sentence down his throat. "Then give it to me."

And he did.

* * *

Life on the home front was blissful, but little by little work was consuming more and more of my time. I was becoming used to that imbalance and used the weekends to even out the work-home equation.

I had conditioned the children to be early risers, getting them up at six, so that we could spend an hour of time together before I caught the train into the city. Lorna, the Jamaican nanny whom we had hired when the children were born, was a sublime blessing, as was her Jamaican friend, Ico, who joined as our housekeeper. By the time our children were three and four, they loved Jamaican food—spicy meat pies, rice and peas, curried goat, stew peas and oxtail—and to this day, those basics of the Jamaican culture are part of my children's own culture.

* * *

LGT's acquisition of Chancellor had been a strategic purchase, the precursor to selling off the combined, and now much larger, entity to a buyer interested in a global presence.

AMVESCAP PLC, the Atlanta-based asset management firm, was looking for just such a global presence, and LGT fit the mold. In the fall of 1997, I was invited, together with Nina Lesavoy who headed the firm's client relationship business, to meet with Charlie Brady, the firm's engaging, unprepossessing and visionary chief executive officer. As Nina and I ate dinner with him, he seemed keen to make the deal—the right deal. We were honest, but we didn't undersell ourselves. Although we were all sworn to secrecy, Wall Street is, at best, a sieve, and it was a secret to hardly a soul when the deal was announced in February 1998, and I was brought on board as a global partner.

I now found myself negotiating incentives for the teams of investment managers that reported to me. There was a recalcitrant member of the group who was demanding guaranteed salaries for himself and his team, which threatened to break the deal. I was unable to talk him down, and eventually, I worked out an arrangement in which I would share part of my salary to make up the difference for him. I had no hard feelings—my objective was to deliver the deal intact. I like to think that a part of that spirit was spawned in those formative years of living in a community where sharing was an essential part of the fabric of life.

The Chancellor culture was epitomized by its geography—New York City. AMVESCAP (or Invesco, the entity that was merging with Chancellor) was bred in Georgia, a different culture that had not seen a company with so many women in decision-making. Except for Charlie Brady, who espoused a cosmopolitan approach to business, the team we were joining was circumspect.

Being a global partner had its rewards, but once again, I was burning the candle at both ends, and I was violating the promise I'd made to myself that I would slow down. Some months later, when John and I were with the children on vacation at the beach, he brought the truth home to me.

"The children and I are in the water all day, and you are on conference calls. This isn't a vacation for you."

He was right. It was the summer of 1999—Labor Day weekend to be precise. I'd just turned fifty-one. That night I lay awake, listening to the sound of the waves crashing against the seawall and thinking about my professional life, our life as a family, and the fact that our children would soon be entering kindergarten. It was time for me to play a more substantial role in their daily lives. I wanted to be there to answer the questions they would have as they progressed through their school years. I wanted to travel with them, without feeling guilty about missing a conference call or two or three every day.

It was a sleepless night but when the sun rose, I was in great humor.

"Darling," I said to my husband, "on Tuesday morning when I get to the office, I'm going to announce my retirement. I promise you I'll be retired by the end of the year." And that's what I did.

I spent much of the last couple of months of my career visiting our offices around the world and bidding farewell to the teams I had come to enjoy working with in Zurich, Geneva, Lugano, Brussels, Luxembourg, and London. I took one final trip to Hong Kong and Tokyo, as well.

I knew it was time to leave, and I felt no remorse over my decision, and when the office in New York threw a lovely farewell party for me before Christmas, I took the microphone and spoke extemporaneously, from the heart, about how much it had meant to me to be part of a team that I had joined in 1980, when it was Citicorp Investment Management. Now, some twenty years later, I was retiring, with a light step and a promise to remain in touch. Many in the audience were tearful. I, on the other hand, was blissfully at peace. The time was right, and I was going home, where I wanted to be.

CHAPTER 44

After Wall Street

2000–2001

I stepped into the new century jobless and excited. At the age of fifty-one, with two children in kindergarten and about to turn six years old, I was bursting with the same enthusiasm that had driven me all my life.

I chose to leave the business world without a definitive plan, but that wasn't to say I was without purpose or had no plans at all. Within a month, I had joined the church choir. From the age of three or four, I'd been taught to sight-read music. As I'd matured into my teenage years, it was Gregorian chant that absorbed much of my musical life. But my career had offered little opportunity to join a choir or choral group—travel and business dinners made it impossible to commit to evening rehearsals.

Time was my new best friend. I reveled in making breakfast for my children, driving them to school, and then coming home and reading the *Wall Street Journal* and the *Financial Times* from cover to cover, accompanied by a cup of tea, a luxury I wasn't always afforded in the office.

In late May, when they completed kindergarten, I gave myself a present by inviting my mother to join me in taking the children to London and Paris—vicariously living the life I craved at their age. Things that Mother and I took for granted, they adored—riding again and again the two-hundred-foot-tall Ferris wheel on the Place de la Concorde; sailing the miniature wooden boats on the pond in the Tuileries Garden, and, despite the oppressive heat, begging to do it again the next day. They were hardly impressed by seeing Queen Elizabeth II on their first day in London, as she rode in an open carriage up the Mall for the ceremony of the Trooping of the Color. The early morning two-hour ride on the high-speed TGV from London to Paris was a thrill for all of us, as were the croissant breakfasts we had each morning in Paris.

The way John and I saw it, travel was education—the more the better. And when our children would, on occasion, complain that we were the oldest parents in the school, we'd remind them of the benefits, which included the opportunities for travel.

* * *

With no idea what the future might hold, I kept close ties with the world of finance. For over a decade, I had been a regular commentator on morning and afternoon business television shows on CNBC, Fox Business News, and CNN, and after my retirement, I continued to be invited to share my thoughts on the markets and economies around the world, allowing me to maintain my visibility in the global world of business and finance.

On a regular basis, the booker would call from CNBC sometime in the midafternoon. "Can you be on *Squawk Box* tomorrow morning at six fifteen? I can have a car at your house at four fifteen," was pretty much the way those calls went, and I never said "no."

Being a regular guest on CNBC's *Squawk Box* felt like a good investment. Wall Street eyeballs were glued to the show, which was co-hosted at the time by Mark Haines and Joe Kernen. While no longer investing billions of dollars of institutional capital, I continued to be very much in the world of investing by managing my own money.

As a habitual early riser, that crack-of-dawn television interview was no hardship, and often by the time the car service dropped me back home, the children were just waking. Frequently, the only way they knew I had been on television was by the makeup that was still caked on my face.

In an effort not to wake the family before dawn, I devised a noise-proof strategy that allowed me to depart undetected for my predawn venture. Having laid out my clothes and jewelry the night before, the process of rising and dressing was reduced to minutes, because hair and makeup would be handled by the early morning makeup crew at the studio, all of whom were immensely talented, as well as cheery and chipper, long before the sun made its appearance.

Without turning on a single light, I would tiptoe my way out of the bedroom on the second floor, go down the carpeted stairs, and then feel my way in the pitch blackness through the dining room, glancing out the window for car lights outside that would indicate the driver's arrival. Using the chairs and the wall as a guide, I'd get to the end of the room and head through the pantry and out into the kitchen, where a small nightlight shed a soft glow on the three stairs down into the garage.

But in life, sometimes the best-laid plans fall short. One morning in the darkness, as I picked up my speed going through the pantry, I tripped over the open dishwasher door and planted my face full force on the kitchen floor. The sound of my cheekbone hitting the tiles still reverberates in my head. The normal silence was broken by my shrieks, fully intended to wake the entire house—which they did, and as bedroom doors opened and feet pounded down the stairs, I lifted my head to see a bloody floor. And then I felt things in my mouth—hard things. I reached my fingers in to discover that my front teeth were shattered.

Looking down on me now were two little seven-year-olds and a man in his early sixties—my family. The children stared in horror as my husband helped to pull me up from the floor. I spat my teeth into my hand, ignoring the pain in my head and cheekbone.

"Let me cancel the car," John said, as he headed toward the garage in his pajamas.

"No," I said in a voice stronger than I felt. "I have to do the show."

"You can't do the show. Your face is swollen, you probably have a concussion, and you have no teeth."

I could see his point, but…

Doing my best to remain composed, I said quietly, "They are counting on me. I need to be there." And putting my teeth into the pocket of my blazer, I walked slowly out of the house and into the waiting car, then texted my dentist to find out how to staunch the flow of blood and to see if I could have an emergency appointment after the show.

Almost immediately, I was remorseful—*It's so early. What if he didn't mute his cell phone?*

Within moments, I had a return text. "Soak a tea bag and put it on your lip to stop the bleeding. Come into the office at nine a.m. I'll fix you up to look like new."

The makeup staff was like a flock of Florence Nightingales, one setting my hair, while the other used exceptional artistry to hide the damage to my face—the puffy lacerated lips, the purple-looking egg that was my right cheekbone—as I told them the tale and prayed they would believe me. When I looked in the mirror, I almost laughed to see the lopsidedness of my face, but the purple bruise was almost imperceptible.

"Thank you, thank you, but I really need to talk to the cameraman before the show starts," I said, as I headed for the green room, and someone made that happen.

"Please," I said, "the camera can focus only on my left side, and I'll keep my head turned to face Mark [Haines] so that I'm only showing a profile. And no close-up of my mouth—please."

The team got it, and we were in the countdown to be on the air. Now all I had to do was concentrate through the concussive headache. *Mind over matter*, I told myself.

Mark seemed oblivious to the physical condition of his guest, as he threw his typical multifaceted questions at me, and I did my best to respond with lips that barely opened. The six- or seven-minute interview ended, and I made my way back to the car as I called one of my sisters, who watched every show I was on.

"How do you think it went?" I asked, not sharing a word of the tribulation of the last few hours.

"Fine," she said. "I liked it."

Disbelieving, I added, "Did I look OK?"

"Yes," and then with a little pause, "but you didn't smile at all."

"Well," I responded, and spilled out my tragedy to a sympathetic ear. "Could you tell anything had really happened?"

"No, nothing like *that!*" was all I needed to hear.

The postmortem that made me laugh was that evening when we were having dinner. My seven-year-old son, looking at my distorted face, opined with an air of seriousness I could only imagine he had learned from his parents—more likely me.

"Mommy, if you'd finished your job last night and closed the dishwasher, this wouldn't have happened."

I had to agree with him as Psalm 8 flashed through my mind, "Out of the mouths of babes, Oh Lord."

CHAPTER 45

Second Career

2002 AND AFTER

T hose early morning engagements on television brought an unanticipated bonus in the form of a telephone call from Martha Samuelson, the founder and CEO of Analysis Group, a firm that offered economic analysis and expert witness testimony to a vast array of industries.

She came to the point. "I see you regularly on television," she said, "and you come across very well. Have you ever thought of doing expert witness work?"

I was taken aback. Expert witness work? My only experience with the term had been watching fictional crime shows on television, but I soon found myself immersed in cases that dealt with investment research and asset management. The scandal of the moment was the bankruptcy of Enron, a company I knew well and had owned in my clients' accounts for several years. It had been one of the hottest stocks in the 1990s because of its prodigious growth in earnings. Then, in a matter of months, the wheels came off, as the company admitted to fraudulent accounting. The stock plummeted to zero when the firm declared bankruptcy in 2001. It was hardly defunct when the lawsuits began.

In a twist of irony, that first expert witness engagement was in defense of Alliance Capital and its renowned portfolio manager, Al Harrison, the most significant competitor I faced over my twenty years as a portfolio manager. Al's long-term track record of investment performance was stellar. For seventeen years, he had managed a sizable portion of the pension plan for the State of Florida, outperforming the market during that period by an average of more than 3 percent a year. Despite that extraordinary record, he and his firm were being sued by the State of Florida for more than $1 billion, far more than the $280 million loss the pension plan incurred in Enron stock.

The case brought to mind my own painful investment experience some fifteen years earlier with Crazy Eddie. As a portfolio manager back then, I'd been duped by much the same kind of fraud. The experience of having relied on the company's fraudulent financial reports gave me confidence as a willing expert witness on behalf of Alliance Capital and Al Harrison, whose reputation was at stake.

My role as an expert was to support the investment process that Al Harrison had created and implemented. That was an easy task intellectually—I was familiar with his style of investing. The defense preparation took three years, as I read thousands of pages of witness testimony—all from the comfort of my home office. Meetings with the defense counsel in Manhattan prepared me for my first of what would become many depositions in my new career.

The jury trial was to be held in Tallahassee, Florida, the state's capital, and in April 2005, I flew there a few days before I was to be put on the witness stand, as one of five experts for the defense. I observed the members of the jury—six people with various levels of education and none who could be called an investment professional—and wondered with concern if my testimony might be overly complex for people who didn't live in the day-to-day world of investing.

The state's lawyer came armed with a huge three-ringed binder that was meant to intimidate. Since fact witnesses and my own deposition had disproved his claim that Al Harrison didn't execute the very investment process he had created, the attorney's tack with me was to challenge the firm's marketing materials as "fraudulent"—his word. It was evident that he knew very little about the workings of the investment business. When his questions to prove his point became almost ludicrous, and I detected confusion by some members of the jury, I took matters into my own hands.

Turning to the jury, I spoke. "I think it would be helpful if I put some things into perspective for you. Marketing materials are meant to simplify and highlight for the client what can be a complex investment process."

And for the next ten minutes I explained in detail to the six members of the jury and the six alternates how the marketing materials that were provided by Alliance Capital to the State of Florida supported Al Harrison's investment process. The nodding heads of many of the jurors gave me confidence that I was helping them understand what the lawyer was deliberately trying to obfuscate.

When I finished, the lawyer, without looking at me, turned a page in his three-ring binder—his hand was shaking. I smiled inside. After one more question, he shut the binder, "I have no more questions."

The trial came to a close a day later and the defense team was pleased. Nevertheless, we were all anxious as the jury received their instructions late on a Thursday afternoon. When no verdict was reached on Friday, we—the team of numerous lawyers, expert witnesses, and employees of Alliance Capital and its recent acquisition of SC Bernstein—spent an uneasy weekend, which the jury had off. And then at about 2 p.m. on Monday, the jury announced its decision—acquitting Alliance Capital and Al Harrison of all twenty-seven counts. And thus I started my twenty-year career as an expert witness.

* * *

In the early 1990s, a couple of years before my children were born, I had been invited to join the board of Amica Mutual Insurance Company, a Rhode Island–headquartered firm that offered automobile and home insurance to individuals and families. Board work had the advantage of being concentrated for a few days, several times a year, and all the preparatory work could be done at home.

Over the next few years after retirement, more board opportunities came my way. I soon found myself fully immersed in a second career—one that would span an array of industries and cover both for-profit and not-for-profit sectors of the economy. This second career burgeoned, and I was grateful for the intellectual stimulation it offered. Equally as gratifying was the flexibility of time that came with it.

My daily routine was now established around the needs of my family. For a full thirteen years—from the day I left Wall Street until both our children graduated from high school and flew the nest as college freshmen—they were the primary focus of my life. I was in my fifties, an age when many women found themselves playing the role of grandmother, with its options to babysit and the liberty to hand the little ones back to their parents, at will. On the other hand, I rejoiced in full-time motherhood.

Each step along the way would invariably bring me back to my childhood and reflections on the dichotomy of the life I experienced growing up and the one I was now able to offer to my children. Such reflections were without rancor on my part; rather, I celebrated the good fortune I now had to provide opportunities never afforded to me.

Traveling the world had been my dream from as far back as I could remember, and I made it a dream come true for our children. Yes, there were Paris and London, but the most memorable trips were to countries with cultures vastly different from ours, places that included Egypt, Zimbabwe, Cambodia, India, and China.

* * *

When my children left home for college, I found myself looking for a way to give back, to share the way in which I had been most supported—through mentoring. I began by working with middle school girls from struggling families at a Catholic school in East Harlem, which was exceptionally rewarding. As those energetic girls shared their outsized dreams and often even wilder ambitions, I was reminded of my own youthful fantasies.

Behind each girl were parents—and most of the girls were fortunate to be living with two parents—who were dedicated to paving a way for their children to attend college and find success and happiness in their careers and their families.

* * *

Mentoring is a two-way street. On the one hand, there is a seeker—someone who is looking for advice, counsel, and direction. To be successful, there must also be a generous giver, someone who will lend an ear and provide the counsel being sought. That's what generates the bond. When that chemistry is in synch, it offers a rich soil for growth.

I am the beneficiary of a long list of exceptional mentors—all but one of whom were men—each of whom helped to pave the way for my journey to success. This book is a tribute to them.

CHAPTER 46

Reflection

2024

A s a child, I had few material possessions. They were forbidden within our community, lest they interfere with what we were told was the sole purpose of our lives—dedication to God.

A couple of months after I had turned seventeen, I received a personal gift for the first time in my life. It was October 1965, and the choir from the University of Valencia was visiting us at the Center. Forty young men and women—students and choristers—had been invited to perform at the opening of the Lincoln Center in New York City. Because the choir director was the brother of a man in our community, they came to visit us before they headed to New York. Mercedes was one of those choristers.

Despite the language barrier—my four years of French fell short as a bridge to Spanish—Mercedes and I bonded immediately. She seemed somewhat like me—energetic and eager to connect. As the younger children shared their ponies and horses with the choir members, Mercedes and I walked through the open fields that stretched across our property.

She spoke, in her faulting English, of the joys in her life—her fiancé, the plans for their wedding the following year, and her looking forward to being a mother.

Her happiness was for me both inspiring and, at the same time, emotionally shattering. This beautiful, dark-haired young woman, with a smile that seemed to emanate from her heart, was forging her own future—an education, marriage, family, a home in which she would raise her children, and years down the road, grandmotherhood. It seemed like a fantasy.

In contrast, I was a postulant, betrothed to Christ and destined to be His bride for the duration of my life. In that role, I was bound by the rules of poverty, chastity, and obedience, forbidden from making a single decision on my own—even to what book I might borrow from our vast religious library. The world was beckoning me to explore it, but I was imprisoned, something I could never say aloud, not even to Mercedes.

On the last day of her visit, Mercedes and I huddled together for a final few moments before she and her companions boarded the bus that would take them to New York City.

"Here," she said. "I give you this to remember me," as she pressed a small item into my hand, almost as though she realized it had to be our secret. Unfolding my fingers, I looked down at a tiny porcelain pitcher, not more than an inch in height—white with a delicately painted stylized flower on the front.

"I'll keep in touch," I promised, as I gave her a final kiss.

Holding the keepsake in my hand, I waved to Mercedes, as tears rolled down my cheeks. How I wanted a friend like her. How I wanted a life like hers.

In the privacy of my cubicle, I hid the memento in the back corner of the top drawer of my dresser, buried under my undergarments, where I trusted no prying eyes would find it and possibly steal it from me—because it broke the rule of "no personal possessions." Day after day, I would peek at it, hold it in my hand, and then return it to its hiding place. Nine months later, when I was kicked out of the Center,

I packed my precious souvenir of friendship in tissue and put it in my small suitcase.

For the fifty-nine years since that day in October, that memento from Mercedes has been my talisman. It traveled with me to Boston, then Philadelphia, then New York, and finally to my home in Connecticut, where today it sits on a shelf in my writing nook, where I spend hours each day. Throughout my adult life, over and over again that memento has brought back the heartwarming experience of walking with Mercedes, as she shared with me visions of a world I thought was lost to me. It served as a vessel of hope.

* * *

Success is the attainment of one's goals. But that makes it sound so intentional and preplanned. The reality is different. There are those who, at a young age, have already established their objectives in life and adhere to a rigid plan for achievement. But others are molded by their workplace experiences and accomplishments and meander their way to success in baby steps that eventually turn into giant steps. The latter was my course.

I entered the "real" world at the age of seventeen as an ingenue and had to tiptoe my way through a frightening maze that was second nature to many but certainly not to me. My first goal was to survive, and doing so may have been the greatest achievement of my young adulthood. The curiosity with which I was endowed from birth was likely the catalyst for much of my drive, complemented by the resilience I found within. I sought help from anyone who would share their time with me and was immensely fortunate and generously rewarded by what I encountered.

As I reached each new rung up the ladder, I still had no grand plan. I simply leapt at opportunities that came my way. In my enthusiasm and drive, I unwittingly ruffled feathers, and in the process, I found myself dubbed "the Witch of Wall Street." Fortunately, many of those who found my office style too intimidating are today good friends.

The long journey was far more rewarding than I had ever envisioned, despite periods of exasperation and frustration. During those trying times, I would sit myself down—metaphorically—and have a heart-to-head monologue.

You have two options but not three. Option one: you can find a new job, with all that entails, and work where you think you will be better appreciated. Option two: you can outsmart the powers that be and put them to shame by proving them wrong. What you cannot do is become a malcontent.

I always chose option two and never regretted it. I was also lucky that for much of my career on Wall Street, I had the wind at my back.

In the end, I turn to my long-held belief in grace. I will be forever grateful that I have been blessed with the grace of optimism, of resilience, of gratitude, and of joy.

In Praise of My Mentors

Sister Ann Mary Cobb

A Catholic nun, you are the only woman who has been a mentor to me. When I was most vulnerable—a teenager about to be tossed out of my home—you defied the rules and used your authority as the principal of our tiny school to take me under your wing, to become my confidante, my adviser, and my cheerleader.

My memories of you as a teacher are myriad and joyous—from reading sessions in the second grade, to English grammar in the sixth, to trigonometry in high school, as well as four years of violin lessons and then four more of trumpet.

There are also special memories I treasure that were outside the classroom. You made a wicked Waldorf salad, and you loved your hot dogs burned almost to a crisp and smothered with mustard.

Your smile, your charm, and your gracious manners were part of your persona until you left this world at the age of ninety-eight.

George Burden

Thank you for hiring me—an eighteen-year-old neophyte just out of secretarial school. In your unassuming way, you read my drive, and you were willing to let me prove myself. Your five-million-dollar challenge was one of the highlights of my life. My gratitude to you is boundless.

I've thought of you often over the fifty-five years that have elapsed since you put your faith in me. Only recently, I discovered that you are buried within one hundred yards of my parents in Mount Auburn Cemetery. I love that family connection with you.

Edwin Taff

For nearly three years, when I was hardly an adult, you were my champion, encouraging me in my studies, giving me all the rope I needed to make headway in my nascent career. You allowed me to be more than a secretary, and I felt the presence of your quiet leadership.

You answered all my questions, you explained concepts I was keen to understand, and you shared your successes with me. I loved our partnership. It was because of you that, when I left Boston for Philadelphia, I was prepared to take some giant steps.

On the less serious side, I enjoyed hearing your stories about escapades with your tangerine Porsche—how once you convinced the state trooper that you needed to be driving one hundred miles per hour because you were testing the tuning that had been done on your car. And the cop let you off. Who ever said that nice guys finish last?

Sherif Nada

You kept your word to me. I was a twenty-three-year-old newcomer to Philadelphia, champing at the bit and keen to move onward and upward when you hired me as an assistant, promising to help me understand the intricacies of stock research.

I remember that interview well and, most particularly, that you stood out in a sea of men with white button-down shirts—yours was blue. I liked that you were unconcerned with following dress code norms.

And then you far exceeded my expectations—first, when you invited me to accompany you on your trip to New York to interview Leonard Stern, the CEO of Hartz Mountain, and second, when you asked me to coauthor the report on the company.

I credit you and thank you for promoting me from assistant to statistician and then for catapulting me across the threshold into the realm of research analyst.

Stew Harvey

We knew each other for less than three months, but you changed the course of my life.

"Go to New York." Those were your words—a command delivered by someone who wanted only the best for me. I heard you and followed your counsel and have never regretted it for a moment.

You may have been gruff on the outside, but you had a heart of gold. I even came to enjoy the smell of chewing tobacco in your office, although I never quite cottoned to the spittoon.

Thank you, Stew, for kicking me out of the nest.

Brad Landon

I knew nothing about machinery stocks, but you offered me a job during my first interview at your firm. You threw me into the deep end of the pool, and you were generous with your time and your counsel.

When I was no longer your employee but your customer, I realized that there was no better machinery analyst on all of Wall Street.

When my children were born in 1994, you sent each of them a present that you admitted they would not likely enjoy for some years—Macallan twenty-year-old single malt scotch—and I knew it was your favorite.

Jay Light

"You have a great future ahead of you." I was a twenty-nine-year-old research analyst at the Ford Foundation who had just been accepted to the Harvard Business School but was torn in my decision whether to accept or carry on in my career as an analyst—one that I adored.

You were a professor at HBS at the time, but you listened to me and then offered me wise counsel I have never forgotten. "You're at a fork in the road," you said. "If you are interested in changing careers, if you want to go into investment banking or become a consultant or run one of those manufacturing companies you follow, the Harvard Business School will be immensely helpful. If, however, you want to continue your career as an analyst and perhaps move on to portfolio management, you don't need the Harvard Business School. You're already a success."

Is it any surprise that you eventually became the dean of the school? Thank you, Jay, for your wise counsel.

Peter Vermilye

You were sixty years old, and I was thirty-one when we met for the first time. It was the spring of 1980, and I had come to your office at Citibank—you were interviewing for an analyst to head the capital goods research team. I was expected to visit the HR department after meeting with you, but you jumped the gun and offered me the job. Thank you.

You were forthright, which led some to stay out of your way. I found that characteristic stimulating. You were a global thinker, and you turned me into one also. You assigned me to be the liaison with our overseas offices, and it changed how I looked at the world. Yours was an open-door policy, and I came close to abusing it, but you never turned me away.

You retired from Citibank at the mandatory age of sixty-five, but you never retired from investing, and you never lost your enthusiasm for stocks.

For four and a half years, you were my mentor, and then for the next twenty-five years, we remained friends. At the age of eighty-nine, you were looking forward to writing a book, and you asked me to share stories from our Citibank days. Sadly, you were felled by a stroke before that dream came true.

I still miss you.

ACKNOWLEDGMENTS

O ne might suppose that writing a second book would come easier than a first one. In some ways that may be true, but as I think back on the last four years of researching, fact-checking, recalling memories, and putting fifty years of life onto paper, I realize how much help I received along the way.

Thank you to my husband, John, who at the drop of a hat would read numerous versions of numerous chapters and write numerous notes in the margins, and to my children, Caroline and Jim, who put up with all the time I dedicated to this second book project. And thank you to my editor, Carolyn Flynn, with whom I spent countless hours over these last four years, and whose invaluable advice can be found in scene after scene. Thank you, also to my copy editor, Gail Harris, whose sharp eye and sharp pencil have smoothed out many rough edges in my manuscript.

My thanks also go to the team at Post Hill Press: Anthony Ziccardi, Maddie Sturgeon, my publisher once again, Donna DuVall, the amazing copy editor, many of whose notations I have saved; Fabien León, who designed the jacket, Cathrine White for the photo, my agent Michael Carlisle, as well as my PR team that includes Susie Stangland, Caitlin Stangland, Lauren Beck, and my book publicist Emi Battaglia.

I am grateful for so many friends for reading and commenting on my manuscript. First, immense thanks go to a special few who took the extraordinary time and effort to not only read my manuscript but also to make recommendations for elaboration and change. They include my dear friend and renowned publisher from Switzerland, Ursula Streit, as well as Phillip Watson, Emilie Deutsch, Rudina Seseri and Chris Grisanti, together with an array of others including Ed Taff, Sherif and Mary Nada, Alexandra Trower, Mary Ellen Markowitz, Robert Ainsley, Chuck and Deborah Royce, Nina Lesavoy, Tania Clark, Susan Mullin, Heidi Pearlson, Tricia and John Boyer, Carly Callahan, and my sister, Cathy Toomey. Each and every one of you offered invaluable advice and made the story better.

And finally a heartfelt thank you to the mentors who were instrumental in shaping the path of my life and my career. Without your guidance, your caring, your willingness to go the extra mile for me, there would be no book, there would be no story with a happy ending. I am eternally indebted to all of you.

Patricia Walsh Chadwick was born in Cambridge, Massachusetts in 1948. She received her BA in Economics from Boston University and had a thirty-year career in the investment business, culminating as a Global Partner at Invesco. Today she sits on a number of corporate boards, and she blogs on issues social, economic, and political. She also mentors young women in high school and college. In 2016, she co-founded and is the pro-bono CEO of Anchor Health Initiative, a health care company that serves the needs of the LGBTQ community in Connecticut. She is married and lives in Connecticut with her husband, John. They have a daughter and a son.